A Hybrid World

ENDORSEMENTS

Prepare to be surprised, perhaps unsettled, to have familiar categories upended. Drawing from Scripture as well as multiple disciplines, the authors of this volume argue convincingly that the world in which we serve is far more complex than our classifications. An appreciation for hybridity opens new windows for insight, creativity, teamwork, pastoral care, and effective missional outreach.

DAVID W. BENNETT, DMin, PhD
Global Associate Director for Collaboration and Content

I like the fact that the contributors are all leading missiologists for whom the topic is a lived experience. Finally, I love this book because it helps me understand my own family better. I am an American raised in the Midwest who served in Japan for twenty years. We now have three adult children in New York City, Cambridge (UK) and London, who are married to a first generation Korean-American, a first generation Latina, and a first generation Englishman who was born in New Zealand to parents of medical missionaries to Africa. I need this book, and I am grateful for it! I commend it to my Lausanne friends around the world!

The contributors in A Hybrid World *are world-class leaders and scholars who have helped to prioritize opportunities, propose solutions with respect to the great sociological reality of our time, and live out what they discuss. Many will not recognize its timeliness and its global significance. However, for those who are ready to respectfully listen to voices from the non-Western world who will lead us into the new realities of a twenty-first century world, this book will prove to be illuminating and indispensable, i.e., "a must read!"*

S. DOUGLAS BIRDSALL
Honorary Chair, The Lausanne Movement

This book is the fruit of an international diaspora consultation, not dominated by Western voices. The insights are enriched by the wide backgrounds and ministries of the contributors, ranging from the challenges facing bicultural families to the all-too-common experience of minority peoples estranged and marginalized in their own countries. The subject matter is as diverse as the contributors themselves. This book has my hearty endorsement and deep hope that it will remind us Christians wherever we find ourselves in the world that only together can we constitute the healthy and whole body of Christ (Eph 4). As the Ethiopian proverb puts it, "Without you there is no me."

JONATHAN J. BONK, PhD
Director, Dictionary of African Christian Biography
Research Professor of Mission, Center for Global Christianity & Mission,
Boston University School of Theology

A Hybrid World *explores biblical, theological, and missional perspectives resulting from the complexities of culture in the context of global migration. Each of the contributors provide insights into issues inherent in the mixing of cultures and the living of life in today's globalized world. This book is a major contribution to diaspora missiology as it calls us to be attentive to what is happening around us in real time. May the insights of this volume move us to further explore the role intentional intercultural congregations have in an increasingly hybridized world.*

CHARLES A. COOK, PhD
Professor of Global Studies and Mission (Ambrose)
Executive Director, Jaffray Centre for Global Initiatives, Ambrose University, Canada

In a world defined by people on the move, this exploration of diaspora and migration, identity, the mission of God, and hybrid cultural identity is a vital contribution to the task of Christian churches in navigating new and frequently perilous waters. If the authors of this excellent and ultimately hopeful volume are correct, the journey may be challenging, but it will be its own reward. I heartily recommend it.

DARRELL JACKSON, ThD
Associate Professor of Missiology, Morling College, Sydney, Australia

Diaspora and people movements are featured prominently in the biblical narrative and Christian history. However, the role of diasporic identity in the process of gospel transmission and appropriation remains understudied. This book fills the gap by highlighting the role of diasporic hybridity in uniquely shaping the identities of individuals, communities, and theologies for missional effectiveness.

STANLEY JOHN, PhD
Associate Professor of Intercultural Studies,
Alliance Theological Seminary, Nyack, NY

This book takes a serious conceptual leap by adopting hybridity as a creative conceptual framework, which allows a wide variety of diaspora experiences and reflections in one table. The dynamic process of hybridization would open an unprecedented space to take live stories into the formulation of contextual theologies. The editors are to be highly commended for this creative work.

WONSUK MA, PhD
Dean and Distinguished Professor of Global Christianity,
College of Theology and Ministry, Oral Roberts University, Tulsa, OK

Hybridity is not only a matter of "cultural mixtures," but has to do also with the consequences of multi-ethnic relationships. The word does not appear in the Scriptures, but the Scriptures are filled with examples. And most of the time, it seems, they highlight the intensity of such intermarriages and their theological consequences. But the Lord never opposed such "mixtures" per se. The problem was never "hybridization," but theological beliefs. Such nuances, however, have been rarely taken into consideration in our missional diasporic studies. Therefore, I am glad for the initiative of Dr. Sadiri Joy Tira, a scholar on diaspora missiology, and Dr. Julie Lee Uytanlet for the publication of this relevant volume: A Hybrid World: Exploring Diaspora Living and Missio Dei.

ELIAS MEDEIROS, PhD
Member of the Lausanne Global Diaspora Network Advisory Board
and of the Brazilian Evangelical Diaspora movement

This book deals with important issues that any serious theologian and missiologist cannot ignore. As the pastor of one of the largest intercultural churches in the world, I affirm the hybridity of the local congregations, and that Latin American, Asian, and African Christians have something to bring to enrich God's mission globally.

SAM OWUSU, PhD
Senior Pastor, Calvary Worship Centre, Surrey, British Columbia

Disunity set in at Babel; the mission of Church is reconciliation with God and restoration of unity among all people. Hybridity is an opportunity and instrument in the age of diaspora mission. This timely collection edited by Dr. Sadiri Joy Tira and Dr. Julie Lee Uytanlet offers biblical, theological, and historical reflections on hybridity as well as expert analyses of the mission strategy. Anyone with serious interest in missions will find much wisdom and encouragement here.

EIKO TAKAMIZAWA
Mongol Kids' Home: Support Manhole Children,
Representative of the Supporting Team SEANET, Steering Committee
Lausanne, Theological Working Core Group

A Hybrid World *is another major contribution from scholars and practitioners to the growing body of diaspora missiology literature. Hybrid diasporas are agents of God and are bridges between cultures and societies. This is a valuable and insightful book.*

TETSUNAO YAMAMORI, PhD
Sr. Vice President, Pyongyang University of Science and Technology, North Korea
Contributing Fellow, Center for Religion and Civic Culture,
University of Southern California

A Hybrid World

Diaspora, Hybridity, and Missio Dei

EDITORS Sadiri Joy Tira & Juliet Lee Uytanlet

WILLIAM CAREY PUBLISHING

Available at missionbooks.org

Published by William Carey Publishing
10 W. Dry Creek Cir
Littleton, CO 80120 | www.missionbooks.org

William Carey Publishing is a ministry of Frontier Ventures
Pasadena, CA 91104 | www.frontierventures.org

Mike Riester, cover and interior design
Damples Dulcero-Baclagon, copyeditor
Melissa Hicks, managing editor

ISBNs: 978-1-64508-288-0 (paperback),
978-1-64508-290-3 (mobi),
978-1-64508-291-0 (epub)

Printed Worldwide
24 23 22 21 20   1 2 3 4 5   IN

Library of Congress data on file with publisher.

DEDICATION

This book is dedicated to
Dr. Joseph Shao and Dr. Rosa Ching Shao,
a couple who is instrumental in shaping many lives, minds, and hands
to serve the Master and the Global Church, particularly in Asia.
For over thirty years, the Shaos have faithfully led the Biblical Seminary
of the Philippines (BSOP), leading it to become a premier seminary
and training ground for kingdom workers.
This volume is a testament to their servant leadership.

CONTENTS

xi   **Foreword**
Michael A. Rynkiewich

xv   **Preface**
Sadiri Joy Tira

1   **Chapter 1: Hybridity in the Old Testament**
Joseph Shao

11   **Chapter 2: Jesus Christ and Hybridity**
T. V. Thomas

19   **Chapter 3: The Challenge of Multiplying Disciples
by Hybrids in Fulfilling Missio Dei**
David Lim

31   **Chapter 4: Hybridity and the Gentile Mission
in Matthew's Genealogy of Christ**
Steven S. H. Chang

45   **Chapter 5: Diaspora, Hybridity, and Theology**
Harvey C. Kwiyani

57   **Chapter 6: Globalization, Hybrid Worlds, and Emerging
Missional Frontiers**
Calvin Chong

75   **Chapter 7: Jewish-Gentile Intermarriage:
A Hybridity Laboratory**
Tuvya Zaretsky

89   **Chapter 8: *Mistizaje* and *Hibridez*:
A Latino Appreciation of Hybridity**
Daniel Álvarez

101 **Chapter 9: Hybridity and Chineseness:
Finding Meaning in Theories**
Juliet Lee Uytanlet

113 **Chapter 10: Becoming *Nikkei*: A Cross-Cultural
Comparative Study of Diasporic Japanese
"Dekasegi" Christian Community in Japan, Brazil, and Peru**
Gary Fujino

133   **Chapter 11: Coconut Generation, Hybridity,
and Hybrid Missions**
Sam George

145   **Chapter 12: Hybridity and Identity Development of
Second-Generation Diaspora**
Kamal Weerakoon

159   **Chapter 13: Bi-National Mixed Marriages:
Contributions and Challenges Affecting Ministry
Among The Diaspora Academic Community**
Leiton Chinn and Lisa Espineli-Chinn

173   **Chapter 14: Helping Hybrid Children Shine:
What the Global Church Can Do**
Miriam Adeney

189   **Chapter 15: Hybridity: A Witness in South Africa**
Godfrey Harold

201   **Chapter 16: Hybridity, Arts, and Mission**
Uday Mark Balasundaram

217   **Chapter 17: Toward a Third Space of Cultures:
Hybridity and Multiethnic Leadership in Christian Mission**
Peter Taehoon Lee

232   **Appendix 1: Manila Declaration**

233   **Appendix 2: Cape Town Commitment**

234   **Index**

FOREWORD

Hybridity, Diaspora, and *Missio Dei*: Exploring New Horizons

The twelve apostles received a call to mission for their time: "You will receive power when the Holy Spirit has come upon you; and you will be my witnesses in Jerusalem, in all Judea and Samaria, and to the ends of the earth" (Acts 1:8). Little could they imagine the dimensions of this call, nor the changes in tactics required to keep up with a changing world and an out-of-control Spirit.

They were immediately tasked with witnessing to hybrid diasporic Jews from every nation with multiple languages and cultures. In their favor, this time the Spirit overcame some of the differences, but new challenges lay ahead: witnessing to half-Jews, then proselytes, and then Gentiles. The transitions were not easy and not without controversy. In the Acts story, as we have it, the Apostles fell behind ("all except the apostles were scattered," Acts 8:1). First the Greek-speaking deacons took up the task; then Paul, Barnabas, Silas, Apollos, Priscilla and Aquila, Phoebe, Timothy, and many others. All had different identities and came from different communities—some related to two or three dissimilar communities.

Somewhere along the way, the church lost the story and the dimensions of mission: from center to periphery, and the reverse;

the constant de-centering and re-centering of the Gospel; the contextualization not only of the message, but the messenger. The young among us, missionaries and missiologists, are rediscovering the dimensions of migration, diaspora, and hybridity in mission. And, once the cat is out of the bag, like the out-of-control Spirit, there is no stopping the movement and the discoveries.

These shifting "scapes" have a quantum-like quality where realities pop into existence and then disappear before we can make their acquaintance. Who has heard of "Peruvian *dekasegi* diaspora," the "third space" (is three enough?), or "*kamishibai*"? Resist the temptation to find the right category for these people and events. Rather, it is past time to move beyond futile attempts to categorize the world and thus pretend to understand it.

What this volume demonstrates is the fleeting particularity of the cultural and social contexts that people pass through. No one can be a generalist, a gadfly in mission to all. But God is able to call someone for each of these multiple dimensions that keep on shifting over time.

How did our hubris come about? When did we come to believe that we could categorize people and thereby quickly understand them? When were we seduced into this false sense of control?

It is due in large part to mission's captivity to colonialism and missiology's failure to break completely out of the box. Missiology fell sway to the never-ending quest of the colonial, neocolonial, and now global order to define and identify race, ethnicity, general publics, resistant populations, Twitter audiences, Facebook followers, niche markets, E2s, windows, UPGs, and other "certainties."

This volume is another step in establishing "hybridity" as being deeply rooted in history and Scripture; not the "new normal," but simply normal. Normal in the sense of: "That's just the way things are, and the way things have always have been."

Does that fact not force us to reconsider our mission theology, history, and anthropology? We might ask whether or not we have understood the *missio Dei* to be whether God has called for purity and clarity, or whether we have called unclean what God has called clean. We must continue the critique of our own history since mission has been sidetracked by the colonial enterprise of "categorize and control." Perhaps we can look at the world in which we live and ask whether we depend too much on the idea that established groups and standard relations form the structure and context of people's lives as much as we thought they did. Are we tied to concepts such as "animism," "tribalism," and "people group," or would we be better off without them?

The second accomplishment of this volume is to make the case for teaching process over method. That is, missiology as a discipline is still tied to preparing missionaries and mission scholars by filling them with content about the place where they are headed and the model of mission that they plan on using. This volume is one more piece of evidence exposing our hubris, because the world is too complex and too rapidly changing for our set of fun facts and amusing anecdotes to adequately prepare people for the day that they arrive in mission. For example, one of our favorite concepts is "heart language," and the claim that people want to hear the gospel in the language that they grew up speaking. I have questioned this elsewhere, and contributors here question the claim again. Newer ideas in linguistics, such as "language ideology" and "language registers," should force us to inquire of the people themselves about translations rather than deciding for others how they will hear the gospel. Reading the chapters here pushes me even more toward teaching method: theological method, historical method, and ethnographic method. I fool myself if I think that I can teach one student what she needs to know to go to a section of Jakarta where migrants live, as well as the student beside her what he needs to know to go to Bangalore to work with university students. However, I can teach them both how to conduct their own inquiry into cultures, languages, and sociality in their place.

Finally, this volume reminds us that with hybridity comes "heterosis" or what we know as "hybrid vigor." When mission students read only missiologists because mission teachers reference only internal missiology literature, then, in this second generation, we lose something. Hybrid vigor in biology refers to the improvement in characteristics and functions of the first generation in the initial cross of parents who, while in the same species, are dissimilar in genetic makeup. The "vigor" refers to the rapidity and extent of growth as well as the "robustness" of the hybrid.[1] The more different the parents are, the greater the effect, which is due to the unlikelihood that each parent will contribute the same deleterious allele and thus permit the expression of something harmful. This is what happens more frequently in the opposite case

---

1 See George Harrison Schull, "What is 'Heterosis'?" in *Genetics* 33:5, 1948, 439–46.

of "inbreeding depression" where the likelihood of recessive gene expression increases.

What is the application? When missiology as a profession does not keep up with the literature in its secular counterparts of literary criticism, historiography, and ethnography, then we miss the opportunity to expand and develop our understanding of the world. Our students end up living in a "missiology bubble" where they talk only to each other and cannot carry on a conversation outside the bubble. The authors of this volume show that they are in conversation with new research initiatives around new concepts from the secular side, concepts such as "reshaped topography," "the history of objects," and "global householding studies." Missiology has already benefitted from the research agenda proposed by such concepts as "imagined communities," "orientalism," "actor network theory," "practice theory," "performance theory," "speech act theory," and "différance." This does not imply a total sell-out to postmodernism, but rather, like the biological analogy, bringing together the two to see what growth and robustness might eventuate from the conversation.

MICHAEL A. RYNKIEWICH
Professor of Anthropology, retired
Asbury Theological Seminary

PREFACE

Hybridity, Diaspora, *Missio Dei*

Diaspora and hybridity are not new phenomena. History, specifically Biblical history, has records of both. Indeed, voluntarily and frequently involuntarily, humans are designed to move. Adam and Eve, the first couple who inhabited the earth, were the only truly homogenous individuals in race and culture. After they were driven out of the Garden of Eden, their "homeland," their family composition was never the same. Succeeding generations would intermarry, forming new ethnicities, adopting and adapting their own languages and cultures, and building their own cities. In terms of population movements and intermixing of peoples, the globalised world of the twenty-first century is not much different from the ancient societies in its hybridity. While it may be a reality of human history and experience, in our time of documentation and observation, "hybridity" is taking centre stage as the world takes note of media celebrities and members of royalty feature "interacial" couples and families. Furthermore, hybrid families and individuals are increasingly visible in communities around the globe.

The Filipino people are a wonderful example of hybridity as evident in their multiracialism and multiculturalism, resulting from centuries of migration into and out of the geographical crossroads that are the

Philippine islands. This hybridity is reflected in the common national language of the Philippines, "Pilipino," a Malay base with a host of Spanish and American English loan words, and in modern Filipino cuisine featuring local Filipino vegetables cooked in Spanish estofados, seasoned with Chinese seasoning (e.g., Five Spice), and served with a side of American salads and canned meats.

In nearly five decades of traversing the globe, I have met Filipinos married to Chinese, to Japanese, to Arabs, to Germans, to Italians, to Koreans, to Scandinavians, to Jews, to Indigenous North Americans, and to European-descent North Americans, etc. The modern "Filipino" is a composition of internationals. A racially and ethnically heterogenous population, modern Filipinos may be, at first glance, difficult to distinguish from other racial and ethnic groups, particularly in diaspora.

My own family has this hybridity on display. My father is of Arab Indonesian descent and my mother is a Spanish Filipino mestiza. From my siblings, our family has Filipino Romanians and Filipino Nigerians. My own wife is of Chinese Filipino ethnicity, and our children married similar hybrid Filipinos. Our daughter is married to a Filipino with Indian and Chinese lineage, and our son is married to a Canadian-born Filipina with Spanish and Chinese ancestors. Our grandchildren identify as 100 percent Filipino Canadian, but look very different from each other.

As a missiologist tasked, in particular by the Lausanne Movement, to interpret current realities through the eyes of missions, I was drawn to the rise of mixed ethnicities in my own context, among Filipino Canadians. Dakshana Bascaramurty reports in the Globe and Mail (Canada) that

> Among Filipinos as a whole, only 22% reported multiple ethnic origins in the 2016 census, meaning the majority had two Filipino parents—but a breakdown by generation tells a different story. For first-generation Filipinos… 14% listed multiple ethnicities. But [by]… the second generation, it was up to 42%. And by the third generation and beyond… it reached 83%.[1]

I became convinced that hybridity is, among urbanization, multiculturalism, and religious pluralism, a major offshoot of migration, and for the Church, an area that needs to be appreciated and addressed.

---

1 Dakshana Bascaramurty, "As Multi-ethnic Population in Canada Rises, Complications Arise for Families," *The Globe and Mail*, https://www.theglobeandmail.com/news/national/multi-ethnic-mixed-race-canada-census-2016/article37475308/.

In 2011, after a visiting lectureship at Asbury Theological Seminary, a Chinese Filipino couple studying at the seminary hosted me for a meal at their apartment in Kentucky. Samson and Juliet Uytanlet would go on to complete their studies. Samson finished his PhD in Biblical Studies at London School of Theology while Juliet completed her PhD in Intercultural Studies at Asbury. She wrote her dissertation on the Chinese Diaspora in the Philippines. Juliet would become a specialist on hybridity, publishing the volume, *The Hybrid Tsinoys: Challenges of Hybridity and Homogeneity as Sociocultural Constructs among the Chinese in the Philippines.* Acutely aware of the diaspora experience and intimately acquainted with the realities of gendered migration, Juliet needed a platform from which her voice would be widely heard. In 2016, with the endorsement of Joseph Shao, general secretary of Asia Theological Association, and president of Biblical Seminary of the Philippines, I asked Juliet to serve the Evangelical church with me, as a diasporas catalyst for The Lausanne Movement.[2] With Juliet in the role of convener, we immediately began planning towards the "Hybridity, Diaspora, and Missio Dei: Exploring New Horizons Consultation," sponsored by The Lausanne Movement and the Global Diaspora Network, and hosted by the Biblical Seminary of the Philippines, in Manila from June 19 to 22, 2018.

This volume is a product of that hybridity consultation which brought together academics and practitioners engaged in research and ministry among diaspora people groups to discuss and discover the implications of hybridity in the mission of God. Though, at the time of this publication, she has moved on to other commitments, Juliet should be credited for her leadership in gathering these experts and doing the bulk of footwork in curating their words of wisdom and expertise for the benefit of global readers. In the last stages of production for this volume, I have the privilege of reading what Juliet has assembled.

The editing and publication of this book, sponsored by the Hallelujah Fellowship Baptist Church in Toronto, ON, Canada, is composed of seventeen chapters, primarily of papers presented at the "Hybridity, Diaspora, and Missio Dei: Exploring New Horizons Consultation," and assembled by theme. Authors include Harvey Kwiyani, Calvin Chong, Tuvya Zaretsky, Daniel Alvarez, Juliet Uytanlet, Gary Fujino, Sam George,

2   In 2016, The Lausanne Movement moved to the title, "catalyst," from the previous title "senior associate" for their issue groups, with each senior associate appointing two co-catalysts. In 2016, I asked Juliet Uytanlet of Biblical Seminary of the Philippines and Sam George of Parivar International, based in Chicago, Illinois to serve with me as the Lausanne Movement's co-catalysts for Diasporas.

Kamal Weerakoon, Leiton Chinn and Lisa Espinelli-Chinn, Miriam Adeney, Godfrey Harold, Uday Balasundaram, and Peter Lee. Included are three chapters presented by Joseph Shao, T. V. Thomas, and David Lim, and a chapter contributed by Steven Chang, presented post-consultation, that give valuable context and meaning to the reader. The volume is multi-disciplinary and the authors, coming from distinct regions of the globe and representing diverse fields of expertise, have been given freedom to write in their preferred style and English spelling (i.e. British and American English). The reader may find this confusing, but it is by design that this book is read through the hybrids' eyes.

Hybridity, like urbanization, multiculturalism, and religious pluralism, is a reality of the human experience and a feature of history. What this volume attempts is to wrestle with the challenges that it presents to global missions and to encourage the global church to celebrate the opportunities that God, in his sovereignty and love, provides, that the "Scattered People" would be gathered to himself.

It is with great gratitude to Juliet, the esteemed contributors of this volume, the Lausanne Movement, the Global Diaspora Network, the Biblical Seminary of the Philippines, the Hallelujah Fellowship Baptist Church, the husband and wife editorial team of Gerry and Damples Baclagon, and the inspirational hybrid men, women, children, and their congregations, that I present this volume. May this be a celebration of, and a challenge for, the Global Church that is, like a hybrid family, composed of all nations, but is one.

Soli Deo gloria,
Sadiri Joy Tira, DMin, DMiss
Edmonton, AB, Canada

CHAPTER 1 | Joseph Shao

Hybridity in the Old Testament

Hybridity is an important topic for missiology and specifically for a new field of missiology called diaspora missiology. Since we live in a globalized world, hybridity is easily observed anywhere in the world. As it is more convenient and faster to traverse in the world, the speed of hybridity will definitely intensify in the near future. With migration, whether it is voluntary or involuntary, different nationalities and people groups will be living in diaspora. The *Missio Dei* in the post-truth era differs from what we have faced before in the missionary task. Previously, we emphasized a "go" strategy, sending missionaries to the ends of the earth. Now with hybridity and diaspora, it is a "from anywhere to everywhere" approach, since many people groups are constantly migrating and they are in our midst in any city, and in any region or country. It is a joy that hybridity, diaspora, and the *Missio Dei* are discussed in this significant consultation.

How should we define hybridity? Should we define it as a mixture of culture, language, and ethnicity? It is quite easy for any people group that would prefer to hold on to purist ideology in maintaining their own uniqueness to separate from others for a time. Is it possible for any people group to maintain its own distinctiveness and exclusivity at all times?

Let us look at hybridity in the Old Testament and see how the people of God handled the condition. With so many people groups surrounding the people of God, are there any principles that we can learn and apply to the *Missio Dei* today? From the nomadic lifestyle during the patriarchal era to the forced diaspora of the Israelites in the Assyrian period and the experience of the exiles in the Babylonian era, are there any challenging values facing the people of God? What should be learned from the experience of the returnees from the exiles? What are the concerns of the post-exilic community, and how does their creativity bring people in multi-cultural contexts back to faith in God?

The purpose of my presentation on hybridity is to provide a diachronic study of hybridity and diaspora in the Old Testament and to explore the *Missio Dei* implications that would be relevant for our twenty-first century.[1] The character and action of God in relation to each era is presented.

Patriarchal Era: Walking with the God Who Leads

There are many examples of hybridity even in the early parts of the book of Genesis. Should we assume that the language, culture, and ethnicity of the people groups represented in the book of Genesis are all the same? Culturally, the people groups, though named differently in the book of Genesis, seem to have some affinity to each other. Biblically, the differences in languages and perhaps ethnicity and even culture come after the dispersion at the Tower of Babel (Gen 11:7–8). In linguistic studies, there is a difference between West Semitic language and East Semitic language.

God walks in the Garden of Eden to search for Adam and Eve. Both Enoch and Noah walk with him (Gen 15:22, 24; 6:9). With the Lord's blessing and command, Abram "walks" as the Lord asks him to do (Gen 12:4). Likewise, the Lord would like Abram to walk with him (Gen 17:1). The action of "walking" implies the intimate relationship of Abraham with the God who leads. The life of the patriarchs is a life of sojourning in the land of Canaan. Their nomadic lifestyle compels them to move around their environment, shepherding their flock. Unless they are aware of their own culture and make a clear decision to separate themselves from

---

1 For studying the Old Testament theme, we can either use diachronic or synchronic approach to bring out the leitmotif. The diachronic approach is usually associated with Gerhard von Rad, *Old Testament Theology* Vol 1–2 (New York: Harper & Row, 1962–65). In the case of hybridity and diaspora, the diachronic approach is the best method to bring out the key themes in the Old Testament.

their environment, it is quite natural for the patriarchs to assimilate the cultures and religious beliefs around them. Hybridity can easily happen in such a context. From Ur of the Chaldeans to the land of Canaan, the Lord chooses Abraham to follow him. When Abraham leaves behind the pagan gods, he worships and serves the God Almighty, El Shaddai. God reveals himself to Abraham with promises of land, heir, and heritage (Gen 12:1–3). Even as Abraham expresses his faith in the Lord, the presence of people groups is a reality. The chosen people are living in the midst of a multi-cultural environment and are easily influenced by the religions of the day. The "sins" of the Amorites constantly influence the patriarchs (Gen 15:16). In principle, Abraham lives in a multi-cultural society.

The first test case of hybridity and diaspora is the incident of Jacob bringing his family with him as he runs away from Laban. Jacob, as a single man, is dislocated to a place other than his paternal home for fourteen years. As Jacob and his family are about to migrate, Rachel his wife steals the household gods and puts them inside her camel's saddle (Gen 31:30–35). With the narrative of how Abraham is so concerned with the faith of Isaac that he arranges the marriage of Rebekah to Isaac (Gen 24:1–4), we would have thought that Laban, who is the brother of Rebekah, would have transmitted true faith to his two daughters Leah and Rachel. The traditions and beliefs in the surrounding culture shaped and influenced Laban, Leah, and Rachel. Rachel steals the household gods of Laban. As Jacob and his family return to Bethel, Jacob leads his family in removing the hybridity of pagan beliefs by burying the foreign gods and the superstitious rings that the family members possessed. True faith in the pluralistic world must remain solid and secure in the One True God. No hybridity is allowed to compromise the worship of the Lord God!

As Joseph rules in Egypt and his father and brothers migrate to Egypt, Joseph makes sure that they settle in Goshen (Gen 46:31–47:3). In light of the Egyptian cultures, Goshen is a place of safety for them. This might be seen as a protection of ethnicity as the Egyptians detest the shepherds (Gen 46:34). With the blessings from God, the place where the Israelites eventually settle is the best part of the Egyptian land. The seclusion allows the people of God to practice their faith without fear.

Hybridity is part of the challenge for Abraham, Isaac, and Jacob as they settle in the land of Canaan. Joseph has married the daughter of an

Egyptian priest On. This might influence the religious beliefs of Joseph. But even with the possibility of hybridity factors that may influence his walk with God, Joseph holds on to his faith, trusting the God of Abraham, the God of Isaac, and the God of Jacob (Gen 50:20). The patriarchal story ends with Joseph walking with the God who leads.

Mosaic Era: Trusting the God Who Delivers

The sojourning of Israelites in the land of Canaan describes their lives in Patriarchal era, whereas diaspora and migration depict their existence in the Mosaic era. In the Mosaic era, God delivers his people and would like them to trust him wholly. Since he knows their predicament, sees their misery, and hears their cry, God shows his greatness through the ten plagues in Egypt and his deliverance of the people at the Red Sea. During the exodus event, aside from the Israelite men and women, many other people follow them (Ex 12:37–38). These "other people" include many non-Israelites. The mixing of races is not an issue, as long as other people groups follow and trust the Lord. At Mount Sinai, he discloses his will for them to be a kingdom of priests and a holy nation (Ex 19:3–6). He reveals his ten commandments and the Covenant Code, giving them a clear instruction on how to live a life pleasing to him in the midst of multi-cultural societies (Exodus 20:1–24:7). Monotheistic faith is demanded. The purpose and reason for such disclosure is to ensure that their faith is in the Lord God who delivered them from Egypt.

The forced diaspora of the Israelites, settling in Egypt, deeply impact the theological practices and beliefs of the people. With Moses staying on the mountain forty days and forty nights, the prevailing Egyptian beliefs come through in the request of the people to make gods who may lead them forward. Casting the shape of a calf is the result of hybrid learning in Egypt. At Mount Sinai, God clearly commands that they shall not have any idols before him. Aaron even explains it as a simple act of throwing all the gold into the fire and the golden calf comes out (Ex 32:22–24). Yet the crafting of a golden calf would take a long time. Is this not the influence of Egyptian beliefs concerning concrete symbols that influence Aaron?

With a new generation about to enter the land, Moses gives them serious teaching on the greatness and love of God. The whole book of Deuteronomy is the sermon of Moses to the younger generation to encourage them to love God. God shows his love by giving them the land that he promised to the patriarchs. The people of God have to remind themselves of the *Shema*, and they are to love the Lord with all their heart, their soul, and their might (Deut 6:4–5). The people of God have to live a different lifestyle than the inhabitants of Canaan. Facing the challenges of the hybridity of cultures, they are to trust the God who delivers.

Pre-Monarchical Era: Serving the God Who Gives

God gives the land to the people. With Joshua leading them into the land that the Lord has promised, they are able to settle in the land and find rest (Josh 21:43–45). The issue facing the people of God during this era is the lifestyle of the Canaanites. As the servant-leader of the people of God, Joshua reminds them to make the right decision to follow and serve the Lord faithfully. He gives them a choice on the issue of hybridity in their beliefs by referring to the gods of the Chaldeans, the gods in Canaan, the gods in Egypt. He sets an example himself with the words: "As for me and my household, we will serve the Lord (Josh 24:15).

During the time of the judges, the people live among the Canaanites. Everyone did whatever pleased them in their own eyes. Hybridity is so prevalent as the people intermarry with the Canaanites (Judg 3:5–6). The religiosity of the Ammonites influences the vow of Jephthah as he sacrifices his own daughter just like what the Ammonites would do for some special request to their gods (Judg 11: 31–35). In the midst of darkness, Ruth, a Moabite widow, dares to proclaim, "Your people will be my people, your God will be my God" (Ruth 1:16).

Facing a strong Philistine culture in the land of Canaan, the people of God trust the power of the Ark rather than the God who created the Ark. The way the Israelites treat the Ark shows the influence of the hybrid culture of the Philistines. At Mizpah, Samuel confronts them to put away their Baals and Ashtoreths and serve God only (1 Sam 7:2). Even as they hope to follow the culture of the day in having a king, Samuel challenges them to take on the right attitude within a hybrid culture. The prophet reminds them to fear, serve, and follow the Lord their God (1 Sam 12:6–17).

The sedentary life differs from the nomadic life in the Patriarchal and Mosaic era. It might be easier for the Israelites to face the onslaught of cultures and beliefs with a patriarch who would be a model for them to follow or with a servant of the Lord like Moses to guide them. With sedentary life, even with the leadership of Joshua and Samuel, the influence of Canaanite cultures brings about hybridity in their religions.

Hence, their ways of trusting God, may include other beliefs of the Canaanites living in their midst. Nevertheless, the people have to be reminded that they ought to serve the God who gives.

Monarchical Era: Praising the God Who Shepherds

The Lord God reminds Samuel that the biblical culture differs from the prevailing culture that looks at external appearance and noticeable height. As Samuel enters the house of Jesse, no one would imagine that David would be selected and anointed as the king. The biblical culture differs from Canaanite worldly cultures. The life of David as a shepherd boy prepares him to be the kingly servant who shepherds the people of God. The fight of David against Goliath illustrates his faith in the living God. Many Davidic psalms express his trust in the Great Shepherd who cares for him (Ps 16, 23). Book 1 in the book of Psalms praises the Creator God who creates the moon, sun, and starry hosts (Ps 8, 19).

The cultural influence of the Philistines affects the transport of the Ark back to Jerusalem. Though they put it on a new cart, this is not the teaching of the Torah (2 Sam 6:3). The Ark of the Covenant, as a sacred symbol of God's presence, is to be carried on the shoulders of the Levites (Lev 4:5–6; 7:9). Living in the land of Canaan, the Israelites found it easy to adopt the influential culture of the day. The thinking and beliefs of the Philistines have deeply persuaded them without checking the teaching of the Torah. The people of God may have followed the Lord inwardly, but outwardly they follow the culture of the day.

The divine blessings for the Davidic descendants, such as Solomon and Rehoboam, must not be shaped with the hybridity of the society by accepting the norms of the Canaanites. Unfortunately, they incorporated the culture of power, sex, and aggression of Canaan. In God's design at the Garden of Eden, marriage means one man and one woman even with the command and blessing of many descendants (Gen 2:22–25). The Lord God as the Shepherd wants the royal king to be different from the power-starved culture of the day. As the servant-king, his role means being an example of not lording it over his brothers (Deut 17:14–20). God wants his people to trust the God who shepherds.

Exilic Era: Worship the God Who Lives

In the exilic era, Ezekiel is the most interesting prophet in relation to hybridity. In Ezekiel, we are introduced to the four living creatures. Clear and vibrant descriptions are given to the four living creatures.

They have legs, wings, and arms, and yet also wheels moving. When the living creatures move, the sound of their wings is like the roar of rushing waters, like the voice of the Almighty. Above the expanse over their heads is what looks like a throne of sapphire. There is neither any prototype of these creatures in Babylonian temples nor in any other Near Eastern art forms. The purpose of the living creatures, contra the death art figures in Babylonian temples, is to point to their even movements under the guidance of the spirit. The Almighty and Glorious God is above and supported by his creation. Instead of worshipping the creatures of Babylon, the four living creatures are worshipping the Almighty God (Ezek 1:22–28).[2]

Many psalms are written reflecting what the psalmists understand and feel during the exilic era. In the Mosaic era, God teaches the people through Moses that he is the only God (Exod 20:1–3). In the earlier era, God is the King of all the earth (Ps 47:7). In contrast to the gods in Babylon, "the Lord is the great God, the great king above all gods" (Ps 95:3). The Lord God is "to be feared above all gods" (Ps 96:4). The gods are to worship the Lord who reigns on high (Ps 97:7). In the context of hybridity, the Lord God is the one and only to be worshipped and feared!

Hybridity, during the exilic era, may have affected the lifestyle and thought pattern of the people of God, who perceive alternatives to their faith. But for most of them, the psalmists remind the people of God to worship the King of kings and the God of gods! Compared with those who follow other gods, the people of God should only worship the God who lives.

Post-Exilic Era: Celebrate the God Who Cares

Malachi the prophet condemns the people for marrying "the daughter of the foreign god" (Mal 2:11). Faith rather than ethnicity is the issue here.[3] Ezra and Nehemiah return to Jerusalem with the two groups of returnees. Both reformists are trying to get rid of the hybridity of the accepted norms

---

2 Iaian M. Duguid, *Ezekiel, NIV Application Commentary* (Grand Rapids: Zondervan, 1999), 56–60, compared the static temple imagery of Isaiah and motion-filled imagery of Ezekiel in Ezekiel 1 wherein the living creatures are the enforcer of God's judgment.

3 The interpretive issue is whether Malachi is condemning marrying a foreign woman, or belief that may result from marrying a foreign woman. See Joseph Too Shao and Rosa Ching Shao, *Joel, Nahum, & Malachi. Asia Bible Commentary,* (Manila: Asia Theological Association, 2013), 112–13. For discussion on other possibility, see Ralph L. Smith, *Micah-Malachi, Word Biblical Commentary* (Nashville: Thomas Nelson, 1984), 321–22.

in marrying the people groups in Jerusalem. The key challenge is to restore them back to real faith in God with a clear understanding.

Looking at it superficially, we may make a quick conclusion concerning the rigidity of the returned community in throwing hybrid cultures away. But checking the names of the first returnees that appear in both Ezra and Nehemiah, we will recognize that there are many people groups other than the Jews that are accepted in their community (Ezra 2, Neh 7).[4]

In the reading of the Torah, Ezra and Nehemiah are practical enough not to tighten down with their traditions of reading at the temple, which was the expected place of worship. Ezra read the Torah at the square before the Water Gate. Before the assembly, in front of men and women and all who are able to understand, the Torah of Moses is read before them. If the Torah were read at the temple, only the men would be able to hear it. Men and women, including the children who understand, should celebrate the God who cares.

Conclusion

For the Israelites, living with so many people groups around them would definitely force them to face the challenge of hybridity. Some hybridity in cultures is good for them. Marrying other people groups, when also bringing them to the fear of the Lord, does not negatively affect the faith of God's people in the Lord God. Hence, the *Missio Dei* is for the people of God to trust the Lord through their daily lives. Across each era, the Israelites are living as God's chosen people amid different cultures. The Lord continues to reveal himself to them as the God who is alive and cares for them.

---

4 See Joseph Shao, "An Asian Reading of the Theological Themes of Nehemiah," in *Light for Our Path: The Authority, Inspiration, Meaning and Mission of Scripture.* Edited by Bruce Nicholls, Julie Belding, and Joseph Shao (Manila: Asia Theological Association, 2011), 119-29.

BIBLIOGRAPHY

Duguid, Iaian M. *Ezekiel. NIV Application Commentary* (Grand Rapids: Zondervan, 1999), 56–60.

Shao, Joseph Too, and Rosa Ching Shao. *Joel, Nahum, & Malachi*, Asia Bible Commentary. (Manila: Asia Theological Association, 2013).

Shao, Joseph. "An Asian Reading of the Theological Themes of Nehemiah," in *Light for Our Path: The Authority, Inspiration, Meaning and Mission of Scripture*. Edited by Bruce Nicholls, Julie Belding, and Joseph Shao (Manila: Asia Theological Association, 2011), 119-29.

Smith, Ralph L. *Micah-Malachi, Word Biblical Commentary* (Nashville: Thomas Nelson, 1984), 321–22.

von Rad, Gerhard. *Old Testament Theology* Vol 1–2 (New York: Harper & Row, 1962-65).

ABOUT THE AUTHOR

DR. JOSEPH SHAO is the President Emeritus of the Biblical Seminary of the Philippines where he served as President from 1990–2019. He earned his PhD at the Hebrew Union College. He was the fourth General Secretary of the Asia Theological Association. He is very much involved in missions, serving as a member of the Board of CCOWE and also serves as the Chair of SIM-Philippines.

CHAPTER 2 | T. V. Thomas

Jesus Christ and Hybridity

We live in a world where there is a growing interest in ancestry. Some are motivated by pure curiosity. Others are trying to find meaning to their personal lives in a world of fractured family relationships and disintegrating trends in society. Then there are others who are seeking significance because they are connected to someone who was significant.

For many, genealogies make a dull subject for reading. To Jews it would have been of the utmost importance. The Jews took genealogy and ancestry super seriously. They kept extensive genealogies to establish a person's heritage, inheritance, legitimacy and rights. After the conquest of Canaan, it was important for Israelites to determine a family's place of residence. God through Moses required the occupation of the land to be according to tribes, families and father's houses. (Num 26:52–56)

In certain cases, the transfer of property required accurate knowledge of one's pedigree. We know that certain offices were hereditary— priesthood and kings, e.g. After the return from the Babylonian Exile, a person had to prove their priestly descent to access their privileges of priesthood.

Genealogy of Jesus

In a tribal community like Israel, it was a man's genealogy that gave the person's identification and location. Therefore, it is not surprising then to see that the New Testament places great emphasis upon the ancestry and genealogy of Jesus Christ.

The apostle Paul explains the ancestry of Jesus in the book of Romans:

> concerning His Son, who was born of a descendant of David according to the flesh, who was declared the Son of God with power by the resurrection from the dead, according to the Spirit of holiness, Jesus Christ our Lord. (Rom 1:3–4, NASB)

The writer to the Hebrews refers to the ancestry of Jesus from the tribe of Judah:

> For it is evident that our Lord was descended from Judah, a tribe with reference to which Moses spoke nothing concerning priests. And this is clearer still, if another priest arises according to the likeness of Melchizedek, who has become such not on the basis of a law of physical requirement, but according to the power of an indestructible life. For it is attested of Him, "You are a priest forever according to the order of Melchizedek." (Heb 7:14–17, NASB)

The story of the earthly life of Jesus of Nazareth is related to Jewish history by a series of genealogies in the Gospels. It is very specific in Matthew and Luke (Matt 1:1–7 and Luke 3:23–38) and it is implicit in Mark's and John's Gospels. (Mark 1:1 and John 1:1) The genealogies of Jesus in Matthew and Luke were compiled from the accessible official public Jewish records which were kept in Jerusalem.[1] They were accessed long before the destruction of Jerusalem in AD 70.

The two genealogies of Matthew and Luke are similar but yet they are also different in at least six ways.

1. Matthew's genealogy is shorter than Luke's because it only goes back to Abraham while Luke's genealogy goes back to Adam. The Gospel of Matthew opens with Christ's family tree.[2] This is quite understandable because Matthew was writing with the Jews as his primary audience. This is why Matthew begins the

---

1 E. M. Blaiklock, *Understanding the New Testament: Luke* (London: Scripture Union, 1966),10.

2 Michael Card, *Luke: The Gospel of Amazement* (Downers Grove, IL: IVP, 2011), 61.

line of descent with Abraham the Patriarch and does not trace it back to Adam as Luke does. Matthew was trying to convince the Jews that Jesus was the prophesied Messiah, and King, the very Son of Abraham. He ties promises and fulfillment. New Testament scholar William Barclay captures it most succinctly:"[3] To Matthew, Jesus was the possession of the Jews; to Luke, he was the possession of all mankind, because his line is traced back not to the founder of the Jewish nation but the founder of the human race." In Matthew, Jesus comes as a son of Abraham—the father of Jews, and in Luke as a son of Adam—the father of all people.

2. Luke pushes the pedigree of Jesus past David, past Abraham, on to the first man, Adam who is literally called the "son of God" in Luke 3:38. Luke wrote for the Greeks who worshipped human perfection. So, Luke presents Jesus to them as "son of man," the perfect man who is also divine. Luke stresses the real humanity of Jesus and He was not a phantom or demi-god.[4]

3. Matthew traces Christ's genealogy through the legal and regal lines of his foster-father, Joseph. Matthew connects Joseph to King David
. by his son, Solomon born of Bathsheba, the wife of Uriah, a Hittite.

4. While Matthew traces the family tree through Joseph, Luke traces the family tree through the line of Mary to David via Solomon's younger brother, Nathan, by the same mother, Bathsheba, the wife of Uriah, a Hittite.

5. Both genealogies of Matthew and Luke diverge after David and converge for two generations in Shealtiel and Zerubbabel. (Matt 1:12, 13; Luke 3:27)

6. What is unique is that Matthew includes women in his genealogy.

Women in Matthew's Geneaology

The most amazing thing is Matthew includes five women in his genealogy of Jesus. Women did not appear in Jewish genealogies. Women were merely the possession of her father or her husband. Often, a woman had no legal rights; she was regarded not as a person but as a thing. This explains why in the regular form of morning prayer, the Jewish man thanked God that he had not been born as a Gentile, a

---

3 William Barclay, *The Gospel of Luke* (Philadelphia, PA: Westminster, 1975), 41.

4 Leon Morris, *The Gospel According to St. Luke* (London: IVP, 1974), 101.

slave or a woman. So, Matthew went counter-cultural in presenting this genealogy with five women.

> *Judah was the father of Perez and Zerah by Tamar, Perez was the father of Hezron, and Hezron the father of Ram. Ram was the father of Amminadab, Amminadab the father of Nahshon, and Nahshon the father of Salmon. Salmon was the father of Boaz by Rahab, Boaz was the father of Obed by Ruth, and Obed the father of Jesse. Jesse was the father of David the king. David was the father of Solomon by Bathsheba who had been the wife of Uriah.*

> *Jacob was the father of Joseph the husband of Mary, by whom Jesus was born, who is called the Messiah.* (Matt 1:3–6, 16, NASB)

What is particularly intriguing is that these women are included when prominent matriarchs like Sarah, Rebekah, Leah and Rachel are omitted from the genealogy of Jesus.

Unlike Luke, Matthew lists women who are Gentiles and sinners. Matthew contains four women … each with something counting against them and with Mary being the exception. All four women contributed to the hybridity in Christ's genealogy.

1. Tamar
Tamar, a Canaanite, was the daughter-in-law of Judah, one of Jacob's sons. She was the widowed wife of Judah's son, Er. Tamar seduced her father-in-law Judah by hiding her identity (Gen 38) One of the twins born to Tamar by Judah was Perez. He was in the direct line of the ancestry of David, and hence of Christ.

2. Rahab
Rahab is the Canaanite prostitute in Jericho who is mentioned in Joshua 2:1–21. She protected the spies from the agents of the king of Jericho in exchange for safety of herself and her family. At the fall of Jericho, Joshua kept his promise and spared Rahab and her relatives (Josh 6:17, 22–25). Rahab became the wife of Salmon and the mother of Boaz. Rahab the Canaanite was the great-great-grandmother of David.

3. Ruth
Due to a severe famine in Judah, Elimelech and his wife Naomi with their two sons from Bethlehem moved into the neighboring country of Moab for economic survival. Unfortunately, Elimelech prematurely dies and Naomi was left with the two sons. The two fatherless sons married

women of Moab (Ruth 1:4).[5] In marrying women of Moab these two Jews sinned against the Mosaic Law which prohibited such practice (Deut 7:3; 23:3). Ruth belonged to an alien and hated people, the idolatrous Moabites. As a Moabitess, Ruth was debarred from the congregation of the Lord until the tenth generation (Deut 23:3). With her marriage to Boaz, Ruth, the Moabite, became an ancestor of King David and Jesus.

4. Bathsheba

Bathsheba was the wife of Uriah the Hittite, a soldier in King David's army. Attracted by Bathsheba's beauty, King David seduced her and had Uriah placed in the forefront of battle so that he would be killed (2 Sam 11). David then made Bathsheba his wife. The child of their adultery died. Then King David had four other sons with Bathsheba, last of whom was Solomon (2 Sam 12:24). Bathsheba was likely a Hittite herself. She was King Solomon's mother. And so, Christ was a descendant of Bathsheba.

The obvious question that arises from this study is why are these women included in the pedigree of Jesus? The only answer is to acknowledge that the grace of God took these women and wove their lives into the ancestry of our Lord Jesus. The blood of these women flowed in the veins of Jesus just as the blood of Abraham and David did. So, several hybridities were in the lineage of the Lord Jesus. In fact, the lineage of Christ is comprised of men, women, adulteresses, prostitutes, heroes and Gentiles. This is the fulfillment of the promise that God made to Abraham in Genesis 12:3 (NASB), "And I will bless those who bless you, and the one who curses you I will curse. And in you all the families of the earth will be blessed."

In Matthew 1:21, Jesus is introduced as Savior of all men and women, regardless of race, ethnicity, language or culture. "She will bear a Son; and you shall call His name Jesus, for He will save His people from their sins." (NASB)

The apostle Paul in Galatians 3:8 concludes:

The Scripture, foreseeing that God would justify the Gentiles by faith, preached the gospel beforehand to Abraham, saying, "All the nations will be blessed in you." (NASB)

---

5 Herbert Lockyer, *All the Women of the Bible* (Grand Rapids, MI: Zondervan, 1967), 145.

Again, in Galatians 3:28, the apostle Paul declares:

There is neither Jew nor Greek, there is neither slave nor free man, there is neither male nor female; for you are all one in Christ Jesus. (NASB)

Hybridity is a Blossoming Phenomenon in Our Times

So, hybridity of races, ethnicities, cultures and languages is a not-so-new phenomenon. Western colonialism expedited the emerging of racial, ethnic, cultural and linguistic hybrids around the world. Therefore, new language has emerged. Words like "biracial" and "multicultural" are commonly used. Terms like "Eurasians" (Malaysia), Anglo Indians (India), *Mestizos* (mixed European, African and Native American descent) have emerged. And because of massive polycentric migration, speedy global travel, growing transnationalism, rapid globalization and digital explosion and other factors, racial, ethnic, cultural, and linguistic hybridity is blossoming significantly.

Four Implications of Hybrity for Missio Dei

1. Christ's Great Commission calls us to reach everyone regardless of origin, ancestry or identity.

2. The inclusion of the four Gentile women in Jesus' genealogy strongly persuades us that hybridity mission is something we must pursue.

3. With increased number of marriages between people of different ethnicities and cultures around the world, we cannot ignore them or their children's generation.

4. Even if the hybridity of races, cultures and languages is not a new phenomenon, its missiological focus is still in its infancy.

Conclusion

This is precisely why the Hybridity Consultation was convened by Global Diaspora Network (GDN) to help the Global Church see the hidden unreached hybrid people in society. As GDN, we want to champion the reaching of the hybrid people to be included in Diaspora Missiology.

BIBLIOGRAPHY

Barclay, William. *The Gospel of Luke*. Philadelphia, PA: Westminster, 1975.

———. *The Gospel of Matthew*. Philadelphia, PA: Westminster, 1975.

Blaiklock, E. M. *Understanding the New Testament: Luke*. London: Scripture Union, 1966.

Card, Michael. *Luke: The Gospel of Amazement*. Downers Grove, IL: IVP, 2011.

Gaebelein, Frank E. ed. *The Expositor's Bible Commentary. Volume 8*. Grand Rapids, MI: Zondervan, 1984.

Just, Arthur A. Jr. ed. *Ancient Christian Commentary on Scripture, New Testament III, Luke*. Downers Grove, IL: IVP, 2003.

Lockyer, Herbert. *All the Women of the Bible*. Grand Rapids, MI: Zondervan, 1967.

Marshall, I. Howard. *Commentary on Luke*. Grand Rapids, MI: William B. Eerdmans, 1978.

Morris, Leon. *The Gospel According to St. Luke*. London, UK: IVP, 1974.

ABOUT THE AUTHOR

*Originally from Malaysia, **DR. T. V. THOMAS** studied in Malaysia, India, Canada and the United States. He is the Founder/Director of the Centre for Evangelism & World Mission (founded in 1984) in Regina, Canada. T. V. is Chairman of the Lausanne Movement's Global Diaspora Network (GDN), and chairs the Ethnic America Network (EAN), Global Mobilization Network (GMN) and InterVarsity in Canada. He is also a member of MECO Canada Board, Perspectives Canada National Team and serves as the Multicultural/Intercultural Ministries Consultant for the C&MA in Canada.*

CHAPTER 3 | David S. Lim

The Challenge of Multiplying Disciples by Hybrids in Fulfilling *Missio Dei*
(Exposition of 2 Timothy 2:1–10)

What role can hybrid Christ-followers play in the mission of God (*missio Dei*) in our post-modern pluralistic world full of people on the move? We live in nations with fast-paced and ever fast-changing cultures that have become more complex in the real, virtual and automated worlds, especially for the millennials today! How can we keep our priorities right, so that the hybrids in our diasporas can use their multicultural gifts for the advance of God's kingdom on earth most effectively and strategically?

Gladly the word of God gives us a clear apostolic model in the life and writings of the multicultural Paul, particularly in his letter to his biracial (Greek father and Jewish mother) and multicultural disciple Timothy on how they should do *missio Dei* in the multicultural and multi-religious world of their time. May I suggest that the best text is 2 Timothy 2:1–10, which shows us the three clear instructions of the apostle Paul on what were required for fulfilling *missio Dei* in their context. It can teach us all (especially diasporic hybrids) the way to fulfill the Great Commission in our times and beyond.

I share this message as a hybrid son of the Chinese diaspora in the Philippines, with the distinct advantage of learning to speak five languages in my upbringing in a provincial city: my mother tongue is Fujianese (the lingua franca of Chinese Filipinos); my second language is Hiligaynon, the local dialect; and I learned English, Filipino/Tagalog (the national language), and Mandarin/Pudonghua in school. I have learned to treasure this multilingual heritage as I have used my multiculturalism in my ministries, especially to mobilize the Filipino diaspora to reach the unreached people groups in Asia (mainly in China).

May I also explain why I will include the word "simple" in the sub-titles of my message? I believe that our God—who loves the whole world and who wants all humans to be saved, free from sin and knowledgeable of the truth (1 Tim 2:3–4; 2 Pet 3:8–9)—must have designed a simple (not complicated) strategic plan to get the good news of His redemption spread to the ends of the earth (Acts 1:8) at the shortest time possible. So Jesus of Nazareth, the perfect God who became the perfect human (Second Adam) modeled for us this simple plan, and trained His disciples (almost all rural folks in remote Galilee) to do the same: "[Like the way] the Father sent me, so I send you" (John 20:21).

Hence, here are the three aspects of doing *missio Dei* that the hybrid Apostle Paul instructed his hybrid disciple Timothy, which can be applied to all of us who seek to do the same in our time: simple spirituality, simple strategy, and simple structure.

1. Simple Spirituality: Focus on Mature Discipleship (v. 1)

Above all, the Apostle Paul reminded Timothy to be a confident mature disciple of Jesus, thus: "You then, my son, be strong in the grace that is in Christ Jesus" (v. 1).

For Paul, true spirituality simply entails two dimensions of mature discipleship: biblical lifeview and Christlike lifestyle: In 1 Timothy 4:4–5 (NKJV), Paul already reminded Timothy of what kind of "full of grace" (*charis*) lifeview that a disciple of Jesus should have: "For every creature of God is good, and nothing is to be refused if it is received with thanksgiving; for it is sanctified by the word of God and prayer." This worldview was highlighted by Paul since he was confronting the false teachings on food and marriage that were emerging in the early church (1 Tim 1–3). Paul had been teaching his disciples that those who grow into "the grace in Christ Jesus" will have a positive or appreciative outlook of the world, and thus they can boldly face the world with hope and confidence.

Paul taught that mature spirituality is to simply be thankful to God constantly for all He has given to all humanity in all generations.

We can perceive God's "common grace" upon all natural resources created and nurtured by God (*creatio Dei*), as well as all cultural artifacts and achievements (including our modern superjets, skyscrapers and smartphones) made, marketed and used by human beings (both Christians and non-Christians alike) made in the image of God (*imago Dei*).

Yet in this sinful world, there will always be sectors and segments that are sinful, messy or evil, but all these can be purified by and consecrated to God (for *missio Dei*) through two means of grace: obedience to the word of God and prayer (to God in Jesus' name). Discipleship is to simply teach every believer to use these two spiritual weapons to break down any (intellectual as well as spiritual) strongholds (2 Cor 10:3–5; Eph 6:10–18) in their lifeviews that hinder their walk with God. In Greek, "be strong" means "be endowed with power (*dynamis*)" or "empowered" to do miraculous or extra-human works for God.

The other dimension of discipleship is to live a Christlike lifestyle: "grace that is in Christ Jesus." In another text, Paul says, "Him we preach, warning every man and teaching every man in all wisdom, that we may present every man perfect in Christ Jesus. To this end I also labor, striving according to His working which works in me mightily" (Col 1:28–29, NKJV). Discipleship aims at producing complete Christlikeness in every believer's life (v. 27; cf. Rom 12:1–2), and this can be achieved simply through training them to develop a good devotional life—to handle the word of God prayerfully (2 Tim 2:15), so they can overcome false teachings and temptations to do wrong, as Paul describes in the rest of this chapter (vv. 11–26). Hence biblical lifeview and Christlike lifestyle constitutes the DNA of the simple spirituality that should characterize all of Christ's mature disciples.

2. Simple Strategy: Focus on Disciple Multiplication Movement (vv. 2–7)

Secondly, Paul reminded Timothy to focus on the main role of any Christ-follower: to become a   disciple-maker (not just to be a disciple): "And the things you have heard me say in the presence of many wit-nesses entrust to reliable people who will also be qualified to teach others" (v. 2). Timothy should be passing on what he has received to others who can be discipled to make disciples with a multiplier effect, hence the phrase "Disciple Multiplication Movement (DMM)," mainly popularized in Robert Coleman's book, *God's Master Plan for World Evangelism*.

Paul then proceeded to give three illustrations of disciple-making (Christ-centered living): "You therefore must endure hardship as a good soldier of Jesus Christ. No one engaged in warfare entangles himself with the affairs of this life, that he may please him who enlisted him as a soldier. And also if anyone competes in athletics, he is not crowned unless he competes according to the rules. The hardworking farmer must be first to partake of the crops. Consider what I say, and may the Lord give you understanding in all things" (vv. 3–7, NKJV).

The task of "making disciples" is tough, for discipleship is a lifelong process (hence it's foolish to try to monopolize the discipling of someone for life). Not only does it entail patience and hard work, there are many distractions to divert us from this most strategic plan in *missio Dei*. Hence Paul used the analogies of soldiers preparing for a spiritual battle (vv. 3–4), athletes competing in a spiritual marathon (v. 5), and farmers laboring to reap a spiritual harvest (v. 6). In all these, "spiritual growth" requires the discipline and the concentration to gain the victory (in winning a war, a race and a good harvest).

Thankfully it is possible (even easy and simple) to multiply disciples, for disciples are made only in small groups, as small as "two or three." Disciples can grow spiritually fast: for the DNA of spiritual maturity can be developed in contexts where intimacy and openness are nurtured regularly by the practice of loving one another, teaching one another, submitting to one another, and even confessing sins one to another (cf. John 13:34–35; 1 Cor 14:26–33; Eph 5:15–21; Heb 10:24–25; Jas 5:16), as they use their spiritual gifts to serve each other in small groups.

Practically, the group should not be more than twelve to fourteen members. What they need to learn from their discipler(s) are: (a) personal devotions: how to experience God and walk with Him daily 24/7 as they grow spiritually through *lectio divina*, the devotional use of the Bible; (b) leading group devotions: how to effectively guide one's family and other small groups of Christ-followers to grow spiritually as they discuss life concerns in the light of the Scriptures; and (c) friendship evangelism: how to do personal witnessing to those who do not have faith in Christ yet. After being discipled in one group for a while, each Christ-follower should be able (and empowered, or given authority) to develop their own disciple-making groups. It is also more strategic to form new groups with each new convert to Christ.

Actually, this was how our Lord Jesus planned to win the world to himself—through this simple disciple-multiplying strategy:

He called twelve ordinary people (rural folks, except for urbanite and educated Matthew and Judas). After discipling them to do what he did (Mark 3:13–15), he sent them out two by two to make twelve disciples each (Matt 9:35–10:16). They succeeded so that he was able to send out "72 others," not the original 12 (Luke10:1–17). If the "72 others" were sent out two-by-two, that's thirty-six pairs going forth to make twelve new disciples each; there would be 432 (36x12) disciples in all! We read in 1 Corinthians 15:6, that after the resurrection, our Lord appeared to more than 500 brethren! If these 500 were to pair off, that's 250 making twelve new disciples each, they would be able to disciple exactly 3,000 new converts! And that's exactly what happened on the birthday of the church at Pentecost: all converts were baptized immediately, since the apostles knew they would all be followed up and discipled in about 250 house churches in Jerusalem ("from house to house," Acts 2:41–47). No wonder their numbers increased DAILY!

I'm glad that I learned this simple DMM strategy while I was a college student (1970–74). With a prayer partner, I started to form "cell groups" and was trained in Kawayan Camp (1972) of Inter-Varsity Christian Fellowship-Phil. (IVCF) on how to multiply them effectively. By the time I graduated in 1974, we had seven cell groups. Without any more contact with our succeeding disciples, I learned five years later that the Light and Salt Christian Fellowship (LSCF) was awarded as one of the top three student organizations and was holding evangelistic concerts in the school's gymnasium!

There are now many DMM programs that can be downloaded from the internet nowadays, especially "Training for Trainers" (T4T). Just go to YouTube or do Google search. My "Effective Tentmaking Made Simple" model may be found at: www.davidlim53.wordpress.com.

3. Simple Structure: Focus on House Church Networks (vv. 8–10)

And thirdly, Paul also showed Timothy that he can do DMM anywhere and everywhere, and through this letter, he taught that DMM can be done even in prison: "Remember that Jesus Christ, of the seed of David, was raised from the dead according to my gospel, for which I suffer trouble as an evildoer, even to the point of chains; but the word of God is not chained. Therefore I endure all things for the sake of the elect, that they also may obtain the salvation which is in Christ Jesus with eternal glory" (vv. 8–10, NKJV). The Word can't be "chained," limited or restrained by space and time; it is omnipresent and eternal!

For Paul and the early Christ-followers, the church is formed wherever two or three are gathered for prayer and the Word (and discipline, Matt 18:15–20). While in prison, Paul evangelized and made disciples there, for he had been forming house church networks (HCN) wherever he "resided." For wherever God's Word is applied prayerfully, God's grace prevails and Christ is present. And where Christ is, there is heaven; and where God's will is done, the kingdom is realized on earth!

For the first three centuries of the Jesus movement, his followers usually met in homes (*oikoi*) and simply met anywhere, anytime, anyhow. *Oikos* is best translated as "household" for it is composed not just of the family, but also of friends, tenants and slaves, as seen in the instructions given in Ephesians 5:22–6:9 and Colossians 3:18–4:1. This means that churches that met in each oikos crossed many cultural barriers, particularly gender, age, class and ethnicity as they gathered and "broke bread" together around the table as equals (cf. Gal 3:28). This is how Christ's reign is to be incarnated in every structure of society, particularly in places of residence (neighborhoods), and especially after the Industrial Revolution, also in places of work, study and/or leisure (in short, workplaces).

DMMs can multiply fast only when we develop and maintain simple structures. Jesus, Paul, Timothy and their contemporaries in the early church did not develop elaborate structures that would need big investments and high maintenance costs, which would have hindered DMMs. There is really no need to develop liturgies, chapels, clerical hierarchy, worship services, etc.; these often result in disempowering the "laity," thereby contradicting the doctrine of "the priesthood of all believers."

The early Christ-followers simply focused on building friendships and making disciples through DMMs. When persecution arose, the first disciples in Jerusalem just brought their faith back to their hometowns (Acts 8:1,4). The first missionaries (Barnabas and Paul) were sent intentionally from Antioch (Acts 13:1ff) as tentmakers as they went mainly to the cities where the Jewish diaspora existed. And other apostles most likely just followed the trade routes which their fellow Jews took as they migrated for business and residence. As priests, every Christ-follower can have direct access to God (through the Word and prayer) and minister in Jesus' name to one another and to the world wherever God sends them.

As a fourth generation Christ-follower who migrated to the Philippines from China, my father showed me that it is possible to be a hybrid disciple-maker who can impact two cultures for Jesus. He migrated as a high school teacher to teach science subjects in a Christian school in Manila, took accounting when he settled in Bacolod, and became an office manager in a car repair shop, while serving as the chief elder of the Chinese Filipino church there. He led our family devotions twice a week (on Tuesdays and Fridays), which included me, my mother's parents and my two siblings. With my mom, who was a second-generation Chinese Filipino who could not read or write in Chinese, they educated me in Filipino schools, and their ministry among Filipino churches exposed me to the local culture and ministries since childhood.

Most significantly, my dad showed that through friendship evangelism, he could lead one Chinese family to Christ at a time until they got baptized at our local church, and then he would find a new head of a family (including the shoe-repair man in our neighborhood) to evangelize and disciple personally. I estimated that 70 percent of the families at our church were won for Christ through his habit of winning "persons of peace" (Luke 10:4b–6) as a diasporic "lay missionary" (v. 7). I later learned that he was the product of the revival ministry of Dr. John Sung (who impacted Chinese Christianity in southern China and southeast Asia) during his teenage years. John Sung grouped his "converts" into teams of three, and sent them to share their testimonies and preach the gospel in the surrounding areas. I believe that like discipleship, revivals are spread also through small groups (especially two or three), as new disciples learn how to share their faith on-the-job!

As a mission mobilizer since 1994 when I organized China Ministries International-Philippines, I have trained ordinary Christ-followers to become cross-cultural disciple-makers, following the "incarnational missions" model of Jesus (Luke 10:1–9) and Paul (in this text). When I was the National Director of the Philippine Missions Association (PMA) from 2011–2014, I had already been working since 2001 to implement our vision and flagship program of mobilizing, training and deploying 10 percent of the overseas Filipino workers (OFWs) to become effective tentmakers (cross-cultural lay missionaries) who can catalyze DMMs in HCNs (we use the model of "companies of three," per our main manual, *A Higher Purpose for Your Overseas Job*) where they live and work.

The "HCN through DMM" mission strategy has been spreading in the HCNs throughout Asia, especially in India, Japan, Thailand, Cambodia and Indonesia—mostly through hybrids! Most especially, it is also being used by the Back to Jerusalem Movements of many HCNs in China nowadays. They learned to do DMM by sending young people in their late teens to go two by two to saturate their respective regions, particularly from 1975–1995. As they now send young adults and couples as professionals and business people to the unreached people groups, they view themselves as "ants, bees and earthworms" to bless the lands and peoples that God will send them to. But most of them would need cross-cultural training, because most of them have mono-cultural upbringing.

Conclusion

Every time we (especially hybrids) move residence or location for whatever reasons (studies, employment, business, marriage, migration, political or economic crisis, natural disaster, etc.), we could be effective disciple-makers wherever God sends and places us. With just a bit more training on specific cross-cultural issues, we can do disciple-making and multiply house church networks among different socio-religio-cultural groups and peoples. After all, that's what our Lord Jesus told all his disciples to do: "to make disciples of all nations" (Matt 28:19). For me, the failure of the global church to focus on following this simple strategic plan for world evangelization is the main reason why there are still so many unreached peoples in the world to this day.

Hybrids have the distinct advantage of being the "bridges of God," as missiologist Donald McGavran originally perceived in his book with the same title, and can serve as excellent "bridge builders," as mentioned by our anthropologist colleague Miriam Adeney at this conference. Though often discriminated against, and also bullied by their peers, hybrids usually grow up naturally with the blessing of being exposed to and immersed in two or more different cultures (each with varied values, lifestyles, and perspectives) from two or more ethnic groups. Thus we can look forward to bigger harvests as our millennial hybrids can be used of God to naturally multiply DMMs in HCNs among more people groups and subcultures.

Sadly, many Christians live non-missional lives today. Instead of living as victorious witnesses of Christ (read: disciple-makers), they remain immature baby Christians who need to be constantly cared for by others. They are still self-centered and self-focused, when in fact they should be serving the Lord and reaching out to others. They fail to enjoy the "abundant life" that Jesus promised: that we should be shining as fruitful, disciple-making Christ-followers in the world (Phil 2:14–16).

We should focus on simply replicating Paul's life goal to multiply disciples in house church networks for Jesus: "I consider my life worth nothing to me, if only I may finish the race and complete the task the Lord Jesus has given me, the task of testifying to the gospel of God's grace" (Acts 20:24). At the end of life, we should be able to say like him, "I have fought the good fight, I have finished the race, I have kept the faith" (2 Tim 4:7). That's the final "victory cry" of a faithful disciple of Jesus who is also an effective disciple-maker for Him!

So let's multiply disciples in simple churches, and just do it! Let's start DMMs and form HCNs. Let's train each Christ-follower to do "friendship evangelism" and to "lead and multiply effective disciple-making groups." May God use each of us to be effective disciple-makers to multiply house church networks in our generation! Most significantly, let's maximize the bridge-building gifts of the biracial and multicultural networks of hybrids to multiply disciples in all nations in our diasporic and multicultural world!

BIBLIOGRAPHY

Addison, Steve. *What Jesus Started: Joining the Movement, Changing the World*. Downers Grove: IVP, 2012.

Allen, Roland. *Missionary Methods: St. Paul's or Ours?* Grand Rapids: Eerdmans, 1962.

_____. *The Spontaneous Expansion of the Church*. Grand Rapids: Eerdmans, 1962.

Claro, Robert. *A Higher Purpose for Your Overseas Job*. Makati: CrossOver, 2003.

Coleman, Robert. *The Master Plan of Evangelism*. Old Tappan, NJ: Revell, 1964.

Gamez, Ana. *Blessing OFWs to Bless the Nations*. Makati: Church Strengthening Ministries, 2012.

Garrison, David. *Church Planting Movements*. Midlothian, VA: WIGTake Resources, 2004.

Gehring, Roger. *House Church and Mission: The Importance of Household Structures in Early Christianity*. Peabody, MA: Hendrickson, 2004.

Hattaway, Paul. *Back to Jerusalem: Called to Complete the Great Commission*. Carlisle: Piquant, 2003.

Lim, David. "Transformational Spirituality: Pauline Spirituality in Asian Contexts." *Asia Theological Association Journal* 7, no. 1. Bangalore: Theological Book Trust, 1999.

_____. "Asia's House Church Movements today." *Asian Missions Advance* 52 (July 2016): 7–12.

McGavran, Donald. *Bridges of God*. London: World Dominion, 1955.

Pantoja, Luis, Jr., Sadiri Joy Tira, and Enoch Wan, eds. *Scattered: The Filipino Global Presence*. Manila: LifeChange, 2004.

Simson, Wolfgang. *Houses That Change the World*. Carlisle: Paternoster, 2001.

Talman, H. and J. J. Travis, eds. *Understanding Insider Movements*. Pasadena: William Carey Library, 2015.

White, Dave. *Anyone Can Lead*. Mandaluyong City: OMF Literature, 2000.

Winter, Ralph, and Stephen Hawthorne, eds. *Perspectives on the World Christian Movement: A Reader*. Pasadena: Wlliam Carey Library, 1988.

Zdero, Rad. *The Global House Church Movement*. Pasadena: William Carey Library, 2004.

ABOUT THE AUTHOR

DAVID S. LIM, PhD, serves as the President of China Ministries International-Philippines (CMI-Phil), which has sent 110 Filipino tentmaker-missionaries to catalyze disciple multiplication movements in the gateway cities of China. He is also the President/ CEO of Asian School for Development and Cross-cultural Studies (ASDECS), which provides post-graduate and certificate level training programs for transformational missions and community development. He is also the Board chairman of Lausanne Philippines, the lead facilitator of the Asian House Church Movement, and serves on the Steering Committee of SEANET, the global network to reach the Buddhist world.

CHAPTER 4 | Steven S. H. Chang

Hybridity and the Gentile Mission in Matthew's Genealogy of Christ

NOTE: This chapter was presented at the Asian Society of Missiology triennial missiological forum in Bali, Indonesia, July 9-12, 2018, and was originally published by Asian Society of Missiology as a chapter in their compendium, Eiko Takamizawa, David S. Lim and Daniel J. Kim (eds), *Christian Mission in Religious Pluralistic Society*, Seoul: East-West Center for Missions Research and Development, 2019. Reprinted with permission.

Biblical scholars have often pointed out that Matthew's genealogy (Matt 1:1–17), far from being a "boring" introduction to the birth of Jesus Christ, is full of significance for the rest of his Gospel. The shape and content of the genealogy invite deeper analysis. Why is the genealogy organized by Abraham, David, and the deportation to Babylon, and by the "fourteen generations" between them? Why are certain women included in the genealogy when other more prominent ones are left out? These problems suggest that Matthew has far more to say in his genealogy of Jesus than most would grasp at first sight.

To dig deeper into the fertile soil of Matthew's genealogy, I propose to consider two perspectives. First, the perspective of missional hermeneutics, a growing discipline that integrates biblical theology and missiology with biblical interpretation, will be intentionally adopted and applied. Second, the perspective of "hybridity," an important concept in diaspora missiology drawn from sociology and postcolonial studies, will be explored in the reading of Matthew's genealogy. It is hoped that a richer understanding of the intention and impact of Matthew's message in a "boring" genealogy will result through this hybridity-mission perspective.

The significance of a hybridity-mission reading of Matthew's genealogy goes beyond biblical studies and should impact how the church thinks about mission to the "other" in a pluralistic setting. This study of Matthew's genealogy shows that from the very beginning, Christian mission understood the importance of inclusion and incarnation in a diverse, hybrid world.

A Missional Reading of Matthew's Genealogy

In a short introductory essay on "Mission and Old Testament Inter-pretation," Chris Wright, a major proponent of missional hermeneutics, outlines four contours of "the Shape of a Missional Hermeneutic."[1] First, a missional hermeneutic relies on the bigger framework of God's mission in the biblical narrative to interpret the various parts of the biblical story. In other words, the grand biblical story bears witness to the mission of God to redeem his creation and thus, how God forms each community in the various biblical stories must be read in the light of the whole. Second, a missional hermeneutic understands that the Bible's purpose is "to equip and shape God's people for their missional witness."[2] That is, the Bible as a missional document served to shape how God's people bore witness to God's mission then, and should be read as such by God's people now. Third, a missional hermeneutic accounts for the "missional location of the Christian community," then and now, giving due importance to the mission location of God's people as they seek to read and understand the Bible. Scripture itself was formed in the missional setting of the first readers,[3] suggesting that readers today should understand Scripture from their missional setting as well. Fourth, missional hermeneutic places the gospel at the center of its interpretive matrix, understanding its critical engagement with cultures in the biblical world and with cultures today.[4] In other words, Scripture, especially the New Testament, is a record of how interpreters engaged their cultures while remaining faithful to the gospel.

In many ways, missional hermeneutic is nothing new. As Wright points out, the New Testament writers themselves were reading the Old

---

1 Christopher J. H. Wright, "Mission and Old Testament Interpretation," in *Hearing the Old Testament: Listening for God's Address*, ed. C. G. Bartholomew and D. J. H. Beldman, (Grand Rapids: Eerdmans, 2012), 180–203.

2 Wright, "Mission and Old Testament Interpretation," 185.

3 Ibid, 186–87.

4 Ibid, 191.

Testament missionally, wrestling with their own mission context, and developing a missional theology along the way. Many of the insights of a missional hermeneutic have been noticed and stated previously by interpreters who seek to listen to what the Bible says about God and his people. Missional hermeneutic has much in common with how the church has read the Scriptures from the New Testament period until today. One can argue that a good biblical theology, wholly requisite for the task of biblical interpretation, has already identified the gospel mission as foundational to the overarching biblical message. Furthermore, a closer look at the world of the first Christians unquestionably paints a picture of a deeply missional community, quite distinct from their pre-decessors, the diaspora Jewish community.[5] Hence, a more intentional missional approach is essential in our reading of Matthew's genealogy.

Traditional readings of Matthew 1:1–17 have focused on the historical features of the genealogy, trying to reconcile the differences with Luke's version or with Matthew's sources. Accordingly, it is thought that Matthew's genealogy focuses selectively on the "royal line" of Jesus while Luke's genealogy on the actual bloodline, or perhaps Mary's line instead of Joseph's. However, a historical reading, while important, does not get at the heart of Matthew's message. Historical conundrums aside, one must admit with David Turner, "Although genuine historical information is provided, the purpose is primarily theological, not chronological."[6] Matthew insinuates much by the distinctive features of his genealogy. Additionally, a missional hermeneutic that sees Matthew as engaged in a missional reading of Israel's Scripture and history (in Jesus' genealogy) for the purpose of equipping the church for God's mission will particularly highlight these distinctive features.

The distinctive features of Matthew's genealogy seem to go in two directions. First, Matthew presents Jesus as the fulfilment of the Jewish messianic hope and the restorer of the Davidic kingdom. Two features point to this message. As most commentators propose, the "son of David" (David being mentioned first and counted twice in the genealogy) speaks to the messianic expectation of the Jews, suggesting

5 Michael F. Bird, *Crossing Over Sea and Land: Jewish Missionary Activity in the Second Temple Period* (Grand Rapids: Baker Academic, 2010), who concludes that Jewish missionary activity was not a "missions movement" and while it formed the backdrop to Christian mission in the first century, the latter was far more intentional about converting the Gentiles.

6 David L. Turner, *Matthew*, BECNT (Grand Rapids: Baker Academic, 2008), 58.

that Jesus is the fulfillment of Jewish messianic hopes.[7] David's kingdom represents something of a highpoint in Jewish history, and certainly, God's covenant with David, that his "throne shall be established forever" (2 Sam 7:16), was a longing of the Jewish people in the first century. In addition, Matthew's insistence on the fourteen generations at each phase of the genealogy, while presenting a difficulty,[8] appears to emphasize the fulfillment of the Davidic kingdom. More than a few commentators have settled with the number fourteen representing David by gematria (dwd in Hebrew amounts to 14 = 4+6+4; David is also fourteenth on the list), indicating a significance similar to the "son of David" reference. Both the title of Jesus as the "son of David" and the fourteen generations between the pivotal persons/events suggest that Matthew portrays Jesus as the Jewish Messiah, who will rescue God's people from their enemies (2 Sam 3:18; Isa 35:4).

Secondly, Matthew presents Jesus as the fulfillment of the universal hope of the Abrahamic promise to be a blessing to all nations. The "son of Abraham" (1:1, 17) points back to the beginnings of God's covenant with the Jewish people (Gen 12:1–3), and perhaps to the priority of faith in God's promise over the law and its requirements (Rom 4:13–25). Viewed from a missional perspective, the reference to Abraham surely anticipates the Great Commission, to make disciples of "all nations" (Matt 28:19), thereby fulfilling the Abrahamic promise that "all tribes" of the earth will be blessed through him (Gen 12:3; 22:18). Further, the reference to the Babylonian exile is often overlooked by commentators. The exile marks the end of David's kingdom, suggesting that what was lost by the exile has now been restored by Jesus. However, from a missional perspective, the exile is also significant for the forced

---

7 E.g., Donald A. Hagner, *Matthew 1–13*, WBC 33a (Dallas: Word, 1998), 9; R. T. France, *The Gospel of Matthew*, NICNT (Grand Rapids: Eerdmans, 2007), 34.

8 The difficulty is more than about historical accuracy (several names are missing and the fourteen generations represent vastly different time periods), but also about what the number implies. Some suggest that three fourteens equal six sevens and thus, Jesus has inaugurated the seventh seven, a period of perfect Sabbath rest. Jesus then is the Lord of the Sabbath (Matt 12:8). Still others suggest that fourteen represents the standard divisions of the line of priests and it may present Jesus as the high priest. The genealogy recognizes Jesus as the Son of God even if the sitting high priest does not (Matt 26:62–63). Still others understand the fourteen as half of the twenty-eight days it takes the moon to wax and wane, suggesting that David's kingdom and the Babylonian exile represent a waxing and waning, with Christ as the new climax. Still others suggest that the number fourteen may simply be a mnemonic device [Craig S. Keener, *The IVP Bible Background Commentary: New Testament*, 2nd ed. (Downers Grove: IVP Academic, 2014), 47.]

dispersion of God's people, in part as judgment but also in part as God's sovereign plan to bless all nations. From this viewpoint, the Babylonian exile may be a reminder to the Jewish Christians that God had sent their forebears to Gentile territories before and for a missional purpose (Jer 29:7). The references to Abraham and to the Babylonian exile then mark the Gentile mission a central theme of Matthew's genealogy, and indeed, signals its importance in the rest of the Gospel.

Matthew's point in the structure around David, Abraham, and the Babylonian exile is missionally significant in that Jesus is the Christ not only for Israel (1:21), but for the Gentiles as well. The universal significance of Jesus is unapologetically signaled from the beginning, and for Matthew, the time of fulfillment has now come. In other words, the generations and numbers point to God's providence "at the right time" (Gal 4:14), especially after the low point of the Babylonian exile. Further, one additional feature, the presence of four women in Matthew's genealogy, supports this reading.

No one doubts that Matthew is saying something important by his inclusion of Tamar, Rahab, Ruth, and Bathsheba in Jesus' genealogy, especially when one considers both that including women in genealogies was unusual and that other more prominent women in Israel's history, such as Sarah and Rebekah, were passed over. While many options have been put forward,[9] the most compelling is that Matthew appeals for Jewish involvement in the Gentile mission. For Matthew, the women represent a Gentile presence in the genealogy of the Jewish Messiah. Tamar, Rahab, and Ruth are well known from Israel's history as good Gentiles who had turned to the faith. Naming Bathsheba as "Uriah's wife" may be a reminder of her Gentile status as the wife of a Hittite. The competing view that these women were included as "sinners" has weaknesses, but then Gentiles by definition were sinners (Matt 6:7; Gal 2:15). Matthew's inclusion of Gentile women may also point to the history of Jewish mission. Unlike the past Jewish attempts to draw in Gentiles, the new faith proclaims the Messiah for all nations with the intention of converting Gentiles. Grant Osborne affirms this missional reading, "The four women were all Gentiles or related to Gentiles, and this leads into a major motif in the first gospel, the preparation of the new community of God to fulfill the Abrahamic covenant (to be a

---

9 See W. D. Davies and Dale C. Allison Jr., *The Gospel According to Saint Matthew*, vol. 1., ICC (London: T&T Clark, 1988), 170–72; Hagner, *Matthew 1–13*, 10–11.

blessing to all nations) by taking the gospel directly to the Gentiles."[10] Matthew's Gospel draws attention to the Gentile mission as the major reason to include these women in the genealogy.

Indeed, the Gentile mission aligns well with the historical circumstances of Matthew's Gospel. If the likely provenance of the Gospel is Antioch,[11] then Matthew is writing to the diaspora Jews of the third leading city of the Roman Empire, behind Rome and Alexandria. It is estimated that some 10 percent of the 500,000 population of Syrian Antioch were Jews.[12] The mission to the Gentile began with the diaspora Jewish church of Antioch (Acts 11) and Matthew was appealing to the diaspora Jewish Christians to "make disciples of all nations" (28:19). In line with this, the book of Matthew, beginning from the genealogy, was written with the dual purpose of demonstrating both that Jesus was the fulfillment of the Jewish messianic hopes, restoring the Davidic kingdom, and that this fulfillment goes beyond Jewish boundaries to include the Gentiles, upholding the promise made to Abraham. Affirming the double purpose of Matthew's genealogy, this chapter will now consider the concept of hybridity.

Hybridity and the Gentile Mission

Hybridity has become an important concept in understanding cultures, especially in post-colonial criticism.[13] The concept is not new. As races and cultures mix, civilizations from ancient times have shown an

---

10 Grant R. Osborne, *Matthew*, ZECNT (Grand Rapids: Zondervan, 2010), 70. See also Sang-In Lee, "Matthew's Concern for Mission by Including the Four Women: Matthew 1:1–17," *Torch Trinity Journal* 10 (2007): 49–74, who concludes, "…by including the four women Matthew's focus is on demonstrating God's plan of universal salvation: everyone, Jews and Gentiles are welcome by illustrating that the Messiah also is connected with Gentile forebears" (69).

11 D. A. Carson and Douglas J. Moo, *An Introduction to the New Testament*, 2nd ed. (Grand Rapids: Zondervan, 2005), 151–52.

12 The population estimate of Antioch in the first century vary widely, as does the number of Jews there. See Eckhard J. Schnabel, *Early Christian Mission*, Vol. 1, *Jesus and the Twelve* (Downers Grove: IVP Academic, 2004), 784–85.

13 Avtar Brah and Annie E. Coombes, eds., *Hybridity and Its Discontents: Politics, Science, Culture* (London: Routledge, 2000), 1, "It has become a key concept in cultural criticism, in post-colonial studies, in debates about cultural contestation and appropriation and in relation to the concept of the border and the ideal of the cosmopolitan." See also Claire Alexander, "Diaspora and Hybridity," in *The Sage Handbook of Race and Ethnic Studies*, ed. P. H. Collins and J. Solomos (London: Sage, 2010), 487–507, esp. 497–98. See also Peter Burke, *Cultural Hybridity* (Cambridge: Polity, 2009).

awareness of and indeed a resistance to hybridity.[14] Much of the discourse against hybridity was fueled by prejudiced views of race and culture that saw one as superior to another. Most likely, one needs to look no further than one's own culture to see the truth of this statement.[15] However, it is now common to think that all civilizations and peoples reflect some degree of hybridity and none can legitimately claim racial or cultural purity. Any claim of homogeneity must be viewed with suspicion because the mixing of races and cultures cannot be avoided in any society.

From the perspective of racial and cultural hybridity, Matthew's genealogy seems ambivalent about lineal purity. Jesus is David's son, but he is also a descendent of Gentile women. The identification of Gentile forebears appears to collapse any claim to respectable Jewishness, especially when one considers that both Jews and Romans adhered to the matrilineal principle.[16] Thus, Matthew's mention of Gentile mothers in Jesus' genealogy would have significant appeal to Gentile readers. Far from being a pure Jew, Jesus is the recipient of a mixed line. As Craig Keener notes, "Matthew seems to highlight the mixed nature of Jesus' lineage purposely!"[17] For Matthew, Jesus was a quintessential Jew as the son of Abraham, and royal heir as the son of David, but he is also of mixed race and Gentile heritage himself, which suggests that God had always intended Gentiles to be included in his plan and people. Matthew's genealogy, offered to a hybrid audience of diaspora Jews among the Gentiles, clearly plays to the inclusion of Gentiles, challenging the Jews to embrace all as they see in Jesus the fulfillment of Jewish messianic hope.

Moreover, the racial and cultural hybridity of Jesus, ultimately as the Son of God (Matt 16:16), may have significance for Matthew's Christology. Jesus was not only the Jewish son of Abraham and David,

---

14 So noted by the diachronic study of hybridity by Amar Acheraïou, *Questioning Hybridity, Postcolonialism and Globalization* (New York: Palgrave Macmillan, 2011), 13–50. As Acheraïou intimates, "In offering a wide-ranging view on métissage reaching back to the ancient civilizations, this study does not merely intend to prove that all cultures are hybrid. This has now become a mere truism. Rather, this diachronic methodology is keen to resituate the power of dynamic and multi-rooted nature of hybridity as both a practice and a discourse overlooked in postcolonial studies." (1).

15 Although these views have thankfully changed in the last decades, it was once common in Korea to demonize (sometimes literally) mixed-race people as undesirable or inferior in some way.

16 I. Levinskaya, *The Book of Acts in Its Diaspora Setting*, BAFCS 5 (Grand Rapids: Eerdmans, 1996), 2–17. Thus, one is a Jew when one's mother is a Jew, and Timothy is a good biblical example.

17 Craig S. Keener, *The Gospel of Matthew: A Socio-Rhetorical Commentary* (Grand Rapids: Eerdmans, 2009), 80, emphasis his.

but he was also the eternal, divine Son of God. He has both a human ancestry and a divine one (cf. Rom 1:3–4). Interestingly, the Gentiles would have been more readily attracted to the claim of divine sonship, a common claim of Roman emperors, while the Jews would have found it blasphemous (John 10:36). To appeal to both groups, Jews and Gentiles, Jesus must be of hybrid origin, in-between Jews and Gentiles, but also in-between human and divine.

Beyond racial and cultural hybridity, Matthew's genealogy must be interpreted within its socio-political context where the concept of hybridity has been profitably applied by empire and postcolonial studies. The literary scholar and postcolonial critic, Homi Bhabha, offers a multidimensional view of hybridity in colonial contexts, where both masters and subjects display ambivalence and complexity in their responses to imperialism.[18] Both are transformed by the mixing of cultures and power. There are now interesting applications of Bhabha's theory of hybridity in studies of ancient biblical texts and worlds.[19] For example, John Marshall applies Bhabha's hybridity theory to a reading of Romans 13, suggesting that Paul's discourse there is "affiliative" as a colonial subject of the Roman Empire, and perfectly in line with more resistant discourse elsewhere in his letters.[20] In another example, Ronald Charles applies Bhabha's theory to the Letter of Aristeas and suggests a reading in that the Jewish author (claiming to be a Greek) displays hybridity when he puts forward a Jewish identity that negotiates and affiliates well with Hellenism.[21] As assumed in these examples, should hybridity be universally a fact of life and therefore applicable to ancient biblical settings, then it is entirely appropriate to apply its perspective to Matthew's genealogy.[22]

---

18 Homi K. Bhabha, *The Location of Culture*, 2nd ed. (London: Routledge, 2004).

19 Tarcisius Mukuka, "Reading/Hearing Romans 13:1–7 Under an African Tree: Towards a *Lectio Postcolonica Contexta Africana*," *Neotestamenica* 46 (2012): 105–38; David A. Kaden, "Flavius Josephus and the *Gentes Devictae* in Roman Imperial Discourse: Hybridity, Mimicry, and Irony in the Agrippa II Speech (*Judean War* 2.345–402)," *Journal for the Study of Judaism* 42 (2011): 481–507.

20 John W. Marshall, "Hybridity and Reading Romans 13," *Journal for the Study of the New Testament* 31 (2008): 157–78.

21 Ronald Charles, "Hybridity and the Letter of Aristeas," *Journal for the Study of Judaism* 40 (2009): 242–59.

22 Note the objection by Christopher Bryan, *Render to Caesar: Jesus, the Early Church, and the Roman Superpower* (Oxford: Oxford University, 2005), 114, that postcolonial perspectives developed in the modern period should not be freely applied to Roman Empire.

In addition, a number of New Testament scholars engaging in empire criticism have understood that the biblical authors responded to their imperial context through some degree of hybrid behavior.[23] Matthew is no exception. For example, Warren Carter argues that the Roman Empire is in the foreground of Matthew's Gospel and so Matthew is a work of "imperial negotiation."[24] For Carter, Matthew's goal is largely to contest the Roman Empire. However, Joel Willitts offers some caution about Carter's thesis and suggests that "Matthew's political vision is not reducible to a single anti-Roman interest."[25] For Willitts, Matthew was not merely anti-Rome, but also pro-"empire of God." He comments on Matthew's genealogy, "Matthew's genealogy with its three pivot points suggests that Matthew was not preoccupied with Rome, which amounted to simply the latest representation (in a long line) of satanic political powers that dominated Israel since the Babylonian captivity (Matt 1:12, 17)."[26] Willitts's point is well taken in that Matthew's genealogy should first be read as a theological effort to establish the kingdom of God. And yet, in terms of hybridity, there appears to be a certain ambivalence to the Roman context.

Reading from the perspective of hybridity, Matthew's genealogy begins to take three-dimensional shape in the first century diaspora Jewish setting under the domination of the Romans. The Jewish Christian audience of Matthew's Gospel are in a "third space" between the larger Jewish diaspora and their Roman overlords. How does Matthew's genealogy that identifies Jesus as the son of David and of Abraham impact this setting? The inclusion of the Gentile women in the genealogy of Jesus, and the challenge to include Gentiles into the promises of the Jewish God's is a form of hybrid negotiation. Under Roman imperial rule, the Jewish Christian community is affiliating themselves to the Romans more than dis-associating with Jews. In this way, Matthew is merely displaying hybridity along with his fellow diaspora Jews. Especially in his desire to see Gentile inclusion in the

---

23 See Scot McKnight and Joseph B. Modica, eds., *Jesus is Lord, Caesar Is Not: Evaluating Empire in New Testament Studies* (Downers Grove: IVP Academic, 2013); Stanley E. Porter and Cynthia Long Westfall, eds., *Empire in the New Testament* (Eugene: Pickwick, 2011).

24 Warren Carter, "Matthew and Empire," in *Empire in the New Testament*, eds. S. E. Porter and C. L. Westfall (Eugene: Pickwick, 2011), 90–119.

25 Joel Willitts, "Matthew," in *Jesus Is Lord, Caesar Is Not: Evaluating Empire in New Testament Studies* (Downers Grove: IVP Academic, 2013), 84.

26 Willitts, "Matthew," 84.

genealogy, in line with other Gentile-friendly features of the Gospel (e.g., Magi in 2:1–12; the centurion's faith in 8:5–12; witness before Gentiles in 10:18; faith of a Canaanite woman in 15:21–28; paying taxes to Caesar in 22:15–22; and the Great Commission in 28:18–20), demonstrates that Matthew's negotiation with imperial Rome causes him to be affiliative. How else would he convince the Gentiles to accept a Jewish Messiah? However, there is another side to this negotiation. Jesus really is the son of a Jewish king (David), which in fact makes him "King of the Jews" (Matt 27:11). Such a claim is resistive and indeed subversive to Roman rule. The very fact of a crucified messiah makes Jesus and his followers enemies of Rome. Further, the reference to the Babylonian exile in Matthew's genealogy was especially significant for the Jews because the exile experience is not over. As other New Testament references to Babylon are associated with Rome (1 Pet 5:13; Rev 14:8 and others), Matthew insinuates that the Jews under Roman rule were in exile even in their own homeland. For Jews who hated their oppressors, the Romans, this reference to the Babylonian exile tells them that Jesus is the restorer of their homeland, ultimately destabilizing Roman rule. Thus, the impact of Matthew's genealogy is hybrid, on the one hand, affiliative and friendly toward Rome, yet on the other, subversive and politically charged against Rome.

Conclusion

A missional reading of Matthew's genealogy understands that Jesus is the fulfillment of both Jewish messianic hopes and the hope of Gentiles to be included in God's promise to Abraham. The inclusion of Gentiles, in the presence of women in the Messiah's genealogy, was God's purpose all along and Jesus was given birth to fulfill this purpose. For the community of Jewish believers, the audience of Matthew's Gospel, the genealogy, far from being a "boring" record of lineage, is a missional call to cross boundaries and include Gentiles into the new Kingdom of God. In addition, a hybridity-mission perspective understands that Matthew's genealogy is a hybrid negotiation of Roman rule within the Jewish diaspora setting, giving it fuller missional expression and significance. Matthew's intention is not only to show that Jesus is the Jewish Messiah, able to re-establish God's kingdom in the face of powerful Roman imperial aspirations, but also that Jesus is the divine Lord whom the Gentiles should worship instead of the emperor. To the Jewish Christian audience of the Gospel, the impact of Matthew's genealogy is to move them toward Gentile inclusion, even in the face of enmity, both from the larger Jewish community and from their Gentile oppressors. The hybridity of Matthew's genealogy appeals to the missional objective that culminates in the Gentile inclusion of the Great Commission in Matthew 28. Yet, the hybridity is also a subtle challenge to imperial aggression that identifies an alternative King, Lord, and Savior, an incarnate Son of God. The inclusion of the Gentiles is made all the more compelling by the incarnation of the God-Man.

And so, what does Matthew's genealogy say to Christians living in a pluralistic world? First, it is a call to cross boundaries and negotiate hybrid settings with the gospel of Jesus Christ because Jesus is universally Lord and Savior of all humanity. The mission of the gospel is the universal inclusion of all, embracing the religious other. Second, it is a call to be equipped for mission by the inclusion and incarnation of Jesus Christ, who goes to the other and seeks to include them into the promises of God. The mission of the gospel is, in essence, the act of inclusion through incarnation. Third, it is a call to love the neighbor and the enemy, even as we seek to lead them to repentance and salvation in Jesus Christ. Hybrid negotiation reminds us that we are called to be at once appealing to those outside and yet offensive to the "rulers of this age" (1 Cor 2:6). In a pluralistic setting, the mission is at heart loving the enemy and praying for those who persecute us (Matt 5:44).

BIBLIOGRAPHY

Acheraïou, Amar. *Questioning Hybridity, Postcolonialism and Globalization.* New York: Palgrave Macmillan, 2011.

Alexander, Claire. "Diaspora and Hybridity." In *The Sage Handbook of Race and Ethnic Studies,* ed. P. H. Collins and J. Solomos, London: Sage, 2010, 487–507.

Bhabha, Homi K. *The Location of Culture.* 2nd ed. London: Routledge, 2004.

Bird, Michael F. *Crossing Over Sea and Land: Jewish Missionary Activity in the Second Temple Period.* Grand Rapids: Baker Academic, 2010.

Brah, Avtar, and Annie E. Coombes, eds. *Hybridity and Its Discontents: Politics, Science, Culture.* London: Routledge, 2000.

Bryan, Christopher. *Render to Caesar: Jesus, the Early Church, and the Roman Superpower.* Oxford: Oxford, 2005.

Burke, Peter. *Cultural Hybridity.* Cambridge: Polity, 2009.

Carson, D. A., and Douglas J. Moo. *An Introduction to the New Testament.* 2nd ed. Grand Rapids: Zondervan, 2005.

Carter, Warren. "Matthew and Empire." In *Empire in the New Testament*, ed. S. E. Porter and C. L. Westfall, Eugene: Pickwick, 2011, 90–119.

Charles, Ronald. "Hybridity and the Letter of Aristeas." *Journal for the Study of Judaism* 40 (2009): 242–59.

Davies, W. D., and Dale C. Allison Jr. *The Gospel According to Saint Matthew, Vol. 1*. ICC. London: T&T Clark, 1988.

France, R. T. *The Gospel of Matthew*. NICNT. Grand Rapids: Eerdmans, 2007.

Hagner, Donald A. *Matthew 1–13*. WBC 33a. Dallas: Word, 1998.

Kaden, David A. "Flavius Josephus and the Gentes Devictae in Roman Imperial Discourse: Hybridity, Mimicry, and Irony in the Agrippa II Speech (Judean War 2.345–402)." *Journal for the Study of Judaism* 42 (2011): 481–507.

Keener, Craig S. *The Gospel of Matthew: A Socio-Rhetorical Commentary*. Grand Rapids: Eerdmans, 2009.

_____. *The IVP Bible Background Commentary: New Testament*. 2nd ed. Downers Grove: IVP Academic, 2014.

Lee, Sang-In. "Matthew's Concern for Mission by Including the Four Women: Matthew 1:1–17." *Torch Trinity Journal 10* (2007): 49–74.

Levinskaya, I. *The Book of Acts in Its Diaspora Setting*. BAFCS 5. Grand Rapids: Eerdmans, 1996.

Marshall, John W. "Hybridity and Reading Romans 13." *Journal for the Study of the New Testament 31* (2008): 157–78.

McKnight, Scot, and Joseph B. Modica, eds. *Jesus is Lord, Caesar Is Not: Evaluating Empire in New Testament Studies*. Downers Grove: IVP Academic, 2013.

Mukuka, Tarcisius. "Reading/Hearing Romans 13:1–7 under an African Tree: Towards a Lectio Postcolonica Contexta Africana." *Neotestamenica* 46 (2012): 105–38.

Osborne, Grant R. *Matthew*. ZECNT. Grand Rapids: Zondervan, 2010.

Porter, Stanley E., and Cynthia Long Westfall, eds. *Empire in the New Testament*. Eugene: Pickwick, 2011.

Schnabel, Eckhard J. *Early Christian Mission, Vol. 1, Jesus and the Twelve*. Downers Grove: IVP Academic, 2004.

Turner, David L. *Matthew*. BECNT. Grand Rapids: Baker Academic, 2008.

Willitts, Joel. "Matthew." In *Jesus Is Lord, Caesar Is Not: Evaluating Empire in New Testament Studies*, ed. S. McKnight and J. B. Modica, Downers Grove: IVP Academic, 2013, 82–100

Wright, Christopher J. H. "Mission and Old Testament Interpretation." In *Hearing the Old Testament: Listening for God's Address*, ed. C. G. Bartholomew and D. J. H. Beldman, Grand Rapids: Eerdmans, 2012, 180–203.

ABOUT THE AUTHOR

DR. STEVEN S. H. CHANG is a professor of New Testament at Torch Trinity Graduate University, Seoul, Korea. He obtained his PhD from University of Aberdeen in Scotland, UK, his MDiv from Trinity Evangelical Divinity School in 1996 and completed his MA in New Testament in 1997. He is a contributor to Scattered and Gathered: A Global Compendium of Diaspora Missiology (Regnum, 2016). He is the pastor of Hallelujah Community Church English Ministries, Seong-nam, South Korea.

CHAPTER 5 | Harvey C. Kwiyani

Diaspora, Hybridity, and Theology

My doctoral research in 2010 explored the theme of theological cross-pollination between African and American Christians attending the same congregations in Minneapolis and St. Paul, Minnesota.[1] In carrying out the research, I sought to inquire if, at all, cross-cultural theological conversations were taking place between the Kenyan and Tanzanian Lutherans and their fellow American Lutherans, especially when they worshipped together in congregations that self-identified as multicultural. I wondered what, if anything, did these African and American Christians talk about when engaging each other in theological conversations—and if cross-cultural conversations were indeed taking place, what were the Africans bringing to the table? I was hopeful that, in asking this question, I would discover the hybrid theology that may emerge in multicultural contexts where Christians from different cultural perspectives engage in conversations about God and God's people in the world, and how this emergent hybrid theology may benefit the wider Body of Christ. Unfortunately, my research discovered that there were no cross-cultural theological conversations taking place in multicultural

---

1 Harvey C. Kwiyani, "Pneumatology, Mission, and African Christians in Multicultural Congregations in North America." PhD Dissertation, Luther Seminary, 2012.

congregations in Minnesota. It actually appeared to me that while they engage in worship together, African and American Christians did not engage with one another. They looked to heaven together but did not look at one another. They did not see one another even though they sought to see God together. The theology in these congregations remained untouched by the entrance of foreign African Christians. It was not affected in any way by the presence of the stranger through whom God might also want to speak. The Africans themselves did not seem keen to make their theologies heard—many did not seem to believe that they had a theological voice, or that they could actually speak theologically to the congregation. Whatever theology was shaping and expressed in those multicultural congregations was exclusively American and was only interested in the American situation. All theological conversations were initiated and led by American leaders and, of course, Africans were always good students, learning at the feet of (white) American apostles. The theological concerns of the Africans were generally of no interest to the wider theologies of these congregations.

There was one congregation in the research, however, that was well integrated both in its demographics and its theology. It embodied the true definition of a multicultural congregation; the membership included a good mix of white Americans and Latinos and African peoples. Their theological conversations were deeply multicultural, always reflecting the mutual influences of African, Hispanic, and American cultures. Even though the senior pastor was American and white, many Africans were deeply involved in various ministries in the church's life— and they were enjoying it. Central to this congregation's hybrid self-understanding was the lead pastor's theological emphasis that every member of the congregation is a foreigner, including the Americans, and that only God was the host. As guests of God, each member of the congregation was required to keep the community as hospitable as possible for everyone. Thus, in doing so, they dethroned the dominant culture and its theology and created a space where the only way forward was hybridity. Together, as equals they shaped a hybrid theology that in turn shaped a hybrid congregation.

Why Theological Hybridity?

As a son of an agriculturalist, I find both the terms "cross-pollination" and "hybridity" fascinating. They are both biological terms that talk about mixing two distinct things to produce something genetically new—usually a better or improved type of a crop (e.g., hybrid maize that is more resistant to drought) or a new species altogether with more needful characteristics (e.g., a mule is a hybrid between a donkey and a horse). The essence of both terms is mixing of two different elements either by nature or by human intentionality to produce something new.[2] Both terms have also come to be used outside the field of biology. We talk about cross-pollinating ideas and drive hybrid cars nowadays. We may, as well, talk about the cross-pollination or hybridization of theology—and this happens when theologies from different cultures or different parts of the world engage one another in mutually critiquing and communally edifying conversations. Indeed, great possibilities of mutual enrichment arise when Christians engage other Christians whose theologies are not native to their own cultures, traditions, and worldview. I would like to explore, even briefly, three factors that I consider very important for the conversation on theological hybridity. The first one is the contextual nature of all theology.

Contextual Nature of All Theology

John Mbiti once said that "the church is kerygmatically universal, but is still theologically provincial."[3] However, even in the "provinces," theology is shaped—and thus divided–by various factors such as denominational persuasions and is always mediated by culture. In addition, this provincial nature of theology means that it is usually difficult to have good and respectful cross-province theological conversations. We live in a world where many believe that Western theology is the theology while every other theology is a contextual theology whose very orthodoxy has to be measured against that of the West. This is the case even in the academic discipline of theology. Andrew Walls lamented the lack of non-Western faculty in Western theological institutions in a 1991 article entitled "Structural Problems in Mission Studies." In his words, "the rule of the

---

2 The dictionary definition of cross-pollination is "the transfer of pollen from the flower of one plant to the flower of a plant having a different genetic constitution," and that of hybrid is "the offspring of two plants or animals of different species or varieties for better characteristics."

3 John S. Mbiti, "Theological Impotence and the Universality of the Church," In *Mission Trends No. 3*, ed. Gerald H. Anderson and Thomas F. Stransky, *Third World Theologies*. (Grand Rapids, MI: Eerdmans, 1976), 8. An earlier edition of the article was published in 1974 in the *Lutheran World*. See John S. Mbiti, "Theological Impotence and the Universality of the Church," *Lutheran World* 21, no. 3 (1974).

palefaces over the academic world remains untroubled",[4] in a world where non-Western Christians far exceed those of the West. He would later argue that, "Western theological leadership of a predominantly non-Western church is an incongruity."[5] Of course, there is still today an unjustifiable theological hegemony by the West over the world as Timothy Tennent observes, "We cannot afford to ignore the theological implications inherent in the demographic reality that Christianity is currently in a precipitous decline in the West and that the vast majority of Christians now live outside the West."[6] Indeed, the theological implications of the worldwide spread of Christianity in the twentieth century deserve a great deal of attention. Craig Ott identifies the problem to be located in four areas: (1) the West's "hegemony postulate," (2) the West's self-perception that it is "the centre," (3) the perception of third world scholars as "purveyors of exotic, raw intellectual material to people in the North," and (4) the "dialogue of the deaf" between the West and the rest of the world.[7] As we stand today, Walls' "rule of palefaces" in theology persists (and is probably worse in missiology). Decades after Mbiti wrote about the provincial nature of theology and Walls talked about the Western stronghold of academic theology (and missiology), non-Western theologians still face uphill struggles to be heard in the West.

However, for most of us in the non-Western world, there has been a change in the way we understand theology. While Western theology continues to scream the loudest, other theologies have emerged and will force the entire discipline of theology to reorganise. Gone should be the days when there existed something called "theology" in Europe and North America that was reflected, rather cheaply, in Latin America, Africa, and Asia as "contextual theology." Many of us now believe that all theology is contextual; there is no such thing as context-free theology. There exists no such thing as theology apart from culture. Even European and North American theologies are contextual, effectively answering

---

4 Andrew F. Walls, "Structural Problems in Mission Studies." *International Bulletin of Missionary Research* 15, no. 4 (October 1991): 152.

5 Andrew F. Walls, "Christian Scholarship in Africa in the Twenty-First Century," *Transformation* 19, no. 4 (2002): 221.

6 Timothy C. Tennent, *Theology in the Context of World Christianity: How the Global Church Is Influencing the Way We Think About and Discuss Theology.* Grand Rapids, MI: Zondervan, 2007. Craig Ott and Harold A. Netland, *Globalizing Theology: Belief and Practice in an Era of World Christianity* (Grand Rapids, MI: Baker, 2006), 17.

7 Craig Ott and Harold A. Netland, *Globalizing Theology: Belief and Practice in an Era of World Christianity* (Grand Rapids, MI: Baker, 2006), 46.

questions that are asked in the West and are, thus, marginally applicable elsewhere. In this context of world Christianity, theology cannot remain Eurocentric. While we celebrate the long heritage of European and American theological inquiry, we must recognise that we now live in a world where Latin Americans, Africans, and Asians also engage in rigorous theological discourse in their own contexts, and that their theological voices are just as valid and important as those of Western theologians. Our theological enterprise must reflect the global nature of the Body of Christ.

Migration

In addition to this emergence of world theologies, we are now living in a shrinking global village where these "provincial" theologies often come into contact with one another as people-movements from one part of the globe to another increase. We live today in the age of migration—people migrate with their religions and theologies. The migration of Christians and the subsequent diasporisation of all sorts of world Christianities create an immense potential for cross-cultural theological encounters between Christians from different parts of the world. Most migrants travel with their "theological backpacks," bringing with them into their diaspora their ways of understanding and talking about God. This is normal for all humans; people travel with their under-standing of their god is and what that god can do. For most Africans, for instance, who love special prayers to be said for visas and anointing oil to be poured on passports as they prepare for travel, God is actively involved in migration. For many Africans, Asians and Latin Americans alike, the process of migration itself is often a theologising experience—it draws people closer to their deities, causing them to reflect on the deity's sustaining power in a foreign land. Migration brings not just foreigners but their theologies as well. Many Western Christians do not need to go to Africa to meet African Christians or to hear African theology; African Christians exist in Europe and North America in large numbers. The same is true for Latin American and Asian Christians in the West—and virtually every major city in the world. We find Christians from many countries in every multicultural city on all continents. In these cities, intentional cross-cultural theological conversations could easily involve Christians from multiple continents at any time. Through migration, God is remixing the nations and revealing the true image of God's son to the world, an image that includes diverse peoples from every tribe and tongue (Rev 7:9–10). Together, in these cross-cultural conversations, we help one another see God better. But for this to be possible, we need to engage one another on a human level through the gift of hospitality.

Hospitality

My Malawian peoples have a proverb that goes *mlendo ndi uyo abwera ndi kalumo kakuthwa*. It translates, "a guest usually comes better equipped to help a community find solutions to its long-standing challenges (because guests can see with a fresh perspective). Another one says *mlendo ndi mame, sachedwa kusungunuka*, which means a guest is like morning dew, before you know it, they will be gone. (They may become one of us or may return where they came from or move on to another place.) Thus, hospitality to the stranger is encouraged—and not only because the stranger may be vulnerable and in need of help, but also because the stranger comes bearing gifts that the community needs. Indeed, even those guests that seem to abuse our hospitality are welcome because they will still bring us gifts, and if it seems like they will stay forever, we take courage in that they are only morning dew. This is possible because in most Malawian cultures, there is an awareness that a community is never self-sufficient. Even when it seems like the community has all it needs, there is always a blind spot that can be easily seen through the eyes of a guest. Among my people group, the Lhomwes of Southern Malawi, hospitality is generally expressed in two ways; sharing (of food) and listening to what the guest has to say. In some cultures, the meal-fellowship does not begin until the guest has been freed to speak.

In the context of the conversation on theological hybridity, it is especially helpful if all Christians from different parts of the world engage one another as if they were all guests, each coming bearing theological gifts for the other. God is the host who gathers us together. Our duty is to keep the fellowship hospitable to all. In such a gathering, people may engage in cross-cultural theological conversations not to correct where the other is wrong, but to hear each other out because it is generally in the spaces of misunderstandings where God reveals himself to us. "God always hides in the cracks," my grandmother always told me. My father, a veteran church leader and a community chief, never misses an opportunity to remind his congregation that if we pay attention to the things we do not have in common, we will discover how much we have to share. Using my research as an example, theological conversations between Kenyan Lutherans and Minnesotan Lutherans could get them exchanging perspectives on how they read "Luther's Works," for instance. Indeed, the British Anglicans and the Nigerian Pentecostals in my neighbourhood in Liverpool could help each other understand the work of the Holy Spirit better. When carried out as an honest conversation among equals, these groups of Christians would help each other see the mosaic that God is in a new light. European Christians whose theology is shaped in the context of modernity and is generally less expressive could both enrich and be enriched by a conversation with African Christians whose theology is pre-modern in its outlook and overly enthusiastic in its expression. North American Christians, with their affluent churches capitalism-shaped ecclesiology, could learn from and teach something to Latin American Christians who live in poverty and yet believe that God has a preferential option for them. No one theology has it all. Every theology will be enriched as it engages other theologies from other parts of the world. As this happens, and as the theologies inform and shape one another, we all get to understand God better—and thus, a new and richer theology that is informed by a multiplicity of perspectives emerges.

Theological Hybridity in Practice

I have seen glimpses of the great theological riches that await us on the other side of these cross-cultural conversations in seminary when, once in a while, we engaged the works of non-Western theologians (with strange names and coming from unknown places in Africa, Latin America, or Asia). All of a sudden, students from those places became our theological experts for the day, directing our attention to issues we would otherwise miss and raising questions that we did not usually think about. Certainly, those intense moments of theological discourse opened our eyes to aspects of God's work in Kenya, or Mexico, or South Korea that we could possibly never hear of if we only depended on European and American theological voices. We came out of those seminars with a better understanding of God—the mosaic of the image of God got a few more colours in it. However, opportunities to engage in cross-cultural theological conversations like this ought not be limited to seminaries. Any congregation that is located in a context of cultural diversity only deprives itself of the gifts of the global church if it chooses the way of monoculturalism or prefer not to engage its Christian neighbours from other parts of the world. Even those who can truly say that they have no access to foreign Christians can access foreign theologies in the libraries or on the Internet. To be formed— or informed—by one theology in our day and age is to risk being theologically misinformed even when we are educated by the best theologians of one's tradition. As a matter of fact, great theologians of our day will be those who have learned to engage the voices of the "other" Christians—women, immigrants, children, Africans, Asians, Latin Americans—not to discredit and dismiss them but to listen and hear what God maybe saying through their voices.

Theological hybridity also happens at a congregational or denominational level. I have seen, in various congregational and denominational settings, different theological camps of Christians choose to engage one another and work together across whatever barriers, be they theological or cultural. I know of two congregations located opposite one another across a busy Birmingham street for decades. They belonged to different denominations and were theologically diametrically opposed to one another. Of course, they disliked each other immensely—each accusing the other of stealing their members and leading them down a wrong theological path. They changed their service times to avoid seeing each other on a Sunday. However, they were forced to work together when a tragedy hit their community and the leaders had to speak to one another. Soon, they discovered that their theologies were actually complementary. They realised that there are some aspects of God that we can only understand when engaged in communion with another. Indeed, my elders in Malawi would actually say that it is not possible to know God without communion with a different 'other'. These two congregations in Birmingham overcame their theological misunderstandings together as they both learned that in God, there is room for difference—and indeed, there is room for everyone—and that race, theology, culture, and whatever barriers there may be cannot stand in the way of true fellowship in the Spirit. They also both learned about the hospitality of God that at the end of the day, we are all guests at God's table. Only God is the host.

Theological Underpinnings

Central to this argument for theological hybridity is the theology of the body—the global body of Christ. Paul's understanding of the *ekklesia* as the Body of Christ is helpful not just for local congregations where members bring their gifts to keep the fellowship going but also to the global body of Christ in which members from different parts of the world bring their gifts together. The body is a collection of members connected together. Each member brings a gift. No member of the body is more important than another. No member of the body is expendable. The eye cannot say to the hand, "I do not need you." Neither can the hand say to the eye, "I do not need you." For, the body is glued together by that which every joint supplies (Eph 4:16). These gifts are the glue that keep the body together in the unity of the Spirit and through the bond of peace (Eph 4:3). Some of these gifts are real life presents that God has given the Body of Christ around the world. However, a good deal of these gifts are theological in nature. What is God revealing about himself in the experiences of the poor in Latin America, or the dying in "Those who have ears need to hear what the Spirit is saying" to the church through their brothers and sisters in other parts of the world.

Sociological Underpinnings

It is widely accepted in the world of business that diversity invigorates society. Forbes Insights called diversity a "formula for success."[8] In their thought-provoking book (published in 2000), *Surfing the Edge of Chaos*, Richard Pascale, Mark Milleman, and Linda Gioja argue that homogeneity is slow death—the absence of variety diminishes life. They state that "the survival of any system depends on its capacity to cultivate and not just tolerate variety in its internal structures."[9] As a result, variety is not just essential for our understanding of who we are; it is critical for our abundant life. Theological homogeneity limits our understanding of the great things that God is doing in the world. It obscures the richness of the entire Body and how its many members speak of and understand God's greatness. Children in Malawi are taught, *kalikokha nkanyama, tili tiwiri ntianthu,* which roughly translates "one who is alone is an animal, those who are a pair are people." That is to say our humanity is always enriched in community with others. We lose our personhood when we chose to live in isolation. My Malawian readers, therefore, understand rather easily that even in our theological identities,

---

8   See Mary Ellen Egan, "Global Diversity and Inclusion: Fostering Innovation through a Diverse Workforce," Forbes Insights, 2011.

9   Richard T., Pascale, Mark Millemann, and Linda Gioja. *Surfing the Edge of Chaos: The Laws of Nature and the New Laws of Business* (New York: Crown Business, 2000), 20.

we need the "other" for us to be. However, this is not just a Malawian message. To be alone, or to engage in our theological endeavours truly without communion with real "others" (who bring different lenses to the reading of the Scriptures) is to limit our own understanding of the texts. Most Africans believe that "I am because we are." This is what the Body of Christ is; it exists because of its many members. This applies to our theologies as well—they only become better in communion with other theologies.

Conclusion

We are living in a world where theological hybridity must happen. Theologies from around the world come into contact with one another with increasing frequency, and they must speak to one another in order to improve each other. The presence of many non-Western migrants in the West (and, in general, the mixing of Christians from different parts of the world through migration) is itself a gift that brings many theological gifts. Multicultural congregations are on the rise. However, their multicultural identity will be betrayed if they can only talk about and understand God from the perspective of one culture. If they do so, they deprive themselves and others the gifts that God sends them in the ministry of the stranger, the immigrant, and the alien. Any theology that is not talking to other theologies in the world will become irrelevant in the near future.

BIBLIOGRAPHY

Cartledge, Mark J., and David Cheetham. *Intercultural Theology: Approaches and Themes*. London: SCM, 2011.

Egan, Mary Ellen. "Global Diversity and Inclusion: Fostering Innovation through a Diverse Workforce." Forbes Insights, 2011.

Haar, Gerrie ter. *How God Became African: African Spirituality and Western Secular Thought*. Philadelphia, PA: University of Pennsylvania, 2009.

Hanciles, Jehu. *Beyond Christendom: Globalization, African Migration, and the Transformation of the West*. Maryknoll, NY: Orbis, 2008.

Kwiyani, Harvey C. *Mission-Shaped Church in a Multicultural World. Mission and Evangelism Series*. Cambridge: Grove, 2017.

———. "Pneumatology, Mission, and African Christians in Multicultural Congregations in North America." PhD Dissertation, Luther Seminary, 2012.

Mbiti, John S. "Theological Impotence and the Universality of the Church." In *Mission Trends No. 3*, edited by Gerald H. Anderson and Thomas F. Stransky. Third World Theologies, Grand Rapids, MI: Eerdmans, 1976, 6–18.

———. "Theological Impotence and the Universality of the Church." *Lutheran World* 21, no. 3 (1974): 251–60.

Niringiye, David Zac. *The Church: God's Pilgrim People*. Downers Grove, IL: IVP, 2015.

Ott, Craig, and Harold A. Netland. *Globalizing Theology: Belief and Practice in an Era of World Christianity*. Grand Rapids, MI: Baker, 2006.

Pascale, Richard T., Mark Millemann, and Linda Gioja. *Surfing the Edge of Chaos: The Laws of Nature and the New Laws of Business*. New York: Crown Business, 2000.

Tennent, Timothy C. *Theology in the Context of World Christianity: How the Global Church Is Influencing the Way We Think About and Discuss Theology*. Grand Rapids, MI: Zondervan, 2007.

Walls, Andrew F. "Christian Scholarship in Africa in the Twenty-First Century." *Transformation* 19, no. 4 (2002): 217–28.

———. "Structural Problems in Mission Studies." *International Bulletin of Missionary Research* 15, no. 4 (1991): 146–55.

ABOUT THE AUTHOR

HARVEY KWIYANI is a professor of African Christianity and Theology at Liverpool Hope University. He received his PhD in Theology from Luther Seminary in St. Paul, Minnesota. He is the author of Sent Forth: African Missionary Work in the West.

CHAPTER 6 | Calvin Chong

Globalization, Hybrid Worlds, and Emerging Missional Frontiers

An Introduction to Movement and Mixing in a Globally Connected World

The impact of globalization on everyday life is a felt but not always readily describable twenty-first century reality. In part, this is so because the effects and conditions that accompany globalization often require new vocabulary and descriptors with which to explain (or make sense) to them. In his primer to help readers understand important phenomena that come with globalization, Eriksen highlights eight key concepts that characterize globalization which are worth noting. These include disembedding, acceleration, standardization, interconnectedness, movement, mixing, vulnerability, and re-embedding.[1] While there are links and overlaps across these eight key concepts, two are singled out as especially relevant to a discussion on the diaspora, hybridity, and globalization: movement and mixing.

Movement is a concept in globalization studies which is both pivotal as well as familiar in the literature. Also known as "circulation,"[2] the idea

---

1 Thomas Hylland Eriksen, *Globalization: The Key Concepts* (Oxford, UK: Berg, 2007), 8–9.

2 Anna Tsing, "The Global Situation," in *The Anthropology of Globalization: A Reader*, edited by Inda Jonathan Xavier and Rosaldo Renato, 2nd ed. (Malden, MA: Blackwell), 66–98.

is strongly featured in Ritzer's definition of globalization—particularly in the attention and the emphasis that he gives to the phenomena of liquidity and flows:

> Globalization is a transplanetary process or set of processes involving increasing liquidity and the growing multi-directional flows of people, objects, places and information as well as the structures they encounter and create that are barriers to, or expedite, those flows.[3]

> It is clear that if one wanted to use a single term to think about globalization today, liquidity (as well as the closely related idea of flows) would be at or near the top of the list. [4]

Predating Ritzer, Appadurai had already proposed describing global flows within the global cultural economy through the lens of five "-scapes": ethnoscapes, technoscapes, financescapes, mediascapes and ideoscapes.[5] Like Ritzer's movement of people, objects, places and information, Appadurai's "five-scapes construct" provides useful categories to describe global movements and their impact on different facets of a nation's landscape.

The concept of mixing in globalization studies has been studied, scrutinized, and debated at great length. Mixing or hybridity is inevitable in a world of liquidity and flows, and it can take on material or nonmaterial expression. It is evidenced in objects and things, individuals and identities, communities and populations, music and media, texts and languages, religions and festivals, art and architecture, fitness and sports.

Yet these mixes happen under a variety of situations. As Burke notes, these situations can involve equals or unequals, depend on the presence of weak or strong traditions of appropriation, occur at urban metropolises or at border frontiers, and transpire within or across social classes.[6] Given the wide range of situations under which hybridity is wrought, it would not be surprising that taxonomies, descriptions of responses, and outcomes of mixes are as varied as they are.[7]

---

3 George Ritzer, *Globalization: The Essentials* (Malden, MA: Wiley-Blackwell, 2011), 2.

4 Ibid., 6.

5 Arjun Appadurai, *Modernity at Large: Cultural Dimensions of Globalization* (Minneapolis, MN: University Of Minnesota, 1996), 27–47.

6 Peter Burke, *Cultural Hybridity* (Cambridge, UK: Polity, 2009), 66–78.

7 Marwan M. Kraidy, *Hybridity, or the Cultural Logic of Globalization* (Philadelphia, PA: Temple University, 2005), 45–71; Eriksen, 107–22; Burke, 79–115.

Canclini defines the term hybridization as "socio-cultural processes in which discrete structures and practices previously existing in separate form, are combined to generate new structures, objects and practices."[8] In that hybrid structures, objects and practices are increasingly observed and experienced in global cities and urban centres, there is need to give attention to frontiers where hybridizing is active and flourishing. At these frontiers, life is being re-ordered and situations birthed which invite missional as well as pastoral responses. It is to these active, re-ordered frontiers that we will turn our attention to in the next section.

The Active Creation of Hybrid Worlds

Hybridity is pervasive and has been observed to be the "new normal" in the many places touched by globalization. In this section, three very different evolving frontiers of hybridity will be explored and briefly described.

The first explores the inescapable and irrevocable reality of a virtual world and how that world has become integrally woven into everyday life. The second focuses on households and explores a situation where traditional household roles are now either occupied or performed by new players from emerging global labour and marriage markets. Finally, the third explores the niche creative frontier of Japanese storytelling traditions and forms that have found global acclaim, influence, and adoption.

The three frontiers are highlighted to illustrate the growing presence and reality of hybrid worlds. In terms of scope and scale, the examples are intentionally varied and dissimilar to shine light on the fact that hybridity is felt and experienced differently on the ground. The final section will then articulate relevance for diaspora missions and call the church to active presence and participation in those emerging hybridizing frontiers.

An Expanded, Integrated Ecosystem of Physical and Virtual Spaces

The opening paragraph of Tsing's essay, "The Global Situation," reads:

> *"Click on world-making interconnections. Your screen fills with global flows."*
>
> *Imagine a creek cutting through a hillside. As the water rushes down, it carves rock and moves gravel; it deposits silt on slow turns; it switches course and breaks dams after a sudden storm. As the creek flows, it makes and remakes its channels.*

---

8 Nestor Garcia Canclini, *Hybrid Cultures: Strategies for Entering and Leaving Modernity* (Minneapolis, MN: University of Minnesota, 2005), xxv.

Imagine an internet system, linking up computer users, or a rush of immigrants crossing national borders, or capital investments shuttled to varied offshore locations. The world-making also flows, not just interconnections but also the re-carving of channels and the re-mapping of possibilities of geography.[9]

Tsing's use of the "reshaped-topography" imagery clearly makes the point that the worlds we inhabit indeed have been subject to globalizing forces and hence have been dramatically re-made. Where the metaphor remains inadequate is in its failure to appreciate that virtual worlds are "new geographies" that have been created ex-nihilo. These are extensions to present geographies, locales, and habitats, not merely "re-carvings" or "re-mapping" of prevailing geographies.

A more fitting imagery to describe virtual world-making would come from architecture, urban planning, and place-making. The virtual world is better described as constructed networks of virtual places, pathways, publics, personalities, and productions, which extend prevailing geographies. Life in the twenty-first century is now lived in an expanded ecosystem of physical and virtual places.

Beyond mere extension, there is increasingly growing integration of both physical and virtual worlds. In his book *The Great Good Place*, sociologist Ray Oldenburg identifies three essential places that people inhabit and live out their lives. The three include the "first place" which is the place we live in, the "second place" where we work at, and the "third place" where we gather to socialize and participate in leisure activities.[10]

By extension, academics and researchers have begun to write about "virtual third places."[11] The rise of the digital age has spawned digital equivalents of second and third places as increasing amounts of work and leisure time is migrated to digital arenas. Given the porosity of the place of boundaries, presence can be maintained in physical first, second, or third places while simultaneously located in virtual second and virtual third places.

What this has resulted in is a situation where feet are firmly planted in physical space, while hearts and minds are deeply buried in virtual space. Within that expanded ecosystem of physical and virtual places,

---

9   Tsing, 66.

10 Ray Oldenburg, *The Great Good Place: Cafés, Coffee Shops, Bookstores, Bars, Hair Salons, and Other Hangouts at the Heart of a Community* (New York: Marlowe and Company, 1999).

11 Farley 2013; McArthur and White 2016; Memarovic, et. al. 2014.

memories, imaginations, identities, habits, intuitions, social practices, self-worth, values, and aesthetic sensibilities are shaped in a culturally rich and diverse environment.

It is at the intersection of the physical and the virtual that a complex, globally connected hybrid world has developed. If we leave our fingerprints at the places we hang out, those places equally leave their fingerprints on us too. Under these conditions, we find the human race becoming more technological and technology becoming more human!

In this hybrid world, individuals and communities flourish as well as flounder. Organizations like the Global Digital Citizen Foundation seek to promote effective as well as ethical global citizens by promoting the development of essential twenty-first centuries' fluencies. These include solution fluency, information fluency, creativity fluency, media fluency, collaborative fluency. Collectively, these fluencies serve the goal of nurturing proficient and responsible global digital citizens who take personal ownership for their own learning, are deeply aware of their place in the world as global and digital citizenships, and care for the world through altruistic service and environmental stewardship.[12]

On the other hand, hybrid worlds are also where folly, fragility, and futility afflict individuals and communities. Near future media installments such as Patrick H. Willems' Black Mirror: Pokémon Go video,[13] Spike Jonze's movie Her,[14] Steve Cutts and Moby & The Void Pacific Choir's animation Are You Lost in the World like Me?,[15] all tell believable tales which portend the dark sides of life in this digital-human hybrid world. As a genre of sci-fi, these extend current realities not into the distant future, but into the near future. As a result of their closeness to home, what is presented is thus very relatable and often unsettling. Even more explicit are the warnings sounded out by technology insiders like Sherry Turkle[16] and Jaron Lanier[17] in recent TED talks. Collectively they suggest that the hybrid digital-human species has allowed technological innovations to

---

12 https://globaldigitalcitizen.org/.

13 https://www.youtube.com/watch?v=v7ugwlcOPPg.

14 https://www.warnerbros.com/her.

15 https://vimeo.com/209248444.

16 https://www.ted.com/talks/sherry_turkle_alone_togethe.

17 https://www.ted.com/talks/jaron_lanier_how_we_need_to_remake_the_internet.

reorder life in a hybrid world faster than the consequences we are prepared to face and deal with.

This hybrid world remains ubiquitous and an integral part of everyday life for a very large proportion of the world's urban population. It is not a world that is easily navigated, controlled, or regulated. Nonetheless, the virtual and the digital has already become a prized, indispensible part of our world and identity. Given how deeply the virtual and the digital has become rooted in daily life for the hybrid self, many will find the idea of unplugging rather disruptive and any suggestion of forced extrication quite unthinkable.

The Growing Phenomenon of Reconfigured Global Households

Households are basic to human reproduction, socialization, material provision, and psychological support. Amongst the fundamental roles for sustaining households include "marriage/partnering, bearing children, raising and educating children (and adults), maintaining the household on a daily basis, dividing labor and pooling income from livelihood activities, and caring for elderly and other non-working household members."[18]

In a globalized world, the nature of household configurations has been observably altered. In developed urban centers, marriage or partnering involving individuals from different nationalities and cultures is increasingly commonplace. In some situations, the role of a spouse is fulfilled by a foreign bride procured at relatively low cost. In other situations, children are adopted into the household from a foreign nation.

The rise of double-income families has resulted in reduced parental involvement in child-minding and child-raising many households. Rapidly ageing populations, higher life expectancy, as well as low total fertility rates also created a growing burden on caregiving for ageing members of households. With more adult family members drawn into the workforce, the responsibility of minding and raising children as well as the responsibility of caring for sick, special needs, and elderly members of the household has been increasingly taken up by low-waged foreign domestic workers or care assistants. While some make long-term contributions to households, many of these domestic workers and care assistants are regarded as expendable and hence only render short-term or mid-term stints in households.

18 Mike Douglass, "The Globalization of Householding and Social Reproduction in Pacific Asia." *Philippine Studies* 55, no. 2 (2007): 157–81.

The descriptions above sketch for us an emerging reality experienced in many urban centers across the globe. Traditional household roles are now being handed over to new players and new arrangements have surfaced to adapt to the changing conditions and growing needs of the modern household.

It is in response to this global, twenty-first century phenomenon of reconstituted household roles that "global householding" studies have developed. Douglass describes this hybridizing phenomenon as follows:

> Global householding is viewed as the interactive process of forming and sustaining the household through global transactions. From a global household perspective, transnational population movement is only partially motivated by and manifested in work and income opportunities. Marriage, bearing, raising and educating children, and caring for the elderly are among the new motives for transnational movements and linkages among people, and all are integral to householding. From a societal level, global householding is also a response to collapsing population growth below replacement, severe labor shortages, rising dependency ratios, welfare systems going broke, and rapidly aging societies. [19]

As a sub-discipline of globalization studies, global householding gives attention to these reconfigured household arrangements, conditions and national policies that govern the movement of foreigners to take on these roles, and the accompanying impact of foreign surrogates on local households. It also explores the experience of surrogates whose services are purchased and who are drafted to serve in key household roles in the host country. In addition, global householding seeks to examine the nature of the links that they maintain with their families and households back home.

Incorporating low cost foreign options from global labour and marriage markets into households opens up more options for life and career choices. It allows gaps in household roles to be plugged and working members of households to pursue job opportunities, maintain extended hours at the work place, travel for business, and enjoy more leisure activities. Scholars writing about global householding however often draw attention to the irony of lowly paid workers leaving gaps in their own households while plugging destination country household gaps. One such scholar, Reiko Karatani, thus notes the phenomenon of "global de-householding" which happens simultaneously with "global householding."

---

19 Douglass, 158–59.

By hiring Foreign Overeas Domestic Workers (FODWs), an employer's family indeed experiences "global householding." It clearly improves their quality of life by having FODWs do the cooking and cleaning, for example. At the same time, however, the FODWs' own families back home face "global de-householding," losing an important family member who could have looked after them and improved their quality of life as well. (Karatani 2012, 142)

...the actual costs of upholding a high level of "security" for those families who opt for "global householding" are simply transferred, in the form of "global de-householding," to the FODWs and the families they leave behind. (Karatani 2012, 143)

Given the fluidity of global people movement, the scale of demand, and the abundance of supply, the phenomenon of global householding is set to grow bigger. While the global householding does not exclude incorporating foreign males to plug gaps in households, the roles have largely been filled by women. Doubtless, in many cases, this has brought great benefit to these women and their families. What has been less highlighted has been the personal cost to them and the destabilization of their families back home.

Women on the move are often subject to challenging working and living conditions in the households they end up at. Despite regulations to protect them, they remain vulnerable to abuse and exploitation. In their time away, families back home commonly suffer estrangement and fragmentation. Hard-earned money regularly sent back has also been known to breed unhealthy financial habits and dependencies amongst family members.

It is thus the growing hybridizing phenomenon of global house-holding as well as its negative counterpart global dehouseholding that should not escape the notice of the global church. Research on this global trend remains occasional and responses by Christian households have been found wanting.

Japanese Storytelling Traditions and Their Global Hybrid Forms

Stories have profound influence over how people feel, think, wish, and behave. Two quotes from Sarah Arthur articulate and elucidate the influence that stories hold over their audiences:

Story has the potential to influence spiritual formation. It does this by facilitating the five activities identified as critical to imaginative health: engagement, synthesis, vision, empathy, and creative response.[20]

Story expresses the beliefs and values of a people by incarnating those values in unforgettable images rather than abstract statements. It preserves cultural memory and gives the hearer a sense of his or her identity within a community...Story shapes worldview, which in turn shapes self-understanding or identity.[21]

In the storyteller's hand, therefore, is the power to shape perception, situate sympathies, focus attention, invite identification, endorse life choices, stoke passions, offer insights into human behavior, and extend horizons of possibilities.

Just as the countries and cultures of the world have their stories and storytelling traditions, Japan too has its share of memorable stories and storytelling forms. Interestingly, many of Japanese storytelling vehicles have strong global appeal and have found global acclaim. Hayao Miyazaki, the principal animator from the world-renown Studio Ghibli, once said:

I do believe in the power of story. I believe that stories have an important role to play in the formation of human beings, that they can stimulate, amaze, and inspire their listeners.[22]

Amongst the many Japanese storytelling vehicles, which have captured the attention of global audiences and adopters, three have been singled out for highlight and elaboration. These include i) *Manga*, ii) *Kamishibai* Street Theatre, and iii) *Pecha Kucha* 20x20.

Manga

"Reading *manga* (comic books and graphic novels) and watching anime (animation) is a significant part of daily life for millions of Japanese." [23] These words by *manga* researcher MacWilliams tell of how this popular Japanese storytelling form is deeply rooted in everyday Japanese life. As a medium, modern manga was aimed primarily at children.

---

20 Sarah Arthur, *The God-Hungry Imagination: The Art of Storytelling for Postmodern Youth Ministry* (Nashville, TN: Upper Room, 2007), 82–83.

21 Ibid., 84.

22 http://www.midnighteye.com/interviews/hayao-miyazaki/.

23 Mark MacWilliams, "Introduction," in *Japanese Visual Culture: Explorations in the World of Manga and Anime*, edited by Mark MacWilliams (London: Routledge, 2008), 3.

Over time, the growing demand for more mature content by *manga* readers and artists birthed the more countercultural, adult-themed *gekiga*. Sometimes translated "dramatic pictures," the latter took a darker flavour than the "whimsical pictures" that *manga* started off as.[24]

To think that Japanese manga evolved as a native storytelling form devoid of foreign influence would be to ignore the facts surrounding its development. Manga historians point to the strong influence of satirical and humorous publications by foreigners in Japan during the mid-1800s. British foreign correspondent-cum-sketch artist Charles Wirgman is credited for having taught Japanese students cartooning techniques and introducing word balloons while French cartoonist-cum-illustrator Georges Bigot is known for acquainting Japanese readers to narrative panels.[25]

The influence of non-Japanese elements is also evidenced in other ways in the body of work produced by Japanese *manga* artists. Amongst the many works of Osamu Tezuka, the famed "grandfather of *manga*," include Shin Takarajima based on Robert Louis Stevenson's *Treasure Island*, Dostoevsky's Crime and Punishment, Goethe's Faust, and Shakespeare's Merchant of Venice. Such is the extent of *manga's* hybridization that already took place on Japanese soil.

Outside Japan, *manga's* popularity has seen explosive, exponential growth on a global scale. On this point, Bryce, Barber, and Plumb note:

> *Recent decades have seen an extraordinary growth in the international reception and consumption of manga and anime. Manga and anime have been central to Japan's popular culture but these powerful narratives, characterized by hybridity and fluidity, have spread out from their local source to achieve global reach and appeal…Once translated, they are capable of connecting people from different cultures and languages, forming a new forum for entertainment, as well as cultural and social communication.*[26]

---

24 Roman Rosenbaum, "Towards a Summation: How Do *Manga* Represent History," in *Manga and the Representation of Japanese History*, edited by Rosenbaum Roman (New York: Routledge, 2013), 6.

25 Helen McCarthy, *A Brief History of Manga* (Lewes: UK: Ilex, 2014), 8–9; Kinko Ito, "*Manga* in Japanese History," in *Japanese Visual Culture: Explorations in the World of Manga and Anime*, edited by Mark MacWilliams (London: Routledge, 2008), 29–30.

26 Mio Bryce, Christie Barber, and Amy Plumb, "*Manga* and Anime: Fluidity and Hybridity in Global Imagery," in *Researching Twenty-First Century Japan: New Directions and Approaches for the Electronic Age*, edited by Timothy Iles and Peter Matanle (Lanham, MA: Lexington, 2012), 323–42.

The British newspaper, *Independent*, ran an arts feature entitled "The Ascent of *Manga*: Japan's Hottest Export Goes Global." In it, its author noted that the adoption of the form has birthed British adaptations as well as fueled growth within a stagnant comics industry.[27]

Beyond noting its global spread, critical scholars have also explored the nature of *manga's* glocalization in different countries of its adoption.[28] Key in Brienza's research on *manga* in America is the identification and discussion of a strong domestication element in the adoption process. Elements in the chain include "licensing, translation, lettering, graphic design, editing, and sales and marketing."[29] On the other hand, her research on *manga's* adoption in other countries of the world broadened the discussion to explore very different purposes, considerations, and histories that have shaped the localization process. The titles of the ten essays found in the contents page of her book *Global Manga: "Japanese" Comics without Japan?* provide fascinating clues and pique curiosity as to the conditions behind their reception:

- The Western Sailor Moon Generation: North American Women and Feminine-Friendly Global *Manga*

- The *Manga* Style in Brazil

- Scott Pilgrim vs. *MANGAMAN*: Two Approaches to the Negotiation of Cultural Difference

- *Euromanga*: Hybrid Styles and Stories in Transcultural *Manga* Production

- "*Manga* is Not Pizza": The Performance of Ethno-racial Authenticity and the Politics of American Anime and *Manga* Fandom in Svetlana Chmakova's Dramacon

- On Everyday Life: Frederic Boilet and the Nouvelle *Manga* Movement

- An American *Manga* Artist's Journey Down a Road Less Drawn

- Sporting the Gothic Look: Refashioning the Gothic Mode in German *Manga* Trends

---

27 https://www.independent.co.uk/arts-entertainment/art/features/the-ascent-of-*manga*-japans-hottest-export-goes-global-1050511.html.

28 Brienza 2015; Brienza 2016; Bryce, Barber, and Plumb 2012.

29 Casey Brienza, *Manga in America: Transnational Book Publishing and the Domestication of Japanese Comics* (London: Bloomsbury Academic, 2016), 39–40.

- Constructing the *Mangaverse*: Narrative Patterns in Marvel's Appropriation of *Manga* Products
- Pinoy *Manga* in Philippine Komiks

From the above, it is clear that mixed circumstances and responses to hybridity have come with global spread of *manga*. To this, we include for discussion *manga's* adoption by Christian artists and publishers to communicate Bible stories. Not surprising, the deployment of this visual storytelling form to communicate with audiences steeped in visual culture has been met with very mixed reviews and reception from the Christian community.

Kamishibai Street Theatre

Kamishibai is a form of theatre performance that was popular in Japan from the late 1920s until the late 1950s. It originated as a form of street entertainment provided by vendors selling candy to children in urban poor neighborhoods.[30] Beyond its origins as street entertainment for children, kamishibai was also used as wartime propaganda aimed at adults.[31]

Orbaugh describes the storytelling form below:

> Kamishibai, *at its most basic, consists of a storytelling performance accompanied by illustrated cards. A set of between ten and thirty cardboard cards ("play cards") about 39 cm by 27 cm constituted one complete play or one episode of a serialized story. An audience would be gathered, and the cards, with an illustration on one side and the script on the other, would be pulled out of a special stage frame one by one as the performer enhanced the script with lively characterizations, songs, and sound effects.[32]*

As noted in the description above, the combination of music, drama, and storytelling all contributed to the appeal of this storytelling form. These elements, coupled with masterly storytelling, fueled its popularity until it's demise with the advent of television.

Even though it's popularity as traditional street entertainment has waned, there are signs that the theatre form has not died out. Instead, the form has found a range of contemporary platforms where it continues to be used.

---

30 Tara M. McGowan, *The Kamishibai Classroom: Engaging Multiple Literacies Through the Art of "Paper Theater"* (Santa Barbara, CA: Libraries Unlimited, 2010), xi.

31 Sharalyn Orbaugh, "Kamishibai: The Fantasy Space of the Urban Street Corner," in *Introducing Japanese Popular Culture*, edited by Alisa Freedman and Toby Slade (London: Routledge, 2017), 348–60.

32 Ibid., 2.

Kamishibai is used today in nightclubs, at political demonstrations, and in a wide variety of edgy venues to communicate affectively rich and often politically charged messages to audiences of all ages.[33]

Contemporary interest in this storytelling form is also reflected in McGowan's recent research which sought to "explore the potential of *kamishibai* as a dynamic 'new' interactive medium for teaching multimodal communication" and to show "how synchronizing oral, visual, and gestural modes develops students' awareness of all modes of communication as potential resources in their learning."[34]

Of interest to the discussion of globalization and hybridity is that the use of *kamishibai* has not been contained to use in Japan, but has spread to many different continents. When Australian oral storyteller Jackie Kerin conducted a *kamishibai* workshop at the International Storytelling Festival 2017 in Singapore, she introduced the form to the participants and told stories from Australia, Indonesia, Thailand, and Japan.[35] A point I recall her sharing with participants was how she used *kamishibai* to tell tales from the Hindu epic *Mahabharata* to Australian high school children because that was the rage amongst teenagers Down Under. Kerin is also an active member of the Australian *Kamishibai* Association, a group which seeks "to raise awareness of *kamishibai* as an art and educational tool, to connect *kamishibai* enthusiasts in Australia and to share events."[36] On Facebook, she is regularly seen performing and connecting with other *kamishibai* performers within Australia and across the globe.

Another example of its use outside Japan is seen in South African entertainer Jemma Kahn's introduction of *kamishibai* to her country. Kahn spent time in Japan and interned under a Japanese *kamishibai* performer before playing successfully in theatres across South Africa telling both local and international *kamishibai* stories in a variety of languages. She has performed for both children and adult audiences and has dished out large doses of innocent as well as raunchy humor. As a theatre practitioner, she has dealt with serious societal and political themes and has incorporated burlesque and other elements of theatre into her shows. Her latest play, which is semi-autobiographical,

---

33 Ibid., 349.

34 McGowan, i.

35 https://storyfestsg.com/2017/programmes/.

36 https://www.facebook.com/pg/AusKamishibai/about/?ref=page_internal.

incorporates the use of four *kamishibai* boxes instead of the traditional one box.[37]

What we thus have is a mixed medium Japanese storytelling form recognized for its value. It has gained a following in various parts of the world, and is presently deployed to tell stories from many different cultures in a very broad range of social settings. These all evidence the hybridization of a storytelling form and the global conditions that have both allowed as well as fueled their movements and mixes.

Pecha Kucha 20x20

Pecha Kucha 20x20 is a slide presentation format that had its origins in Tokyo, Japan. It was devised in 2003 by Astrid Klein and Mark Dytham, expatriates who were running the architectural firm Klein Dytham Architecture. As a format, it was designed to help young designers move away from traditional bullet-point presentations and to keep them brief and visually eye-catching.[38] Garner provides a description of Pecha Kucha below:

> Pecha Kucha, *which means "chit chat" in Japanese, is an electronic presentation format composed of exactly 20 PowerPoint slides with exactly 20 seconds of narrative for each slide (for a totally presentation time of 6:40)...Given a topic to explore and present, students must consider the facts and concepts to include (or to omit) and then create visual and auditory displays within the time constraints of the Pecha Kucha format.*[39]

Since its inception in the early 2000s, *Pecha Kucha* has been adopted by different professional and educational communities. Amongst them include artists, designers, architects, entertainers, and students in schools and universities. The success of this presentation format is seen in its widespread global adoption and the emergence of *Pecha Kucha* events in major cities around the world. There, anything from personal introductions, self-descriptions, lessons of life, groundbreaking ideas, pub entertainment, and business proposals have been presented.

---

37 https://sarafinamagazine.com/2017/06/01/a-conversation-with-jemma-kahn/.

38 Steve Ingle and Vicky Duckworth, *Enhancing Learning through Technology in Lifelong Learning: Fresh Ideas; Innovative Strategies* (Maidenhead, England: Open University, 2013), 45.

39 Brad Garner, *Engaged Learners and Digital Citizens. Newcastle upon Tyne* (Cambridge Scholars, 2016), 127.

One educator proposed using it to assess how well students have grasped as well as can demonstrate their learning of content in the allocated six minutes and forty seconds.[40]

Pecha Kucha has now been firmly established amongst creatives in urban centers around the world and used to communicate stories and ideas from different cultures, academic fields, and professional industries. Besides developing a global following, the 20x20 format has also developed various adaptations. These include Ignite, which uses a five-minute format with a shorter, fifteen-second limit for each of the twenty slides used. Then there is also Talk20 which follows the *Pecha Kucha* format but lines up ten speakers for every event. The speakers are carefully selected with the goal of leaving audiences with diverse learning experiences and resources for personal or community enrichment.

The Evolving Frontiers of Hybridity and Their Relevance for Diaspora Missions

What are the threads that run through and hold the three evolving frontiers of hybridity described above? What relevance do they hold for diaspora missiology? While it is true that the work of missions focuses on people, it cannot be divorced from the worlds they move and live in. The world's peoples on the move enter new spheres which they have to negotiate and navigate. As they move and mix, they spawn hybridization and are themselves hybridized.

On another level, the forces and effects of globalization are also introducing new frontiers of hybridization. These can be globally widespread and ubiquitous as in the example of the expanded, integrated ecosystem of physical and virtual spaces. They can also be globally located within a specific pillar of society as in the case of the growing phenomenon of reconfigured global households. Otherwise, they can be globally situated within niche arenas as in the case of creatives deploying Japanese storytelling traditions to communicate in an age of visuality and visual culture.

Whether they are felt at all levels or only by one sector of society, the three examples offered representative fronts of innovation and rapid change. These are but a few of the evolving culturally mixed worlds that the world's people will inhabit and where perspectives, intuitions, and social practices are being reordered.

---

40 Ingle and Duckworth, 46.

When we consider activity at these fronts, what is disconcerting is that the church remains slow to adapt or respond there. The church has little influence at frontiers of change and innovation. At times, it remains unaware and ignorant. At other times, it remains resistant and reactionary. Otherwise, it remains silent and absent. Yet, it is a matter of missional imperative and pastoral responsibility that the church serves to, through, beyond, and with the peoples on the move at new hybridizing worlds and frontiers. These frontiers are expanding and redefining the contexts within which diaspora missiology needs to be situated. In response, the call is for bearers of the gospel of Jesus Christ to engage, to be mobilized, to be active, and to be present at these missional frontiers.

BIBLIOGRAPHY

Appadurai, Arjun. *Modernity at Large: Cultural Dimensions of Globalization.* Minneapolis, MN: University Of Minnesota, 1996.

Arthur, Sarah. *The God-Hungry Imagination: The Art of Storytelling for Postmodern Youth Ministry.* Nashville, TN: Upper Room, 2007.

Bland, Archie. "The Ascent of *Manga*: Japan's Hottest Export Goes Global," December 4, 2008. https://www.independent.co.uk/arts-entertainment/art/features/the-ascent-of-*manga*-japans-hottest-export-goes-global-1050511.html, 2008.

Brienza, Casey, ed. *Global Manga: "Japanese" Comics without Japan?* Surrey, UK: Ashgate, 2015.

———. *Manga in America: Transnational Book Publishing and the Domestication of Japanese Comics.* London: Bloomsbury Academic, 2016.

Bryce, Mio, Christie Barber, and Amy Plumb. "*Manga* and Anime: Fluidity and Hybridity in Global Imagery." In *Researching Twenty-First Century Japan: New Directions and Approaches for the Electronic Age,* edited by Timothy Iles and Peter Matanle, 323–42. Lanham, MA: Lexington, 2012.

Burke, Peter. *Cultural Hybridity.* Cambridge, UK: Polity, 2009.

Canclini, Nestor Garcia. *Hybrid Cultures: Strategies for Entering and Leaving Modernity.* Minneapolis, MN: University of Minnesota, 2005.

Douglass, Mike. "The Globalization of Householding and Social Reproduction in Pacific Asia." *Philippine Studies* 55 (2): 157–81, 2007.

Eriksen, Thomas Hylland. *Globalization: The Key Concepts.* Oxford, UK: Berg, 2007.

Farley, Ashleigh. *Digital Third Places: Using Online Spaces to Connect to Community.* Charlotte, NC: Queens University of Charlotte Knight, 2013.

Garner, Brad. *Engaged Learners and Digital Citizens.* Newcastle upon Tyne: Cambridge Scholars, 2016.

Ingle, Steve, and Vicky Duckworth. *Enhancing Learning through Technology in Lifelong Learning: Fresh Ideas; Innovative Strategies.* Maidenhead, England: Open University, 2013.

Ito, Kinko. "*Manga* in Japanese History." In *Japanese Visual Culture: Explorations in the World of Manga and Anime*, edited by Mark MacWilliams, 29–30. London: Routledge, 2008.

Karatani, Rieko. "Female Domestic Workers on the Move: Examining Global Householding and Global De-Householding in Today's World." In *Multiculturalism and Conflict Reconciliation in the Asia-Pacific: Migration, Language and Politics*, edited by Kosuke Shimizu and William S. Bradley, 137–61, 2012.

Kraidy, Marwan M. *Hybridity, or the Cultural Logic of Globalization.* Philadelphia, PA: Temple University, 2005.

MacWilliams, Mark. "Introduction." In *Japanese Visual Culture: Explorations in the World of Manga and Anime*, edited by Mark MacWilliams, 3–25. London: Routledge, 2008.

McArthur, John A., and Ashleigh Farley White. "Twitter Chats as Third Places: Conceptualizing a Digital Gathering Site." *Social Media + Society*, September, 2016.

McCarthy, Helen. *A Brief History of Manga.* Lewes: UK: Ilex, 2014.

McGowan, Tara M. *The Kamishibai Classroom: Engaging Multiple Literacies Through the Art of "Paper Theater."* Santa Barbara, CA: Libraries Unlimited, 2010.

———. *Performing Kamishibai: An Emerging New Literacy for a Global Audience* (Routledge Research in Education). New York: Routledge, 2015.

Memarovic, Nemanja, Sidney Fels, Junia Anacleto, Roberto Calderon, Federico Gobbo, and John M. Carroll. 2014. "Rethinking Third Places: Contemporary Design with Technology." *The Journal of Community Informatics 10* (3).

Oldenburg, Ray. *The Great Good Place: Cafés, Coffee Shops, Bookstores, Bars, Hair Salons, and Other Hangouts at the Heart of a Community.* New York: Marlowe and Company, 1999.

Orbaugh, Sharalyn. "Kamishibai: The Fantasy Space of the Urban Street Corner." In *Introducing Japanese Popular Culture*, edited by Alisa Freedman and Toby Slade, 348–60. London: Routledge, 2017.

———. *Propaganda Performed: Kamishibai in Japan's Fifteen Year War.* Leiden, Nederland: Brill, 2015.

Ritzer, George. *Globalization: The Essentials.* Malden, MA: Wiley-Blackwell, 2011.

Rosenbaum, Roman. "Towards a Summation: How Do *Manga* Represent History." In *Manga and the Representation of Japanese History*, edited by Rosenbaum Roman, 251–58. New York: Routledge, 2013.

Tsing, Anna. "The Global Situation." In *The Anthropology of Globalization: A Reader*, edited by Inda Jonathan Xavier and Rosaldo Renato, 2nd ed., 66–98. Malden, MA: Blackwell, 2008.

ABOUT THE AUTHOR

DR. CALVIN CHONG is Associate Professor of Practical Ministries at the Singapore Bible College. His teaching and research interests include Church Engagement with Culture, Urban Missions, and Diaspora Missions. Dr. Chong also serves on the boards of the migrant NGO Healthserve and the Evangelical Fellowship of Singapore.

CHAPTER 7 | Tuvya Zaretsky

Jewish-Gentile Intermarriage: A Hybridity Laboratory

Us and them: That is a classic Jewish worldview. It is simple and straightforward. World Jewry identifies as an ethnically singular nation in distinction to all the other nations. It is expressed as *Am Yisrael*, the nation Israel, and *Kol Ha-goyim*, all the nations. This simple ethnocentric classification, as one nation versus all the others, presents an interesting "petri dish" for an anthropological missiological study of hybridity. We aim to show some of the implications and opportunities for disciple-ship of the next generation of Jewish-Gentile couples and families.

We will first examine the dramatic shift toward Jewish-Gentile intermarriage since 1990.[1] We will note how the broader Jewish community has reacted to the phenomenon. To seek understanding of that reaction we will consider some issues, challenges and implications regarding Jewish national development and Jewish intermarriage in the Bible.

From these two perspectives, we see within the current Jewish-Gentile intermarriage trend, a laboratory for the study of hybridity and some of the missiological implications.

---

1 Throughout this chapter, I use the term Gentile to mean "the other nations" in distinction from Jewish people, descendants of Israel. Grammatically, I recognize "gentiles" as more correct reference to nations. Here I am using "Gentile" to denote other nations as a proper noun for the people group that is in parallel with the Jewish people.

The Changing Demographic

Over the past thirty years, intermarriage has been a dominant pattern of Jewish life in the Diaspora. The 1990 National Jewish Population Survey (NJPS) was the first citation of the seismic sociological shift among American Jewry. The American Jewish intermarriage rate rose slowly from 6 percent in the 1960s to 12 percent in the 1970s. By 1990, the NJPS reported the "bad news" that the Jewish-Gentile intermarriage rate was continuing to double every decade, finally reaching 52 percent. This was the first time in American Jewish sociological reports that Jewish-Gentile exogamy exceeded endogamous Jewish marriage.

In 1997, then Harvard law professor, Alan Dershowitz, in *The Vanishing American Jew: In Search of Jewish Identity for the New Century*, warned the trend would lead to American Jewrys' assimilation, except for the Orthodox community. In the same year, American diplomat, educator and legal expert, Elliott Abrams, warned of the threat to Jewish survival in *Faith or Fear: How Can Jews Survive in Christian America*. Before the next decadal report, Jewish Theological Seminary historian, Jack Wertheimer, warned Jewish exogamy had become "self destructively... accommodated" by American Jews.[2] The fact of Jewish intermarriage signaled a dramatic change in the identity of American Jewry and the increased hybridity of the next generation.

Jewish sociologists and religious leaders responded with anguish and aggression. Jewish institutions increased funding and programs designed to promote Jewish reattachment to Judaism and conversion of Gentile spouses. At the same time, American sociological studies continued showing a 63 percent Jewish disaffiliation from Jewish institutions. American Jews were turning their backs on traditional Judaism, disconnecting from synagogue life and trending toward assimilation.

The 2001 NJPS demonstrated none of those efforts were having the desired impact. The trend was not slowing or turning back. Jewish intermarriage registered at 54 percent. At that point the American Jewish Federation discontinued providing decadal studies. In 2013, the Pew Research Center's, "A Portrait of Jewish Americans," found that fully 44 percent of all American Jews today are married to non-Jewish spouses. The Jewish rate of exogamy continued to rise to 58 percent

2 Jack Wertheimer, "Surrendering to Intermarriage," *Commentary Magazine,* https://www.commentarymagazine.com/articles/surrendering-to-intermarriage/.

by that year. Further, if you were to remove the small community of Orthodox or *Haredi* religious Jews from the American Jewish population sample, the intermarriage rate is actually a whopping 73 percent.[3] The demographic trend toward Jewish exogamy was anticipated by the Lord and addressed in history. We now turn attention to briefly look at those considerations as presented in the Bible.

Intermarriage in the Bible[4]

Within Biblical history, God demanded the Jewish people remain separate from the Canaanite nations they encountered in the Promised Land. Historically, rabbis have taught that, for the preservation of Judaism, Jews must not intermarry and assimilate.

The subject of intermarriage in the Bible is first introduced after the young nation of Israel was redeemed from slavery out of Egypt. After 40 years together in the Sinai wilderness, the Jewish people were about to enter the Land of Promise. The God of Abraham, Isaac and Jacob was visibly present with the nation in a pillar of fire by night and the cloud by day, residing among them over the Tent of Meeting. They received instruction in Torah and a promised blessing if they would look to Him daily with trust and obedience.

God also prohibited the Israelites from marrying the Canaanite people in the land they were to inherit. The issue was not racial, but a warning about spiritual character. That ban was to protect the Hebrews against religious perversion and idolatrous influences of Canaanite religions.[5]

The Lord God was jealous for the hearts of the Israelites. Therefore, He warned them against exposing their families, and the generations of children yet to come, to spiritual practices that would lead them away from *Adonai*. They could endure harm to their faith through intimacy with people who did not share their love and faithfulness in the one true God. This same principle ought to be applied today by the partners in Jewish-Gentile couples that believe in Messiah Jesus. They ignore their sanctification at the cost of spiritual well-being.

---

3 Luis Lugo, Alan Cooperman, and Gregory A. Smith, principal investigators. "The 2013 Pew Research Center Survey of US Jews: A Portrait of Jewish Americans," *Jewish Federation of North America*, http://www.jewishdatabank.org/Studies/details. cfm?StudyID=715.

4 Tuvya Zaretsky, *He Said…then She Said: Helping Jewish-Gentile Couples Find Spiritual Harmony*. Appendix 3: "Intermarriage in the Bible." (San Francisco: Jews for Jesus), 121–26, 2016.

5 Exodus 34:10–17 and Deuteronomy 7:1–4

Today, many Christians are aware of Paul's teaching in 2 Corinthians 6:14 against being "unequally yoked." Still, too many forget purity for the sake of contemporary trends toward the embrace of passion. The "unequally yoked" warning is from Deuteronomy 22:10, "You shall not plow with an ox and a donkey together." Jewish people have been preserved as a unique nation, sanctified as a testimony of God's faithful covenant, to show the nations His indelible Word of promise to Abraham, Isaac and Jacob. *Adonai*'s character is displayed in His faithfulness to sustain Israel.

Even King Solomon, the son of David, took about 700 wives, many from foreign nations.[6] The Scripture is powerfully direct in charging that Solomon allowed his heart to be turned away from the God of his father and his people. He was "not loyal to the Lord his God, as was the heart of his father, David."[7] Solomon's bad example caused the Jewish nation to pay a terrible price in the centuries that followed. His disregard for God's instruction allowed the idols of those other nations to pollute the hearts and faith of Israelites. They turned from the Lord and subsequently split from one another as the Northern and Southern kingdoms.

Their diminished faith in *Adonai* of that era eventually led to separate deportations of Jewish exiles to Assyria and then later to Babylon. Both Ezra and Nehemiah describe their dismay at the compromised faith and assimilation of their nations' religious leaders who brought foreign wives back with them from captivity.[8] The issue was then, and is today as well, God's jealousy for the hearts of those who are His people. The identity of the Lord's chosen ones, from whatever nation, depends upon their abiding trust in Him. This is a contemporary issue as we look at how Jewish-Gentile couples and their children establish new hybrid identities today. Here, we can consider missiological implications and opportunities.

Intermarriage Implications and Opportunities: Jewish Responses

The 2013 Pew Research into American Jewry found that, over the past three decades, 83 percent of the children from Jewish-Gentile marriages have also married a spouse who is not Jewish. A generation

---

6 1 Kings 11:1–5.

7 1 Kings 11:2–5.

8 Ezra 9 and 10 and Nehemiah 13:23–27.

of Jewish-Gentile children from these intermarriages are now adults presenting a new hybrid Jewish identity. They are the American Jewish Millennials. They now proceed through higher education and move into the professional workplace. Jewish leaders, like Rabbi Aaron Lerner, Executive Director of Hillel at UCLA, observed a totally new self-identity among American Jewish college students. To the wider Jewish community, these children from Jewish intermarriages do not look like past Jewish generations. Lerner cautioned, "If we don't give these men and women a right to be part of our Jewish community, we risk losing them forever."[9]

Institutional American Jewish opinion has trended toward the viewpoint that Jewish hybridity from intermarriage is bad for the Jews. Emma Green wrote in The Atlantic, "But what's at stake is actually the future of Jewish identity and pluralism."[10] In our Missiological laboratory, we see implications and opportunities for ministry rising from the cross-cultural experiences and hybrid identities found among Jewish-Gentile couples and their Jewish Millennial children.

A Hybridity Picture of Jewish-Gentile Identity

The 2013 Pew Research Center Survey of US Jews also highlighted the impact of intermarriage and secularization on the children of Jewish-Gentile marriages. They are a generation known as Millennials, born between 1981–1997. More than half of them, reflecting the intermarriage rate of their parents, are from Jewish-Gentile couples.

The Pew study found only 19 percent of Baby Boomers, the parents of Millennials, self-identify as Jewish without any religion: or "nones". By contrast, 32 percent of Jewish Millennials self-identify as Jews of no religion. That is a 13 percent increased change from the identity of their parents. And 62 percent of all Pew respondents said that being Jewish is more about culture and ancestry—not about religion.[11] The hybrid Jewish identities, particularly in America, reflect a disconnect from religious identity. Whereas traditional Judaism maintained a high

---

9 Aaron Lerner, "On College Campuses, the Intermarriage Debate is Already Over." *The Jewish Forward Online*, http://forward.com/opinion/spirituality/386405/we-asked-22-rabbis-is-intermarriage-a-problem-or-an-opportunity/?attribution=tag-article-listing-3-headline.

10 Emma Green, "We're Headed Toward One of the Greatest Divisions in the History of the Jewish People," *The Atlantic*, https://www.theatlantic.com/politics/archive/2017/07/intermarriage-conservative-judaism/533637/.

11 Lugo, Cooperman, and Smith, 2013.

"hedge" to prevent Jewish curiosity about Christian faith, the non-religious trend implies a greater openness to other expressions of spirituality. That has greater implication for younger American Jewry.

Over the past ten years, Barna Group has interviewed 27,140 Millennials in 206 studies. They are commonly finding Millennials making a distinction between spirituality and self-identity according to religion. This was one characteristic found in the Barna Group study of American Jewish Millennials in 2017.[12] That religion doesn't necessarily now mean affiliation with any religious organization is just one of the new facets of Jewish identity that Barna highlighted.

The Barna Group 2017 Study on American Jewish Millennials

Perhaps the most exciting barometer of the opportunity for ministry to Jewish-Gentile couples is revealed by the October 10, 2017, Barna Group study on American Jewish Millennials.[13] A few significant observations of that study point toward opportunities for ministry:

- Jewish Millennials are open-minded to spiritual conversations and do not find them scary.

- Millennial Jews see a difference in affiliating as opposed to believing. They are asking, "What will work for me?" and "Where is my community?"[14]

- Jewish Millennial relationships are often experienced through one-dimensional contact such as social media and digital devices. Millennials tend to crave meaning and connection as one result of such social isolation.

- Jewish Millennials are discovering value in Jewish wisdom literature in the Bible. Examples include:

  - Ecclesiastes says a lot about ambition: "Young person, think about what it means to live a long and meaningful life."

12 Barna Group, *Jewish Millennials: the Beliefs & Behaviors Shaping Young Jews in America*, Ventura, CA: Barna Group, 2017. See https://resources.barna.org/collections/millennials-generations/products/jewish-millennials.

13 Ibid.

14 Ben Sales, *"Jews for Jesus Commissioned a Study on Jewish Millennials. Here's What it Found."* New York (Jewish Telegraphic Agency) https://www.jta.org/2017/10/31/news-opinion/united-states/jews-for-jesus-commissioned-a-study-on-jewish-millennials-heres-what-it-found.

- Lamentations sees ways to express deep sorrow in the horrific events and relational models present in life.

- Song of Songs has a lot to teach about sexuality.

- Proverbs, the original Twitter feed, has good advice to offer about wise living.

Some specific findings for our consideration: The Barna Group report found that while 38 percent of American Jewish Millennials say they are not religious, 82 percent said they were "somewhat" or "very interested" in spirituality. What kind of spirituality? Surprisingly, 73 percent were interested in learning about the spirituality of other faiths besides Judaism, including Christianity.

One of the biggest surprises was the new perspective of Jesus among Jewish Millennials. Even the *Jerusalem Post* took notice, reporting, "The survey found that 21 percent of Jewish Millennials believe Jesus was 'God in human form who lived among people in the 1st century.'"[15] Evidence of hybridity is certain since demographics indicate more than half of Jewish Millennials have one non-Jewish parent. There are implications for spiritual influence from Gentile parents that may have been Christians and exposed their children to Jesus' teaching.

Jews for Jesus was commissioned as a mission organization, but did not influence the 2017 Barna Group study. The mission produced a missiological analysis of the study along with a series of articles based on the most significant Barna Group findings. It is titled, *7 Myths about Jewish Millennials*. Examples include Myth #1 The Rebel Millennial; Myth #4 Spirituality is Just Yoga and Unicorns. You can find the Jews for Jesus report available online at www.j4j.co/barnamyths.

American Jewish leaders have been doing their own analysis of the Barna Group findings and are adjusting to the evidence of identity changes among American Jewish Millennials. Ari Kelman, Jewish Studies professor at Stanford University, responding to the Barna report said, "These don't look like Jews I recognize...maybe these are Jews we've never seen before."[16]

The *Jerusalem Post*, besides noting that 21 percent of Jewish Millennials believe that Jesus was God, reported 42 percent of

---

15 Ibid., "Study: One-fifth of Jewish Millennials Believe Jesus is the Son of God," http://www.jpost.com/Diaspora/Study-One-fifth-of-Jewish-millennials-believe-Jesus-is-the-son-of-God-512015.

16 Ibid., "Jews for Jesus Commissioned a Study on Jewish Millennials," 2017.

respondents celebrate Christmas.[17] Barna also found a majority of Jewish Millennials said they could "hold other faiths and still be Jewish."[18] Thirty-four percent said "belief in Jesus as the Messiah was compatible with being Jewish," which also reflects a growing awareness and acceptance of Messianic Jews in Israeli and American Jewish cultures.[19]

Sara Weissman, editor of the web-zine New Voices, is one of the younger Jewish editors to opine regarding the significance of the Barna Group study.[20] She expressed both incredulity, but also familiarity with American Jewish Millennial culture. Weissman opined how the assessment is true, because she knows that Jewish Millennial the Barna study described. Nevertheless, she found the survey descpription disquieting:

> The young adults describe themselves as religious, and practice Jewish ritual, but are unaffiliated. They value tradition and family, but don't plan on marrying only Jews. They are proud to be Jewish, but don't feel that contradicts with practicing other religions.[21]

At the same time, Weissman offers an ethnographic description from her experience of the American Jewish Millennial who could be "dating a Buddhist," "laying tefilin daily even though he couldn't find a synagogue" or goes "clubbing on Friday nights, but insisting on turning off her phone and the computer." They say that being Jewish is "very important" to them. In fact, 80 percent would self-identify as "religious Jews." Weissman conceded, "the point is, our Judaism looks different… as millennials stray from traditional Jewish institutions and movements."[22]

These Jewish Millennials are the next growing wave of Jewish-Gentile couples. The Barna data indicates their hybrid identities lead them to be more spiritually open to new ways of defining Jewishness, spirituality and love of God. The missiological perspective on hybridity among contemporary Jewry, especially in America, indicates new and exciting opportunities for Gospel presentation among Jewish-Gentile couples and their families.

---

17 Ibid., "Study: One-fifth of Jewish Millennials Believe Jesus is the Son of God," 2017.

18 Ibid.

19 Ibid.

20 Sara Weissman, "Did Jews for Jesus Get Jewish Millennials Right?" New Voices: News and Views for Campus Jews, http://newvoices.org/2017/11/06/did-jews-for-jesus-just-get-something-right-about-jewish-millennials/.

21 Ibid.

22 Ibid.

Challenges and Opportunities

While American Jewish leaders lament that assimilation, secularization and intermarriage are dangerous to Jewish survival, the Christian community has been strategically unresponsive to this spiritual opportunity. Within half of those Jewish intermarriages are Gentiles. Often those are the partners who are familiar with the Bible, who desire to maintain an abiding faith in the Lord Jesus, and concurrently seek a deeper understanding of Jewish history and customs.

Studies by sociologists and psychologists report that interfaith couples experience greater threat to marital stability and satisfaction than same faith couples.[23] Studies indicate that 75 percent of mixed-faith couples experience marital dissatisfaction or divorce. Christians have a message of potential hope for this situation. It is the potential for spiritual harmony.

Finding Spiritual Harmony

It is important to state at the outset that we have a perspective about *the way* to find spiritual harmony. It is based on the biblical belief that the one Creator God accomplished reconciliation with Himself through His Messianic redeemer Jesus. When marital partners find vertical relationship with the same God through the same faith, they are then able to find horizontal intimacy and shared spirituality with one another.[24] God, in the Scriptures, promised He would answer anyone who earnestly opens their heart to Him and invites Him to be known. God has given everyone the gift of free will and the ability to understand His truth. If anyone is open to the words of Jesus, it is important that they know His offer, "Ask and you will receive. Seek and you will find. Knock and the door will be opened to you."[25]

In the ministry to Jewish-Gentile couples, we believe that if each partner would seek God in the way He wants to be known, He will lead them to Himself through the person of Messiah Jesus. My confidence is founded on biblical statements by Jesus and the apostles. See for examples John 14:6; Acts 4:12 and 1 John 5:11 & 12.

---

23 R. A. Call Vaughn, and Tim B. Heaton, "Religious Influence on Marriage Stability." *Journal for the Scientific Study of Religion* 30, no. 3 (1997): 390.

24 Enoch Wan, "The Paradigm of 'Relational Realism,'" *Evangelical Missiological Society* 19, no. 2 (2006).

25 Matthew 7:7.

Issues and Challenges

There seem to be at least three contemporary issues that drive the conversation around Jewish-Gentile intermarriage. Those are survival, enculturation of children and finding spiritual harmony.

Survival is an imperative core value for world Jewry. That impulse was intensified by the extermination of one third of the people during the Holocaust. Contemporary rabbis in America are especially concerned about the massive dis-affiliation from Judaism and Jewish institutions. In their perspective, intermarriage is a direct threat to the survival of the religion. That is because they define Jewish identity according to religious attachments, connecting religious culture to ethnic makeup. No similar impulse exists within the Christian community. Christians who marry a non-believer are regarded as making a personal choice to put their spiritual well-being in jeopardy. However, intermarriage is not viewed as a global, national or cultural threat to Christian faith.

Enculturation of children of Jewish-Gentile marriages is a second pressing issue. Couples all too often avoid the choices around the process of enculturating the next generation. Marianna Calahan at USC identified four strategies of enculturation and included 1) Delegation to one partner, 2) Cooperation-where both partners share in the enculturation of their children in one or both faith traditions, 3) Abdication-where they intentionally choose not to offer religious training so the children "may decide for themselves", 4) Avoidance-the failure to adequately discuss the process of enculturation usually results in tension, mistrust, frustration and anger. The choices come down to one faith, two faiths or none.

A third issue is an inability to find spiritual harmony. As we will show, American Jewish Millennials are rejecting religion, while showing an interest in tradition and a hunger for spirituality. This, I believe, is an opportunity with Missiological implications related to identity hybridization occurring in the subsequent generation of Jewish-Gentile couples.

An Approach

A 2004 ethnographic study of the cross-cultural challenges reported by Jewish-Gentile couples identified five key challenges.[26] Underlying all of them was the inability to find a satisfying spiritual harmony. I suggest a Missiological approach that utilizes tools of cultural anthropology.

---

26 Zaretsky, "The Challenges of Jewish-Gentile Couples," 2004.

We seek greater understanding of the cross-cultural challenges that Jewish-Gentile couples report from their experience. While spiritual rebirth or renewal is the desired goal, this ministry does not start with a conversionary agenda. We absolutely believe that salvation in Christ can lead to satisfaction and stability in marriage through spiritual harmony, following the methodology presented by Donald K. Smith in *Creating Understanding: A Handbook for Christian Communication Across Cultural Landscapes.*[27]

Missiological cultural anthropology seeks to understand how partners use words, concepts and presuppositions that inform their world view. We can serve them in being cross-cultural translators, helping build bridges between their two identities, cultures and world views. At the same time, we must be mindful of our own intervening culture during this process. Specific practices have been developed and presented as a training manual for Christians desiring to engage in Jewish-Gentile couples ministry.[28]

The 2017 Barna study describes religious outlook and identity of American Jewish Millennials. It begins their description as, "… free-thinking and flexible in their spiritual and religious identity, yet they gravitate toward formal customs and ancient expressions of faith." This population is the majority of American Jewry today: a hybrid identity coming out of the Jewish-Gentile marriage phenomenon dating back to the last thirty years. A key issue for them is where can they find community? A beginning point is to inform them that they are the majority of American Jewry today. A booklet is now available to introduce couples to discussion around Jewish-Gentile spiritual harmony. It is intended for them to read together and complete a self-assessment section at the end of each chapter, which they share with one another.[29]

The Barna Group Report on American Jewish Millennials found a third would say they are not religious, and yet more than two thirds are interested in spirituality. They have turned away from religious conventions, while respecting traditions that convey history, story and meaning.[30] Jewish-Gentile intermarriage has significant implications for

---

27 Donald K. Smith, *Creating Understanding: A Handbook for Christian Communication Across Cultural Landscapes* (Grand Rapids: Zondervan Publishing House), 1992.

28 Zaretsky, *He Said…Then She Said,* 2016.

29 Ibid., *Finding Spiritual Harmony in Your Jewish-Gentile Couple Relationship*, 2017.

30 "We're not Religious, but we are Spiritual" *Gospel-Life*, https://jewsforjesus.org/articles/?_sft_category=newsletter-jul-2017.

Gospel ministry to a new spiritual interest among Jewish hybrid identities. Their forms of identity expressions may appear unconventional, but they include a desire for a relationship with God. It is the right time to get out of the laboratory and into fruitful spiritual engagements.

BIBLIOGRAPHY

Barna Group. *Jewish Millennials: the Beliefs & Behaviors Shaping Young Jews in America* (Ventura, CA: Barna Group), 2017. See https://resources.barna.org/collections/millennials-generations/products/jewish-millennials.

Green, Emma. "We're Headed Toward One of the Greatest Divisions in the History of the Jewish People." *The Atlantic.* https://www.theatlantic.com/politics/archive/2017/07/intermarriage-conservative-judaism/533637/.

Lerner, Aaron. "On College Campuses, the Intermarriage Debate is Already Over." The Jewish Forward Online, http://forward.com/opinion/spirituality/386405/we-asked-22-rabbis-is-intermarriage-a-problem-or-an-opportunity/?attribution=tag-article-listing-3-headline.

Lugo, Luis, Alan Cooperman, Gregory A. Smith, principal investigators. "The 2013 Pew Research Center Survey of US Jews: A Portrait of Jewish Americans" (Jewish Federation of North America) http://www.jewishdatabank.org/Studies/details.cfm?StudyID=715.

Sales, Ben. "Jews for Jesus Commissioned a Study on Jewish Millennials. Here's What it Found." New York (Jewish Telegraphic Agency) https://www.jta.org/2017/10/31/news-opinion/united-states/jews-for-jesus-commissioned-a-study-on-jewish-millennials-heres-what-it-found.

Smith, Donald K. *Creating Understanding: A Handbook for Christian Communication Across Cultural Landscapes.* (Grand Rapids: Zondervan Publishing House), 1992.

Vaughn, R. A. Call, and Tim B. Heaton, "Religious Influence on Marriage Stability." *Journal for the Scientific Study of Religion* 30, no. 3 (1997): 390.

Wan, Enoch. "The Paradigm of 'Relational Realism.'" Evangelical Missiological Society 19, no. 2 (2006).

Weissman, Sara. "Did Jews for Jesus Get Jewish Millennials Right?" New Voices: News and Views for Campus Jews. November 6, 2017. http://newvoices.org/2017/11/06/did-jews-for-jesus-just-get-something-right-about-jewish-millennials/.

Wertheimer, Jack. "Surrendering to Intermarriage." *Commentary Magazine.* https://www.commentarymagazine.com/articles/surrendering-to-intermarriage.

Zaretsky, Tuvya. He Said…then She Said: Helping Jewish-Gentile Couples Find Spiritual Harmony. Appendix 3: "Intermarriage in the Bible." (San Francisco: Jews for Jesus), 121–26, 2016.

Zaretsky, Tuvya. "The Challenges of Jewish-Gentile Couples: A Pre-Evangelistic Ethnographic Study." A Dissertation and partial fulfillment of the Doctor of Missiology Degree at Western Seminary; Portland, Oregon 2004.

ABOUT THE AUTHOR

DR. TUVYA ZARETSKY has pioneered and served for over four decades with the Jews for Jesus ministry. He earned a Doctorate in Missiology at Western Seminary. His work focuses on Jewish-Gentile couples. He presently serves as president of the Lausanne Consultation on Jewish Evangelism, the longest standing Lausanne issue network.

CHAPTER 8 | Daniel Álvarez

Mestizaje and *Hibridez*: A Latino Appreciation of Hybridity

Currently, there is a noticeable gap in the literature of a Latino[1] perspective on hybridity. In what follows, I review Latino literature that mentions hybridity. Most of it is written from a non-theological vantage point. Latino theological literature uses another term, *mestizaje*, to describe intercultural and interracial realities. *Mestizaje* is a theological term that affirms Latino identity and worldview. Its usage is very similar to hybridity, but specific to the Latino experience. As such, Latino theological discussions engage culture, agency, nationality, and race through *mestizaje*. In the latter part of this chapter I build bridges from *mestizaje* to hybridity in order to, first, describe an inter-cultural and interracial dialogue within the Latino community, and secondly, to engage the larger context outside this community. My conclusion is that Latino theology must dialogue with hybridity in order to contribute to it and to learn from it.

---

1 Because of the gendered connotations of the term in Spanish, many prefer to write the word "Latino/a," "Latin@," or "Latinx" to specify the inclusion of females. The author wishes to clarify that he is conscious of the need to have inclusive language in the academy and that his use of "Latino" is intentionally inclusive of all genders.

Hybridity in Latino Literature

In the breadth of theological literature from the Latino community in the US it is very difficult to find literature considering hybridity. One particular author that is helpful is Néstor García Canclini, an Argentine author that refers to hybridity and hybridization. He is a well-known social theorist that writes about the issues of modernity and modernization in Latin America.[2] In a primordial sense, García Canclini's usage is biological in nature: it is space between two zones of biological purity distinguishing between two discrete species and hybrid pseudo-species that result from these combinations.[3] Secondly, he uses hybridity in relationship to culture as "the ongoing condition of all human cultures, which contain no zones of purity because they undergo continuous processes of transculturation (two-way borrowing and lending between cultures)."[4] An example of this double function of hybridity is in an essay in which he discusses the adjustment of indigenous cultures to mainstream Mexican culture post NAFTA.[5] There are many streams that enter into dialogue racially and culturally: Amerindian cultures, Latino culture, and the introduction of dominant US culture. García Canclini's efforts are worth mentioning; nonetheless, his study is not related to theological discussion or to the work of the church.

Another author that uses these two concepts is Antonio Cornejo Polar, a social theorist from Perú.[6] Cornejo Polar states that in Latin American theory, hybridity has to do more with the biological dimension of humanity.[7] However, he points out that Latin American intellectual discussions and literature prefer to use another term, *mestizaje*. For Cornejo Polar, *mestizaje* recognizes a difficult coexistence in Latin America between Spanish, Portuguese and Amerindian-language cultures with English or other European cultures. Cornejo Polar is conscious of the various racial and cultural influences affecting Latino cultures. Cornejo

---

2 Néstor García Canclini, *Hybrid Cultures: Strategies for Entering and Leaving Modernity* (Minneapolis: University of Minnesota, 1995).

3 Ibid. xv.

4 Ibid.

5 Néstor García Canclini, Néstor, "Culturas Híbridas y Estrategias Comunicacionales," *Estudios Sobre las Culturas Contemporáneas 3.5* (June 1997): 109–128.

6 Antonio Cornejo Polar, "*Mestizaje* E *Hibridez*: Los Riesgos De Las Metáforas. Apuntes," in *Revista Iberoamericana*, LXVIII, Núm. 200 (Julio–Septiembre 2002): 867–70. Originally published in Spanish in 1997.

7 Ibid., 867.

Polar points out that while these two terms, hybridity and *mestizaje*, do not converge, the two terms can complement one another.

In an interesting turn, Latino theological literature picks up on *mestizaje* and not hybridity. The material dealing with *mestizaje* is abundant in theological literature. However, there was minimal dialogue with post-colonial notions of hybridity.[8] The dominant theological motif explaining US Latino identity is *mestizaje*. Authors such as Virgilio Elizondo, Ada María Isasi-Díaz, and Néstor Medina consider *mestizaje* as the locus theologicus of the Latino community in the US.[9] While social theorists dialogue between both terms, and sometimes equate the two, theology could incorporate hybridity.

Mestizaje

Mestizaje points to the origins of Latin America and its various cultures. Primarily, this concept carries biological or racial connotations because of discussions in the US context. Latino theology had to deal with issues of identity as being racially and culturally different to mainstream US culture.[10] For this reason, Latino theologians looked at their own community to come to terms with their identity. However, a close look of Latino identity reveals powerful streams of racial intermixture.[11]

Mestizaje is the Spanish term for mixture. It can also be translated as inter-mixture or as miscegenation. This last term has connotations of something being wrong, as in misspelled, or misconstrued. Initially it was a pejorative term used to demarcate social and power structures in colonial societies defined along racial lines. In these societies, European-born "white" Spaniards were considered the top of the socio-cultural and colonial system.[12] These were followed in the hierarchical scheme by *criollos/as*, or Europeans born in the Americas. Furthermore,

---

8   Daniel Orlando Álvarez, Mestizaje e Hibridez: *Identidad Latina en Perspectiva Pneumatologica* (Mestizaje and Hibridez: *Latin Identity in Pneumatological Perspective*) (Cleveland: Centre for Pentecostal Theology, 2016).

9   Virgilio Elizondo, *Galilean Journey* (Maryknoll: Orbis, 2000); Ada María Isasi-Díaz, *Mujerista Theology* (Maryknoll: Orbis, 1996); Néstor Medina, *Mestizaje* (Maryknoll: Orbis, 2014).

10 Ibid., 24.

11 Virgilio Elizondo, The Galilean Journey, ii–iii.

12 Michelle A. González, "Who Is Americana/o," in *Postcolonial Theologies: Divinity and Empire*, edited by Catherine Keller, Michael Nausner, and Mayra Rivera (St. Louis: Chalice, 2004), see especially her discussion on pages 64–65. Furthermore, many of the European Spaniards had already experienced racial mixture with the invasion from the Moors.

the Europeans encountered Amerindians in the colonies. These were considered inferior due to their race as well as their lack of contact with European culture.

In the conquest of colonial territories and due to the lack of Spanish women in Latin America, Spanish men took native women as wives and *hetaerae*.[13] This dimension of colonial life was not a pleasant reality because of the violence and exploitation these women experienced at the hands of the Europeans.[14] González states that one cannot sanitize the history of this mixture.[15] Furthermore, with the decimation of the Amerindian people due to disease and slavery, the Europeans imported African slaves. Over time, the Europeans also intermixed with Africans and this resulted in what the Spaniards called *mulatez*.

These intermixtures were primarily perceived as interracial or biological mixtures. However, these intermixtures also included intermixture of culture and *cosmovisiones* (worldviews). The new people who emerged in the American continent were called *mestizos* and *mulatos*. In the grand scheme of society they were considered above the Amerindians and blacks, but inferior to European-born Spaniards and *criollos*. Over time, the result was a society that incorporated dimensions of Amerindian, African, and European cultures, with an overarching dominant motif of the Iberian influence.[16] In theological literature *mestizaje* thus denotes the unique experiences of Latin America. It describes racial miscegenation and cultural mixtures that occurred throughout Latin America since 1492.[17]

Mestizaje is central to Latino identity. It not only serves as an ethnic and racial descriptor, but also serves as dynamic philosophical identity descriptor. As such, it reveals a way of being, thinking, and acting in the world as Latino. There can be negative or positive readings of these mixtures. In many ways, Latinos are in and of themselves an expression of social taboos in mainstream North American culture where local laws prohibited miscegenation. However, there is also a

13 Ibid., 66.

14 Juan Rivas Moreno, "La Ley de Matrimonios Mixtos Que Cambió la Colonización de Latinoamerica," *El Mundo* June 10, 2014, http://www.elmundo.es/la-aventura-de-la-historia/2014/06/10/5396e7af268e3e54428b4587.html.

15 Ibid.

16 See also Eldin Villafañe, *The Liberating Spirit* (Grand Rapids: William B. Eerdmans, 1993), 3–11.

17 Elizondo, *The Galilean Journey*, 1–2.

positive reading as Latinos have moved to incorporate Amerindian, African and European traditions. By nature, Latinos are diverse. They embody a multicultural ethos.

Theologians like Elizondo and María Isasi-Díaz embraced *mestizaje*. They used this term to make sense of their context and their respective Mexican and Cuban heritages despite their sociocultural marginalization in the US.[18] Furthermore, they sought to affirm their identity and carve out space for their communities by using *mestizaje*. During the time that they wrote, scholarship was fixated exclusively on a Black versus White racial discourse. The Latino experience challenged such rigid racial delineations.[19] *Mestizaje* thus affirmed the uniqueness of Latinos and allowed them to resist assimilationist tendencies. It also demonstrated the complexity of a Latino identity when it comes to ethnic and racial markers.

Mestizaje Critiques

More recent writers have critiqued the usage of *mestizaje* in theology and literature. One of these authors is Manuel Vásquez, a social ethicist from the University of Florida.[20] The other is Miguel De La Torre, a social ethicist at the Iliff School of Theology who wrote a book on rethinking Latino identity.[21] Their main point of contention is that *mestizaje* is currently being used to generally describe Mexico, Central and South Americans, a region covering over twenty different countries. While all these nations have experienced *mestizaje*, each of these nations has its own history with equally diverse peoples and cultures. Such diversity prompts both of them to question this universal and totalizing implementation of the term *mestizaje*.

Vásquez, in particular, describes his journey in El Salvador, a country with an unfortunate and painful history of violence. In this nation the term mestizo was used as a grand meta-narrative to excuse violence

---

18 Medina, *Mestizaje*, xi.

19 Ibid., x.

20 "Manuel Vásquez," by the University of Florida, http://religion.ufl.edu/files/2012/11/Vasquez.pdf (last accessed May 21, 2018). Vásquez wrote, "Rethinking *Mestizaje*," in *Rethinking Latino(a) Religion and Identity*, edited by Miguel A. De La Torre (Cleveland, OH: Pilgrim, 2006),145.

21 "Miguel De La Torre," by the *Iliff School of Theology*, https://www.iliff.edu/faculty/miguel-de-la-torre/ (last accessed October 25, 2018). See De La Torre's chapter, "Rethinking Mulatez," in the book *Rethinking Latino(a) Religion and Identity*, edited by Miguel A. De La Torre (Cleveland, OH: Pilgrim, 2006): 158–71.

against the poor, women, and Amerindians in order to build a unified nation. Vásquez describes this violence with his case-in-point being La Matanza de 1932 in which the military massacred 10,000 peasants (most of indigenous descent) in order to bring order to a chaotic nation-state.[22] In the years that followed the massacre an extreme form of violence ensued that led thousands to immigrate to the US and other countries. Currently, it is estimated that Salvadorans are the third-largest constituency of Latinos in the US.[23]

Vásquez argues that we need to be careful in implementing *mestizaje*. His reason is that *mestizaje* was used as an educational tool to explain that El Salvador was a *mestizo* (emphasis on masculinity here also) nation. Thus, the ideal Salvadoran was a male person mixed with whiteness. Consequently during the country's Civil War, those in power moved to wipe out minority groups in order to build this *mestizo* nation. Vásquez states, "*mestizaje* functioned as the nation-building myth that has helped link dark to light-skinned hybrids and Euro-Americans, often in opposition to both foreigners and indigenous others in their midst."[24]

Thus, *mestizaje* reveals an inherent contradiction because it calls for a common Latino identity at the expense of forcibly harmonizing Latinos. De La Torre also offers a similar reading of this unfortunate history in Cuba in using the term mulatez.[25] Vásquez and De La Torre argue that Latinos are much diverse than perceived. They also resist blanket cultural assimilation and acculturation because the particularities of each of these groups cannot be subsumed or lost in their interactions with each other.

Dialogue with Hybridity or *Hibridez*

Authors such as Vásquez, De La Torre, and Néstor Medina begin to talk of *mestizaje*s, *mescolanza*, or other terms such as *mestizaje*-intermixture.[26] However, Vásquez also points towards an intra-ethnic solidarity based on *mestizaje*'s de-centering of self and a world traveling that hybridity encourages.[27] It is at this point where there is further opportunity

---

22 Vásquez, 155.

23 Mark Hugo López and Ana González Barrera, "Salvadorans May Soon Replace Cubans as Third-Largest US Hispanic Group" *Pew Center*, http://www.pewresearch. org/fact-tank/2013/06/19/salvadorans-may-soon-replace-cubans-as-third-largest-u-s-hispanic-group/.

24 Manuel A. Vasquez, "Rethinking *Mestizaje*," 145.

25 Miguel De La Torre, "Rethinking Mulatez," 158–71.

26 Medina, 134; Vasquez, 155.

27 Vásquez, 155.

for dialogue and engaging hybridity.[28] Obviously much work has been done to explain and describe Latino identity through *mestizaje*. The purpose here is not to jettison the term, *mestizaje*.

However, there is an opportunity to create further dialogue in two directions—first, between different Latino communities, and secondly from Latino communities to multicultural realities in the US, Canada, and beyond. It is here where hybridity can aid the church as diverse Latino cultures interact within themselves and with the dominant North American culture in the US.

For example, Latinos vary in culture when it comes to their countries of origin. However, they are all labeled as "Hispanic" in the United States. While they may speak Spanish, some speak Portuguese (Brazil) or another Amerindian language. Latinos comprise a vast variety of cultures and histories. Mexican culture, for example, is different from Guatemalan, Honduran, Puerto Rican, or Cuban cultures. Sometimes, going to church can be a difficult transition for some, because the Spanish-speaking church they join may be composed of Latinos from different Latin American nations. Different countries have different accents and will speak with regional jargon. As such, a person from one nationality may feel left out or uncomfortable in a church with a majority of members from another culture.

Secondly, hybridity may also help Latinos understand their relationship to the majority culture. For example, many Latinos no longer primarily speak Spanish or Portuguese in the United States. Many of them choose to communicate to one another and within their family systems through Spanglish, a communication that uses both Spanish and English at home or with friends. In more cases, including Brazil, they may communicate in Port-Spanglish. Life in the US forces them to adapt and they now have a culture that is similar to that of first-generation immigrants but distinct in many ways.

Consequently, a dialogue with hybridity does two things: first it recognizes diverse experiences, through terminology that does justice for each unique Latino identity. There is common ground and a way to dialogue with each other through *mestizaje* and *mulatez* as forms of hybridization. Secondly, it recognizes difference. Each nationality in Latin America has its unique characteristics. To speak of a Latino in the US necessarily means speaking of diversity in constant dialogue. Finally, including hybridity they

---

28 Álvarez, *Mestizaje* and *Hibridez*, 61–81.

allow us to engage those outside Latino communities because Latino immigrants live side by side with different communities in the US, whether they are Caucasian, African American or other.

Furthermore, a dialogue with hybridity reveals tensions between the self and the other. These are in dialogue through *encuentros, encontronazos, reencuentros* and *desencuentros*.[29] These in turn continue to shape this Latino hybridity. Thus hybridity includes a movement to decenter the totalizing universal self or the dismantling of totalitarian tendencies. This opens the door to a continual process of hospitality. Theologically we may speak of the Spirit of God as dwelling in liminal spaces and inviting humanity to dialogue and orient us after the *orthopathos* of God.

A second reason to dialogue with postcolonial hybridity is because the dialogue between the self and the other is a major concern for postcolonial theory. *Mestizaje* must be informed by the struggle between the self and the other, or what I call identidad and otredad.[30] This dialogue and an emerging hybridity should inform our understanding of *mestizaje*. Nonetheless, there is the concern of merely absorbing hybridity uncritically and still preserve the origins through *mestizaje*. I prefer to use the term *hibridez*, both a Spanish and Portuguese term, because it points to the Latino community's unique experiences through *mestizaje*.[31]

Some have issues with this dialogue. For example, discussion with hybridity could collapse into an exclusive argument of biology.[32] This could derail a conversation on Latin American realities because it may collapse into a discussion on mere racial delineations. It could also collapse into a negative reading because it points to sterility, like a mule.[33] Furthermore, its usage may connote a strict scientific determinism that does not necessarily capture Latin American cosmovisiones.[34] For example, its association with scientific determinism could potentially collapse into a closed scientific worldview that rejects spiritual possibilities. Such is a position that contradicts the cosmovisiones of Amerindians and others in Latin America.

---

29 Álvarez, 78. This may be translated as, "encounters, collisions, second encounters, and encounters that lead to conflict or broken relationships."

30 Vásquez, 155.

31 Álvarez, 78.

32 Canclini, "Culturas Híbridas y estrategias comunicacionales," 110.

33 Cornejo Polar, 868.

34 Canclini, *Hybrid Cultures*, 265.

However, if we connect *hibridez* to *mestizaje* and the visceral every day reality of Latino peoples, the resulting understanding of *hibridez* may be redeemed for theological use because it is a term that points to a place of creativity and creation in liminal space. People negotiate forms and meanings in this space.[35] It may also help move stagnant dialogue forward in order to expose intra-Latino dynamics, such as ethnocentrism and racism within Latinos. It may also simultaneously point to those dynamics towards the outside of the Latino community. Such dialogues between different Latino communities in the US and dialogues with those outside the Latino community help us to nuance alternate currents.[36] For instance, it may help us explain the case of second, third, fourth, etc., generation Latinos in the US who find more affinity with US mainstream culture than with those who come from Latin America. It also helps an intolerant mainstream culture understand that for the recent immigrants it takes time to adapt, learn a language, and that many times they negotiate meanings—this requires patience, longsuffering, and love (Gal 5:22–23).

Conclusions: *Hibridez* and the Church

Hibridez points to a place or a reality where such disparate realities converge. This is a place of encounters between the self and the other. It is a liminal place where we see the negotiation of identity in which a person identifies with the two distinct realities. Homi Bhabha describes this type of existence as being on a bridge where one can communicate to both sides of a river's banks despite their inhabitants speaking different languages or having different customs.[37]

There is no other place that needs this more than the body of Christ. We are facing critical times where there is much-needed interracial and intercultural dialogue. The current political climate pigeonholes individuals, when in reality culture is dynamic and has potential to make adjustments and change. Humans are called to be in a united relationship with one another (Ps 133:1). This discussion between *mestizaje* and *hibridez* may help navigate multicultural realities.

---

35 Anjal Prabhu, *Hybrdidity: Limits, Transformations, Prospects* (Albany, NY: SUNY, 2007), xi.

36 Chiara Donadoni and Eugenia Houvenaghel, "La *Hibridez* de la tradición judeocristiana como reivinidicación del sincretismo religioso de la nueva España: El divino narciso de Sor Juana," *Neophilologus* no. 94, (2010): 474.

37 Homi K. Bhabha, *The Location of Culture* (London: Routledge, 2004), 37–38.

BIBLIOGRAPHY

Álvarez, Daniel Orlando. Mestizaje *and* Hibridez: *Latin@ Identity in Pneumatological Perspective*. Cleveland, TN: Centre for Pentecostal Theology, 2016.

Bhabha, Homi K. *The Location of Culture*. London: Routledge, 2004.

Chomsky, Noam. *Turning the Tide: US Intervention in Central America and the Struggle for Peace*. Chicago: Haymarket, 2015.

Cornejo Polar, Antonio. "*Mestizaje* E *Hibridez*: Los Riesgos De Las Metáforas. Apuntes." *Revista Iberoamericana*. LXVIII, Núm. 200 (Julio–Septiembre 2002): 867–70.

De La Torre, Miguel. "Rethinking Mulatez." In *Rethinking Latino(a) Identity*. Edited by Miguel A. De La Torre. Cleveland, OH: Pilgrim, 2006: 158–71.

Donadoni, Chiara and Eugenia Houvenaghel. "La *Hibridez* de la tradición judeocristiana como reivinidicación del sincretismo religioso de la nueva España: El divino narciso de Sor Juana." *Neophilologus* no. 94, (2010): 459–75.

Elizondo, Virgilio. *The Future is Mestizo: Life Where Cultures Meet*. Boulder, CO: University Press of Colorado, 2000.

_____. *Galilean Journey: the Mexican-American Promise*. Maryknoll, NY: Orbis, 2000.

García Canclini, Néstor. "Culturas Híbridas y Estrategias Comunicacionales." *Estudios sobre las Culturas Contemporáneas*. Colima, Mexico, Junio, Año/Vol. III, no. 5, 1997, 109–28.

_____. *Hybrid Cultures: Strategies for Entering and Leaving Modernity*. Minneapolis: University of Minnesota, 1995.

González, Michelle A. "Who Is Americana/o." In *Postcolonial Theologies: Divinity and Empire*. Edited by Catherine Keller, Michael Nausner, and Mayra Rivera. St. Louis: Chalice, 2004: 58–78.

López, Mark Hugo, and Ana González Barrera. "Salvadorans May Soon Replace Cubans as Third-Largest US Hispanic Group." Pew Center. http://www.pewresearch.org/fact-tank/2013/06/19/salvadorans-may-soon-replace-cubans-as-third-largest-u-s-hispanic-group/.

Medina, Néstor. *Mestizaje: (re)mapping Race, Culture, and Faith in Latina/o Catholicism*. Maryknoll, NY: Orbis, 2009.

Prabhu, Anjal. *Hybrididity: Limits, Transformations, Prospects*. Albany, NY: SUNY, 2007.

Rivas Moreno, Juan. "La Ley de Matrimonios Mixtos Que Cambió la Colonización de Latinoamerica." *El Mundo*. http://www.elmundo.es/la-aventura-de-la-historia/2014/06/10/5396e7af268e3e54428b4587.html.

Vasquez, Manuel A. "Rethinking *Mestizaje*." In *Rethinking Latino(a) Religion and Identity*. Edited by Miguel A. De La Torre. Cleveland, OH: Pilgrim, 2006: 129-57.

Villafañe, Eldin. *The Liberating Spirit*. Grand Rapids: William B. Eerdmans, 1993.

ABOUT THE AUTHOR

DANIEL ÁLVAREZ is Assistant Professor of Theology at the Pentecostal Theological Seminary. He has written Mestizaje and Hibridez: Latina Identity in Pneumatological Perspective. *He has also written chapters and articles dealing with Latino identity from a Honduran perspective. Daniel is also involved in the Society of Pentecostal Studies and in the Fraternidad Teológica Latinoamericana.*

CHAPTER 9 | Juliet Lee Uytanlet

Hybridity and Chineseness: Finding Meaning in Theories

Who is More Chinese?

"Who is more Chinese?" asked Michael Rynkiewich. "If a Chinese Filipino born of pure Chinese parentage sits in a cafe, and then a Chinese fresh from the Mainland enters the place, who is considered more Chinese? Whose Chineseness is more authentic?" His questions penetrated my heart as I sat inside Solomon's Porch in the quiet town of Wilmore discussing my dissertation topic with my mentor back on August 25, 2011. I have always thought that I am very Chinese in my cultural practice and mindset since I grew up in Binondo Chinatown and of "pure" Chinese parentage. My father was from Fujian, China and my mother is a Cantonese whose parents came from Guangdong. Rynkiewich's question challenged my identity and Chineseness. I realized I needed to confront myself that as a third-generation Chinese in the Philippines, my Chineseness or Chinese culture is no longer "pure" after all.[1]

---

1 The immigrant is the first generation, the children with one or both immigrant parents will be the second-generation, and the grandchildren will be the third generation. The ethnic Chinese's generational categories or immigrant generations in the Philippines usually based on the father or paternal lineage since most of the early immigrants were male. However, the classification of generational categories must be based on which ethnicity and which traced to the farthest or earliest time frame of immigration. See also Brian Duncan and Stephen J. Trejo, "The Complexity of Immigrant Generations: Implications for Assessing the Socioeconomic Integration of Hispanics and Asians" in *ILR Review* 70, no. 5 (October 2017): 1149–50.

Hybridity is often associated with the idea of crossbreeding or of mixed "blood." Jan Nederveen Pieterse broadens its definition by explaining that it is a process of crossing categories. The categories can be "cultures, nations, ethnicities, status groups, classes, genres."[2] He explains that hybridity "carries different meanings in different cultures, among different circles within cultures and at different time periods…Hybridity is entirely contextual, relational."[3] In the context of cultural anthropology, hybridity is the mixing of "blood" or inter-ethnic marriages or the mixing of cultures and/or cultural elements within a culture. Therefore, for the Chinese in the Philippines, hybridity is not solely in the context of inter-ethnic marriages or being Chinese *Mestizos*, but it is the mixing of the Chinese and the Filipino cultures or the mixing of cultural elements.

> *The mixing of cultures is about being bicultural or multicultural. In the mixing of cultures, it can be a mix of one or more cultural elements in varying degree of influence like languages, religions, traditions, customs, and stories within a culture or cultures.*[4]

The phenomenon of mixed languages (*Minnanhua*, Filipino, and English) in communication among the Chinese Filipinos is an example of mixing of cultures or cultural elements. In religion, the Chinese Filipinos tend to mix Roman Catholicism, Daoism, and Buddhism.[5] This chapter seeks to discover whether a Chinese Filipino who practices cultural mixing is still considered a Chinese? What degree of Chineseness must one has to be identified a Chinese?

Who is a Chinese?

Who is a Chinese? What does it mean to be a Chinese? What is Chineseness? For those Chinese born and residing in China, this is obviously not an issue to contest. However, for the millions of Diaspora Chinese scattered in 130 countries, what does it mean to be a Chinese?[6]

---

2 Jan Nederveen Pieterse, *Globalization and Culture: Global Mélange* (Oxford: Rowman and Littlefield, 2004), 72.

3 Nederveen Pieterse, *Globalization and Culture*, 106.

4 Juliet Lee Uytanlet, *The Hybrid Tsinoys: Challenges of Hybridity and Homogeneity as Socio-Cultural Constructs Among the Chinese in the Philippines* (Oregon: Pickwick, 2016), 65.

5 Uytanlet, *The Hybrid Tsinoys*, 65–67.

6 "The population data of Overseas Chinese is very difficult to determine. The number varies. There are estimates of 57 million by Henry He and 60 million according to Woods and Yeh. However, the Overseas Community Affairs Council estimates in

The Chinese immigrants may maintain that they are Chinese since they were born and raised up in the Mainland. However, the descendants of the Chinese immigrants may have difficulty identifying as Chinese if they lose or are losing their Chineseness with adaptation and adoption of cultural practices of the host country they live in.[7]

Why do we preserve Chineseness or Chinese identity? Ethnic minorities who preserve their cultural practices are often charged with ethnocentrism and disloyalty to the host country. Teresita Ang See and the *Kaisa Para Sa Kaunlaran* emphasize that the Chinese Filipinos loyalty remain in the Philippines and their continuous adherence to Chinese cultural practices is simply an expression of their celebration and preservation of their ethnic heritage. The term *Tsinoy* means Tsinong Pinoy, or literally a Filipino of Chinese ethnicity or ancestry.[8]

There were labels and names given to them throughout the Philippine history. These names are the result of prejudices and stereotyping. There were also names and labels given by various sectors of the society. Lastly, the Chinese Filipinos lay out their own identities with the names they prefer to be called.

> *The Spaniards called them Sangleys then Chinos. The Americans called them Chinamen and Coolies. They were also classified as non-Christian Tribe and Aliens. The Filipinos called them* Tsino, Kabise, Tsekwa, Intsik, Beho, Barok, Bulol, Butsekik, Singkit *or* Singkot, Tsinito *or* Tsinita, Chinky-eyed, Chinks, Tsinoy, *or* Chinoy.

2015 that there are 43 million ethnic Chinese living beyond China, Taiwan, Hong Kong, and Macau. The Chinese people is then the largest group dispersed in the world, having the largest world population of 1.39 billion in China in 2015." Juliet Lee Uytanlet, "Transit, Transient, Transition: How the Lexington Chinese Christian Church became an Instrument of Conversion" in Reaching New Territory: Theological Reflections (ed. Samson Uytanlet, et al; Valenzuela City: Biblical Seminary of the Philippines, 2017), 24. See also Peter S. Li and Eva Xiaoling Li, "Chinese Overseas Population" in Routledge Handbook of Chinese Diaspora (ed. Tan Chee Beng, London: Routledge, 2013), 20–21.

7 The term *huaqiao* 華僑 refers to the Chinese immigrants "living as permanent residents in foreign countries." *Huaren* 華人 refers to all Chinese in diaspora. Uytanlet, "Transit, Transient, Transition," 25–26.

8 Teresita Ang See, "The State and Public Policies, Civil Society And Identity Formation In Multi-Ethnic Societies The Case of The Chinese In The Philippines" in *The State, Development and Identity In Multi-Ethnic Societies Ethnicity, Equity and The Nation* (eds. Nicolas Tarling and Edmund Terence Gomez, London: Routledge, 2008), 162–63. See also Kaisa Para Sa Kaunlaran, "About Kaisa," http://www.kaisa.org.ph/?page_id=2.

The social scientists categorized them as huáshāng 華商 *or merchants,* huágōng 華工 *or Coolies,* huáqiáo 華僑 *or overseas Chinese,* Jìjū 寄居 *or Sojourners,* huárén 華人 *or Chinese people in diaspora, and* huá-yi 華裔 *or of Chinese descent. They were also labeled as Jews of the east, immigrants, transnationals, essential outsiders, market-dominant minorities, flexible identities, cosmopolitans, cosmopolitan capitalists, or global cosmopolitans.*

Missionaries and missiologists have referred to them at different times as heathens, pagans, unbelievers, enRAWGen, split-level Christians, syncretistic, folk evangelical Christians, or chap chay lomi *(mixed belief system).*

In academics, proper reference to the Chinese in the Philippines has evolved as well from mere "Chinese" to "Philippine Chinese" to "Filipino-Chinese" to "ethnic Chinese" to "Chinese-Filipino" to "Chinese Filipino," dropping the hyphen.

The Chinese Filipinos referred to themselves in Minnanhua *as* lanlâng, Tiong kok lâng, Banlam lâng, Hua-din, Hua-è, Chinese, Tsinoy, *or* Chinoy. *There were those who called other Chinese or even themselves* hoan-á.[9]

Richard T. Chu acknowledges how globalization and trans-nationalism as well as the past exclusion tendency of the Philippine government toward the Chinese Filipinos led to the construction of the Tsinoy identity and reconstruction of the female gender role in the traditional Chinese family. He discusses Chineseness as portrayed in the Filipino movie *Mano Po*. He writes,

Political loyalty to the Philippines, however, does not preclude the maintenance of certain "Chinese" cultural practices. The Mano Po *films give viewers a glimpse of what "Chineseness" means to diasporic families, including the ability to speak Chinese languages, particularly Hokkien.[10]*

According to Teresita Ang See, an expert in Chinese Filipino studies, sociologically speaking an ethnic Chinese must have the following traits.

1. A measurable degree of Chinese parentage

2. Working knowledge of Chinese language and education

3. Some form of education in Chinese schools

---

9 *Minnanhua* 閩南話 is also known as the Amoy language or Hokkien, Uytanlet, The Hybrid Tsinoys, 1 and 73.

10 Richard T. Chu, "Strong(er) Women and Effete Men: Negotiating Chineseness in Philippine Cinema at a Time of Transnationalism," *Positions* 19, no. 2 (Fall 2011): 374.

4. Retained some Chinese practices

5. Enough to call themselves or be called by neighbors as ethnic Chinese or *Tsinoys*[11]

Older immigrants would consider those who cannot speak the Minnanhua or Mandarin not ethnic Chinese. Their children struggle with identity with the fusion of two or more cultures operational in their day to day lives. They are challenged with their ethnicity as Chinese and their nationality as Filipinos. Is hybridity a problem or can hybridity solve this problem of ambiguity? See find that the third, fourth, or fifth generation Chinese Filipinos who do not speak the Chinese language or studied in Chinese schools may no longer be called ethnic Chinese. They may be of Chinese descent but not ethnic Chinese in practice and identity. They have completely assimilated into the Filipino society.[12]

Finding Meaning in Hybridity Theories

Michael Rynkiewich believes that to understand people, we must study their culture, society, ecology or environments, and history. The Chinese Filipinos face the challenge of discovering their identity or identities in light of being in diaspora and in this culturally hybrid global age. It is crucial that they revisit their history in consideration of their present reality. Culture is contingent as people take what is available around them; constructed as people pick and choose which cultural elements to use daily; and contested as people challenge the culture being practiced. Culture is a system of knowledge, values, and feelings that help peoplze understand and interpret their reality.[13]

Rynkiewich's definition of culture helps us understand the adoption and adaptation process of culture and cultural mixing. It all starts with a story or an idea. A person will choose to accept or reject the idea. When accepted, the idea can be adopted as is or adapted with modification. As time goes by, the idea is practiced and was discovered to be of value to his/her life. This is the point where it became a worldview.

---

11 Teresita Ang See is one of the founders of Kaisa Para Sa Kaunlaran, Inc. The institution is created to serve as the bridge between the Chinese and Filipinos in the Philippines. Teresita Ang See, individual interview by author, 29 July 2012. Uytanlet, *Hybrid Tsinoys*, 101. *Tsinoy* means Tsino (Chinese) and *Pinoy* (Filipino).

12 Teresita Ang See, individual interview by author, 29 July 2012.

13 Uytanlet, *Hybrid Tsinoys*, 111. Michael Rynkiewich, *Soul, Self, and Society: A Postmodern Anthropology for Mission in a Postcolonial World* (Eugene, OR: Cascade, 2011), 38–39.

It became part of his/her beliefs. The idea believed and practiced became a custom that eventually was shared with his/her family and community as a tradition. This idea then becomes a cultural practice that gives meaning to their reality and identity. Therefore, in cultural hybridity or cultural mixing, the Chinese Filipino will have to decide which of the cultures and cultural elements of a culture they want to apply in their daily lives.

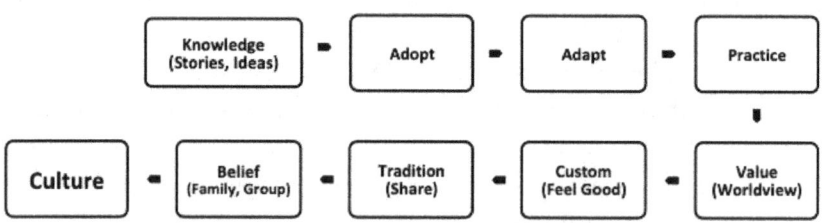

Chart by Juliet Lee Uytanlet based on Michael Rynkiewich's definition of culture

There are 1.5 million Chinese Filipinos in the country. Less than 2 percent are evangelical Christians. An ethnographic research was employed from 2012 to 2014 to create a profile of the present Chinese in the Philippines. The objective of the profile is to help us understand them better and how we can do better mission among them. There are six groups of Chinese Filipinos.

1. Old Immigrants—They are the immigrants who entered the country between 1898 to 1975. They originally wanted to come to the Philippines to find greener pastures or evade the war in China. Unexpected circumstances like tight immigration laws and the Cultural Revolution in China led them to settle and unable to return back to their home country.

2. New Immigrants—They are the immigrants who entered from 1976 onwards. They came to follow after the footsteps of their ancestors, finding greener pastures. They also seek to reconnect with family and loved ones.

3. Tsinoys (second, third, and fourth generations)—They are mainly the descendants of the immigrants. They struggle with identity and cultural hybridity. They grew up speaking at least three languages but English is the medium for reading and writing.

4. Chinese Citizens and Overseas Chinese Filipino Workers—They are the minority among the minority. Those with Chinese citizenships

are born and raised in the country but are marginalized with their citizenry. Those who worked overseas experienced strangeness and unbelongingness.

5. Spouses of Mixed Marriages (Chinese and Filipino spouses)— These people go against the tradition of endogamy. They desire acceptance from their spouses' side of the family.

6. Chinese Mestizos (first, second, and third generations)—They are in a liminal state wherein they struggle with identity and acceptance by both Chinese and Filipinos. They experienced prejudices with their being mixed "blood".

I employed three hybridity theories to understand their identity and the reality of cultural mixing instead of cultural purity. The first is the unhomely theory of Homi Bhabha. The second is the situational theory of Fredrik Barth. The third is the theory of mixed yet unmixed of Joel Robbins.

Bhabha's Unhomely Theory: Finding Meaning in Being Unhomed

Homi Bhabha discusses liminality and coining the term "unhomed" as someone who has a home but does not feel at home.[14] The unhomed theory is fitting for the immigrants whether old or new immigrants with their sojourning situation. They find themselves in unhomely situations as they try to adapt to the host country. Surprisingly, even the other groups also find themselves unhomed in different contexts and situations.

The *Tsinoys* are unhomed with prejudices and stereotyping. They feel unhomed with dual identities, Chinese and Filipino. The *Tsinoys* with Chinese citizenships may hold Taiwan passports or China passports.[15] They feel unhomed with their imaginary citizenships since these ethnic Chinese still need to acquire visas to enter Taiwan with their Taiwan passport. They desire to find their identity and belonging. The Overseas Chinese Filipino Workers feel unhomed upon arriving in foreign lands to work and usually are separated from their loved ones. The Chinese and Filipinos spouses in inter-ethnic marriages experienced unhomely feelings when prejudices and rejection arise from either side of the spouse's family. The Chinese *Mestizos* feel unhomed with language

---

14 Homi Bhabha, *Location of Cultures* (London: Routledge, 2004), 13.

15 I refer to the Chinese immigrants and specially their children as Tsinoys even though they hold Chinese citizenships since they consider the Philippines as their country.

fluency or physical appearance (look more Filipino or Chinese).[16] Bhabha's unhomely theory helps give explanation to the liminal and "in-between" situations of the Chinese Filipinos.

Barth's Situational Theory: Finding Meaning in Pragmatism and Syncretism

Fredrik Barth discovers two things about ethnicity: (1) it is exclusive not just because of no contact with outside world; (2) it persists despite contact with other ethnic groups. This may sound essentialist, but Barth is presenting the fact that ethnicities are not "boxed or immune from outside world" yet they continue to persist or remain exclusive.[17] Barth's situational theory led to ideas like transnationalism, negotiations, and flexible identities.

> The Chinese Filipinos apply Barth's situational approach in their everyday lives as they negotiate their way into the mainstream society or co-mingle with Filipinos. Their acquired knowledge of Filipino language and culture through education, exposure to Filipinos, media, and the internet enabled them to apply appropriate responses in different situations to avoid conflict and problems. They have adapted in their residence in the country. They even adopted the Filipino language as one of their languages.[18]

The pragmatic Chinese Filipino will negotiate identities and cultural practices for the sake of prosperity or survival. They will adapt to their host country and adopt cultural norms and practices to maintain unity and harmony as they coexist with the majority. Their pragmatism extends to their practice of religion with the syncretistic tendency as they add on different religions. The deities are functioning more like genies or prosperity gods that grant their prayers and hearts' desires than as their master and lord of their lives. Barth's situational theory enables us to understand the pragmatic and syncretistic tendency of immigrants and ethnic minorities.

---

16 Uytanlet, *The Hybrid Tsinoys*, 69, 99–118, 163–64.

17 Fredrik Barth, *Ethnic Groups and Boundaries: The Social Organization of Culture Difference* (Bergen, Norway: Universitesforlaget, 1969), 9–10.

18 Uytanlet, *The Hybrid Tsinoys*, 162. See also Barth, *Ethnic Groups and Boundaries*, 162–63.

Robbins' Mix yet Unmixed:
Finding Meaning in Compartmentalization

Joel Robbins challenges the idea of hybridity as a way of mixing but maintaining their respective distinctiveness.[19] This is like the missionaries who adapted to the country of their mission field without losing their original culture. Paul Hiebert calls this compartmentalization.[20] It is also similar to the popular Filipino dessert called *halo-halo*. The *halo-halo* is a mix of sweetened fruits and beans like bananas, shredded coconut, corn, mung-beans, garbanzos with finely crushed ice, milk, custard, purple yam, and a scoop of ice cream. All these ingredients were mixed together and yet somehow you can still identify each ingredient while eating it.

The Chinese Filipinos may employ different cultural practices and different languages in their day to day life as they relate to the majority Filipinos or other ethnicities. However, they may continue to uphold the Chinese culture as their dominant cultural adherence. The hybridity theory of Robbins enables us to see that it is possible for us to have a dominant culture that one adheres to and yet knowledgeable and adaptable to other cultures.

Conclusion

A Chinese Filipino is an ethnic Chinese whose dominant culture practiced in the home or even in the social sphere is the Chinese culture. The most evident cultural practice is what language they use at home aside from the Chinese traditions or customs. The sociologically accepted traits laid out by Teresita Ang See can be helpful in measuring one's Chineseness. The higher the degree of practice or applicability of each trait will also determine the degree of adoption and affinity to the Chinese culture or ethnic identity.

However, the hybridity theories provide meaningful explanations to the actions and responses of the Chinese Filipinos co-mingling with Filipinos. They will be unhomed in situations where their difference is heightened and emphasized, but this can also lead to opportunities to help the others better understand them. They will generally be pragmatic as they negotiate with two or more cultures in their everyday

---

19 Joel Robbins, *Becoming Sinners: Christianity and Moral Torment in a Papua New Guinea Society* (Berkeley: University of California, 2004) 3–4.

20 Paul Hiebert, *Anthropological Insights for Missionaries* (Grand Rapids: Baker, 1985), 106–7.

life. They seek unity and harmony as they adapt and adopt cultures. They will be mixed and yet unmixed in their culture and cultural practices as they adhere to a dominant culture.

The hybrid nature of the Chinese Filipinos enables us to realize that in reaching the Chinese in the Philippines, we cannot simply use one style or one method of evangelism for all of them. We need to understand what kind of Chinese Filipinos they are; to which group or generation they belong to; which is their preferred language; and how best to minister and reach out to them. The fact that they continue to persist in their cultural heritage despite applying cultural hybridity in their lives shows that ethnic Chinese churches are still important vehicles in reaching these Chinese in diaspora. Lastly, in view of the hybridity theories, knowing that they are unhomed provides opportunity for us to point them to Christ in whom they will find eternal home; knowing that they tend to be syncretistic provides us opportunity to emphasize that there is only one true God; and knowing that they adhere to a dominant culture provides them opportunities to choose the kind of church that will best suit them.

BIBLIOGRAPHY

Barth, Fredrik. *Ethnic Groups and Boundaries: The Social Organization of Culture Difference Bergen*, Norway: Universitesforlaget, 1969.

Bhabha, Homi. *The Location of Cultures*. London: Routledge, 2004.

Chu, Richard T., "Strong(er) Women and Effete Men: Negotiating Chineseness in Philippine Cinema at a Time of Transnationalism." *Positions* 19, no. 2 (Fall 2011): 365–91.

Duncan, Brian and Stephen J. Trejo. "The Complexity of Immigrant Generations: Implications for Assessing the Socioeconomic Integration of Hispanics and Asians." *ILR Review* 70, no. 5 (October 2017): 1146–75.

Hiebert, Paul G., *Anthropological Insights for Missionaries*. Grand Rapids: Baker, 1985.

Kaisa Para Sa Kaunlaran, "About Kaisa." http://www.kaisa.org.ph/?page_id=2.

Li, Peter S. and Eva Xiaoling Li. "Chinese Overseas Population." In *Routledge Handbook of Chinese Diaspora*, edited by Tan Chee Beng. London: Routledge, 2013.

Nederveen Pieterse, Jan., *Globalization and Culture: Global Mélange*. Oxford: Rowman and Littlefield, 2004.

Robbins, Joel. *Becoming Sinners: Christianity and Moral Torment in a Papua New Guinea Society*. Berkeley: University of California, 2004.

Rynkiewich, Michael. *Soul, Self, and Society: A Postmodern Anthropology for Mission in a Postcolonial World*. Eugene, OR: Cascade, 2011.

See, Teresita Ang. "The State and Public Policies, Civil Society And Identity Formation In Multi-Ethnic Societies The Case of The Chinese In The Philippines." In *The State, Development and Identity In Multi-Ethnic Societies Ethnicity, Equity and The Nation*, edited by Nicolas Tarling and Edmund Terence Gomez. London: Routledge, 2008.

Uytanlet, Juliet Lee. *The Hybrid Tsinoys: Challenges of Hybridity and Homogeneity as Socio-Cultural Constructs Among the Chinese in the Philippines*. Oregon: Pickwick, 2016.

___. "Transit, Transient, Transition: How the Lexington Chinese Christian Church became an Instrument of Conversion." In *Reaching New Territory: Theological Reflections*, edited by Samson Uytanlet, et al. Valenzuela City: Biblical Seminary of the Philippines, 2017.

ABOUT THE AUTHOR

DR. JULIET LEE UYTANLET, PhD, teaches Global Missions and Urban Missions at the Biblical Seminary of the Philippines. She also teaches Ethnographic Research Methods at Asia Graduate School of Theology. Her dissertation entitled "The Hybrid Tsinoys: Challenges of Hybridity and Homogeneity as Sociocultural Constructs among the Chinese in the Philippines" (American Society of Missiology Monograph Series Book 28) was published in 2016.

CHAPTER 10 | Gary Fujino

Becoming *Nikkei*: A Cross-Cultural Comparative Study of Diasporic Japanese "Dekasegi" Christian Communities in Japan, Brazil, and Peru

The *dekasegi* or "migrant worker" phenomenon of the late twentieth and early twenty-first centuries had a profound impact upon the economies and cultural perceptions of their respective immigrant populations in Japan, Brazil, and Peru. It also affected and contributed to the Christian presence in these countries. Defined as South American residents of Japanese[1] or *Nikkei*[2] identity "who returned temporarily to live and work in Japan, where they often had a separate identity from that of the larger Japanese population,"[3] these *dekasegi* lived, worked, raised children, and worshipped in Japan, as well as in their native Peru or Brazil during the decade of the 90s and much of the early 2000s.

---

1 "Japanese": used here as a descriptor, *Nihonteki*: 日本的 *lit., 'Japanese-y' or 'Japanese-like.'* I sometimes use this term as an adjective, although with the same spelling in English; it has broad application and can be used to describe things Japanese, whether they come from or are related to Japan itself or whether they are associated with *Nikkei* expatriates abroad, e.g., in Brazil or in Peru.

2 *Nikkei* : 日系 *lit., "of the Japanese system, lineage or group."* A person or persons of Japanese descent, and their descendants, who emigrated from Japan and who created unique communities and lifestyles within the societies in which they now live…*Nikkei* also potentially encompasses people of part-Japanese descent, to the extent that they retain an identity as a person of Japanese ancestry. Being *Nikkei*, in other words, has primarily, but not exclusively, to do with ethnic identity." Lane Hirabayashi, Akemi Kikumura-Yano and James Hirabayashi, *New Worlds, New Lives: Globalization and People of Japanese Descent in the Americas and from Latin America in Japan* (Stanford, CA : Stanford University, 2002), 19–20, 25.

3 Hirabayashi, Kikumura-Yano, and Hirabayashi,19.

As a Japan-based church planter with a North American mission agency, I was tasked with researching, visiting, and helping to establish networks for evangelism and mission in these disparate locales among sections of the *dekasegi* diaspora of Japan, Brazil, and Peru. Over the course of a four year period (2009–2012), I visited Brazil and Peru several times as well as various *dekasegi* communities inside Japan, where I was living. Based on participant observation, on-site research, and informal interviews conducted during these visits, I was able to observe and study local historical factors, religious affections, different views of personal identity, and the socio-cultural impact of trying to adapt to a specific society in particular but also fluid and globalizing contexts like car manufacturing plants in Nagoya, Japan, or the cities of Sao Paolo, Brazil, or Lima, Peru. I also saw the effects of Japanese, Portuguese, Spanish, and even English language use in these various contexts. During the time frame of this research, I personally experienced and witnessed some of the effects of hybridity and globalization upon select *Nikkei dekasegi* diasporic communities in these areas.[4]

What follows are partial findings and missiological implications from this long-term ethnographic research.[5] It is beyond the scope of this chapter to present a comprehensive and exhaustive analysis. Only reflections are contained here, and they may not be generalized beyond the populations studied.

The thesis developed from my research is that *Nikkei* identity in the *dekasegi* diaspora mentioned above is formed by an individual but with the influence of a community (which may or may not be *Nikkei*—or both) as well as variegated other influences. As such, this type of hybrid identity necessitates a unique missiological, evangelistic, and pastoral approach, which I shall suggest in the implications section. Among implications detailed are the understandings that 1) the pathway of

---

4 I have been asked why I did not also cover other Japanese populations for this research. The answer is twofold: 1) the specific assignment I had with my agency was only with these countries so my focus of study was only on these nations initially. Also, 2) the *Nikkei dekasegi* populations in both Brazil and Peru created measurable and visible communities and sub-cultures that affected local areas in Japan in a significant manner. Other possible *Nikkei* dekasegi populations were not so visible or prevalent within Japan during this same time period. Further research should be done in other areas of the global Japanese diaspora but that was beyond the scope of this particular project.

5 I presented my research details and methodology at the June 2018 consultation in Manila, The Philippines. This paper has been edited to only show the final conclusions and missiological implications because of space considerations.

Nikkei and *dekasegi*[6] identity formation is multi-faceted, that 2) *Nikkei* and *dekasegi* are the same but different in each of the three nations studied, that 3) "triadic" convergence[7] is what helps to form identity and also creates a hybrid identity as well as that 4) the effects of the *dekasegi* movement, even in the present day, should not be ignored. Finally, 5) there are various ways for reaching *dekasegi* populations including language outreach but what works in one place may not apply in the same way for another place.

Basic Demographics and Short Histories

To begin, in order to better understand the implications, it is necessary to give a brief overview of the three countries featured in this paper—specific to their Japanese[8] and *Nikkei* populations. These are not meant to be comprehensive or even complete summaries. What has been included here only relates to the phenomenon of the *dekasegi* diaspora.

Japan: A short history on its Brazilian and Peruvian immigrants

The history for Japan on this topic of Latin American *dekasegi* is fairly recent, dating back to the Immigration Control and Refugee Recognition Act of 1990 and its revision in 1998 and then again in 2015 and 2018. What this law did, in part, was to open the doors for Brazilians and Peruvians of Japanese descent to leave their home countries and enter into Japan to live and work. The response was overwhelming, peaking at nearly 300,000 Brazilian *Nikkei* and roughly 100,000 Peruvian *Nikkei* in Japan through the late 1990s.[9] But there was a marked decrease from the end of 2008, because of downturns in the global economy. Many *dekasegi* from both Brazil and Peru lost their jobs and domiciles in Japan, some even a way back to their homelands. Language barriers,

---

6 In this paper, I do not use "dekasegi" as a category of ethnicity. Rather, it is a descriptor of a type of *Nikkei* identity that is manifested in these various contexts by nature of migration.

7 See Hirabayashi, Kikumura-Yano, and Hirabayashi, 2002.

8 Here, I use "Japanese" as a noun: for a people, *Nihonjin*: 日本人 *lit., 'a Japanese person or the Japanese people.'* In this paper, I sometimes use "Japanese" as a noun to describe only a Japanese citizen who lives in Japan or is temporarily living outside that country but intends to return, who speaks the Japanese language as their only or first tongue, who "looks" Japanese physically, and who is regarded by other Japanese individuals or the larger society as a Japanese person. The term may also be applied in a plural form toward a group of individuals.

9 A 4/25/2009 *New York Times* article estimated a combined population of 366,000 Brazilian and Peruvian immigrants in Japan.

xenophobia, low or non-employable skill sets, etc., contributed to making it difficult for people to make ends meet.

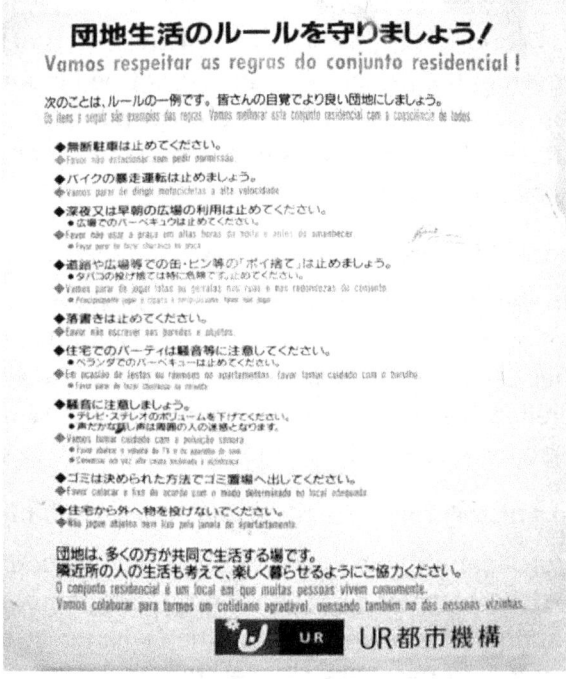

Symbol representing the Latin American dekasegi diaspora in Japan: The polarization of cultures

A sign, in the Portuguese and Japanese languages (ca. 2010), showing rules that Brazilian workers living near the Toyota plant in Homi-city, Aichi prefecture, must follow in order to live in their own community. These Brazilians are surrounded by disgruntled Japanese residents and the sign represents how rules have been established to keep these communities strictly separated.

Brazil: A short history of its Japanese immigrants

Brazil opened its doors to immigrants from Japan in 1908. The one hundredth anniversary of Japanese immigration to Brazil was celebrated in 2008. Japanese laborers originally went to Brazil to replace slave laborers brought in from Africa; the former group had dreams of making it rich and then returning to Japan. Most stayed and made names for themselves as a people by farming the most difficult hinterlands, including the Amazon, against great odds and hardships. After World War II, some pro-Emperor protests and an internal terrorist-like activity from both *Nikkei* and Brazilians alike erupted and polarized society for a couple of decades after the war. Gradually, the *Nikkei* population gained status and acceptance in society and moved from the farm to the city. The majority of *Nikkei* are now part of the Brazilian middle class. But assimilation has come with a cost and many *Nikkei* still do not feel completely Brazilian nor do all Brazilians completely accept them. The *Nikkei* in Brazil remain a largely unreached people group of between 1.3–1.8 million according to various estimates.

Symbol representing the Brazilian dekasegi *diaspora: A Japanese 'torii'—The fusion of cultures*

Highway exit leading into *Mogi das Cruzes* marked by a *'torii'*, the traditional gate used in Japan to demarcate the entrance to a Shinto shrine. Forty-five km outside of Sao Paolo city, *Mogi das Cruzes* has a sizeable *Nikkei* population. This symbol of Japan over a major road in Brazil illustrates how *Nikkei* Brazilians who erected this torii seek to co-exist there in an unusual mix or "fusion" of cultures.

Peru: A short history of its Japanese immigrants

Peru welcomed Japanese immigrants a decade earlier than Brazil and hosts one of the oldest "new worlds", behind Hawaii and Guam. In 2019, Peruvian *Nikkei* celebrated its 120 years of immigration. World War II was a watershed event for the Japanese in Peru because of negative circumstances flowing out of Peru's military alliance with the United States, i.e., incarceration and deportation for those with Japanese "blood", caused Peruvian *Nikkei* to become less strict about cultural preservation. This is reflected in present day trends where over 60 percent of *Nikkei* are said to marry outside their community. The modern day rise of Alberto Fujimori to power as erstwhile president of Peru, the effects of his three consecutive administrations, and his subsequent decline from power, imprisonment and loss of favor in Peruvian society profoundly affected the resident *Nikkei* communities in both Peru and Japan, even in the United States. Despite the *dekasegi* phenomenon of massive *Nikkei* emigration that was instigated under Fujimori, the effects of enculturation and globalization have weakened or even caused some *Nikkei* in Peru to lose their traditional ties to Japan.

Painting for art class by a *Nikkei* woman at the Peru-Japan Cultural Center in Lima:

The cartoon characters from Japanese children's stories in the original (top right) were originally depicted with wide, round eyes. But, for her own art class project (bottom left), this lady of Japanese descent chose to draw these same characters with narrow, slanted ones—even though wide, round eyes were initially drawn by Japanese animators in Japan.

Symbol representing the Peruvian dekasegi *diaspora:* Nikkei *artist's rendition of Japanese cartoon—The embedding of cultures*

Missiological Implications Based on Data Interpretation

Missiological implication #1:
The pathway of Nikkei dekasegi *identity formation is multi-faceted*

The model depicted below illustrates my conception of *Nikkei* identities of the various people I met and interviewed while in Japan, Brazil and Peru on research trips between 2009–2012. Additionally, several extended in-country visits were made to various Peruvian and Brazilian communities throughout Japan during that same time period. This schema is a generalization, an amalgamation, of my interview data and responses separated into categories and designations which shall be explained further below in this section:

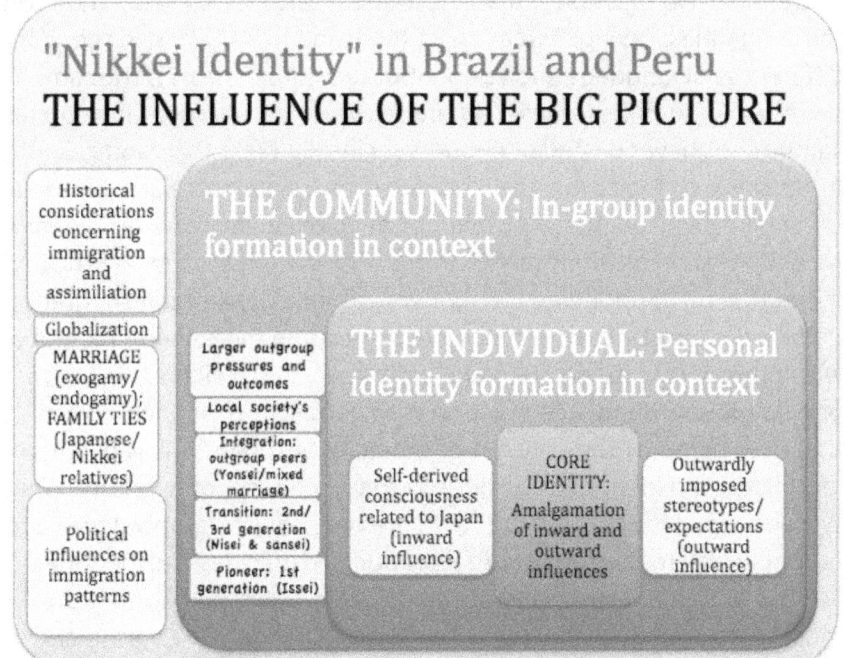

The following is my explanation for the contents of the graphic above:

The Individual: I view one's core identity as an amalgamation of inward and outward influences. Here, and specific to our topic, "self-derived consciousness" means what one thinks about oneself as it relates to Japan, i.e., an intrinsic, psychological state of mind or influence. That is, the thinking, "I am a 'Japanese', a *Nikkei*, a *dekasegi*, or a combination of all. It speaks to the question, where do I come from? Or, who am I?

For example, in the course of my research of these various communities, I found that many *Nikkei* from both Brazil and Peru seemed to suffer from identity crises when they went to live and work in Japan because of confusion between the meanings of *Nikkei* and "Japanese." These are not synonymous terms. On the other side of this, some *Nikkei* did not suffer from identity crises when they went to live and work in Japan simply because they were able to discern and decide for themselves the differences of meanings behind their identities as *Nikkei* or "Japanese" and how those terms might apply to them. At the same time, some non-*Nikkei* respondents might even generalize the differences based on ethnicity, i.e., saying, "we are all Brazilian" instead of admitting that one could be "a *Nikkei* from Brazil." Contrary to the first two examples, these respondents chose to focus more on the similarities, saying, "we all have the same heart" or, "yes, there are differences of language and culture but the human heart is the same."

Adachi describes these different types of self-identification as something "beyond-the-state" and specifically hints that "some South American *Nikkei* and other Latin American transnational migrant workers are creating a new sense of ethnic identity by claiming to be simply Latin American, aligning themselves along non-Japanese Latin Americans." [10]She goes on to underline that because of mobility and transmigration patterns, "boundaries of ethnic groups become more fluid in a global world...People can create various homes and origins...The more people move around—connecting with people from various 'homes'—the more complex the concept of ethnicity becomes." [11] This fluidity of "ethnicity" and identities ties directly to the concept of hybridity. What Werbner and Modood call the "transgressive power", "ambivalence and the sheer efflorescence of cultural products, ethnicities and identities." [12]

DeVos and Romanucci-Ross call ethnicity a "self-perceived group," [13] more than being based upon "common lineage." Thus, ethnicity is always being made and remade, especially because of political and social boundaries as "a subjective sense of continuity and belonging." [14] This agrees with Hirabayashi et al's definition of '*Nikkei*' above. I also

---

10 Adachi, 19.

11 Ibid.

12 Werbner and Modood, 2015.

13 DeVos and Romanucci-Ross, 18.

14 DeVos and Romanucci-Ross, 25.

concur with anthropologist Michael Rynkiewich who notes that, in reality, *all* cultures are contingent, constructed and contested.[15] Ethnic and cultural (*Nikkei*) identity naturally proceed out of all of the aforementioned manmade constructs.

In plain terms, what this means regarding the ethnic identity of *Nikkei* is that, in part, one "becomes *Nikkei*" because one chooses to be with a "self-perceived group" who call themselves *Nikkei* or even that the person himself prefers to think as such. This selection of self-identification is not primarily nor even necessarily contingent on ethnicity, language or cultural surroundings. Rather, it is based on how one thinks and feels about oneself, internally and individually, as well as from how one might be described or thought of by outsiders of a given group, which create for the insider "a subjective sense of continuity and belonging."

Self-perception can also be influenced by what others say about oneself, the extrinsic influences of culture, society, even racial prejudice or unconscious profiling, etc. In other words, this is the externally imposed concept of "the other" which says "you're so (not) Japanese" or "you don't look Japanese" or even "all Japanese are like you..." etc. In sum, the combination of what people may think of you, along with what you think of yourself regarding your own ethnic identity is what makes or doesn't make a person identify himself as a *Nikkei*, a "Japanese" or a *dekasegi*.

The Community: The category, "the community" in the graphic above encompasses topics too broad and expansive to be properly covered in a paper this size. However, they are worth mentioning in passing, and include generational heritage and societal pressures from both the larger *Nikkei*, Japanese or Latin societies surrounding these communities. That is why I include four generations of Japanese immigrants in the graphic above, as well as perceptions of one's local societal setting (the area where one grows up), plus, larger outgroup pressures (nationally, from within Japan, Brazil or Peru).

A helpful visual illustration of this is an unpublished generational chart of immigration and social perceptions of *Nikkei* in Brazil. It was

---

15 Rynkiewich, Michael A. Rynkiewich, *The World in My Parish: Rethinking the Standard Missiological Model*, *Missiology* 30, no. 3 (2002): 315–16.

created by Dr. Jurandir Yanagihara, a third generation Brazilian Christian of Japanese descent:

TIME PERIOD	SITUATION	OBJECTIVE	LOCATION	IDENTITY	FORM OF IDENTITY	FEELINGS TOWARD LARGER CULTURE
1908–1941	Accommodation/ adjustment	Become wealthy enough to be able to return to Japan	In colonies, on the farms	Japanese	Similar to what they had in Japan	As a stranger
1942–1962	Adaptation	New motherland	On the farms and in the city	Japanese-Brazilian	Constructed	Dualistic: being both Japanese and Brazilian at the same
1963–1980	Integration	Individualized recognition	In the city and on the farms	Nikkei-Brazilian	Fragmented	Double "non-citizenship"
1981–2000	Identification	Roots	The city	Brazilian-Nikkei	Self-acceptance	A "non-native" Brazilian
2001–	Acculturation	Enjoyment and influence	Upper middle class	Brazilian with Nikkei roots	Acknowledged	A type of a Brazilian with an ethnic consciousness

The historical process of migrant integration for the Nikkei into Brazilian society
(Source: Jurandir Yanagihara)

It should be noted that a taxonomy such as this one is not static or unidirectional, especially in a discussion involving hybridity. *Nikkei* identity in Brazil should not be viewed as being on a continuum where self-perception neatly moves from point A to point B and so forth. Rather, it should be visualized as a child's Lego block structure where colors and "levels" overlap and go in directions they should not, i.e., not rationally or orderly. Thomas Kuhn's (1962) idea of paradigm shifts, where new "shifts" overlap with old ones, is helpfully analogous to Yanagihara's insightful classifications here. This taxonomy helps one to historically understand the hybrid constructs and re-makings of Brazilian and Japanese *Nikkei* identity over eras and circumstance. Each of these time periods should be seen as connected to each other, continuing into the present, even more than one hundred years later. Brazil is used here as one example but a model like this would differ for Peru, Japan, North America or anywhere else since each are independent, unrelated societies with varying histories of Japanese immigration.

The bi: This final categorization which includes the influences of history, globalization, marriage and family ties, as well as political concerns are, again, beyond the scope of this paper to cover in detail. It is not possible to comprehensively cover each country and its immigrant populations in this way.

So, once more, we will only touch on one specific example from recent history: the 1990 immigration law enacted by Japan to open its borders to *Nikkei* abroad which forever changed the relationship between not simply Brazil and Peru but with the families who went from those countries as well. It illustrates the impact of the "big picture" quite well. A Wall Street Journal op-ed column December 6, 2018, noted that these South American *dekasegi*, "ethnic Japanese who live abroad…were welcomed to Japan throughout the 1990s. But during the financial crisis (of 2008 and beyond) the government offered them cash grants to leave lest they displace native workers".[16] What this historical and societal example underlines is how governments can easily both instigate and then obviate the very same immigration patterns they commence. The 1990 Immigration Control and Refugee Recognition Act was specifically directed toward migrant workers of "Japanese" identity. So, the impact on both the individual and the community of *dekasegi Nikkei*, not only in Japan but in Peru and Brazil as well, is germane concerning the implementation of that law and its various changes in 1998, 2015 and 2018. The implementation of its most current revision in November 2018 by the current Japanese government raises many questions as to Japan's capability to receive and "welcome" non-Japanese immigrants. In one news article, the *dekasegi* movement of the 1990s is cited as a specific example of such challenges to Japanese law and immigration policies.[17] Beyond historical and political machinations, we would be remiss to not also mention the persistence of both in-group (endogamous) marriages—to "preserve" identity—and out-group (exogamous) marriages—in conforming with social mores— to the degree that some of my respondents in Peru, for example, feared the total loss of their *Nikkei* identity because of high intermarriage rates.[18] These and other of the "big picture" items mentioned above in the graphic affect individuals and communities at the "grassroots level" which also influences and causes a hybridization of *Nikkei* identity, whether these persons are in Japan, Brazil, Peru or elsewhere.

---

16 I would add that one condition of those grants was a signed contractual promise never to return to Japan.

17 "Making Sense of Japan's New Immigration Policy: A Controversial New Regulation Will Allow More Foreign Workers into Japan. But Can Japan Take Care of Them Once They Arrive?" https://thediplomat.com/2018/11/making-sense-of-japans-new-immigration-policy/.

18 See the following links for miscegenation statistics in Brazil among *Nikkei*: https://en.wikipedia.org/wiki/Mixed-race_Brazilian#Japanese/non-Japanese https://www.labeurb.unicamp.br/elb/asiaticas/japones.htm (this link is in Portuguese).

Identity is a fundamental aspect of personality formation even though it is a cultural and social construct. And as we have seen, in the case of *Nikkei* and *dekasegi* identity, how it is formed in a globalized and migratory context could also deeply influence the practice of ministry in terms of evangelism, discipleship and the structure of worship and church attendance. Thus, in seeking to minister to the disparate populations and generations of each nation mentioned in this paper, the pathway of identity formation along which a *Nikkei* must pass is something that must be taken into account as the gospel is shared with them.

Missiological implication #2:
Nikkei *is one and the same, yet different in three countries*

Closely related to missiological implication #1 that *Nikkei dekasegi* identity formation is multi-faceted and complex, and there is also the notion that *Nikkei* is the same yet different in each of the three nations and even within their own communities, as Jurandir Yanagihara's taxonomy demonstrates.

On the one hand, many similarities exist. *Nikkei* everywhere share a common heritage with Japan and/or the Japanese community in their localities, as well as a common original language (Japanese)—except sometimes with immigrants from Okinawa (Okinawa dialect). Immigration a century ago took place only a decade apart for the original ships departing to Brazil and Peru, and recent "re-emigration" to Japan from Brazil and Peru started once more for *Nikkei* in both countries at the same time, beginning in 1990 because of the enactment of the Japanese law mentioned above. The inherited cultural heritage from the *Meiji* era brought by the original pioneer settlers a hundred years ago is shared and has been transformed as successive waves of immigrants who, in turn, 'brought' the accoutrements and behaviors of their successive eras to these adoptive homelands. For example, many traditional Japanese values such as restraint, hard work, pensiveness, a focus on education and being true to oneself were still emphasized among the *Nikkei* I met in Japan, Brazil and Peru.[19]

On the other hand and at the same time, differences are also considerable. The biggest difference I saw was how *Nikkei* were treated in the various local communities of each country. For example, in Aichi,

---

19 Nobuko, Adachi, *Japanese and* Nikkei *At Home and Abroad: Negotiating Identities in a Global World* (Amherst, NY: Cambria), 2010.

Japan, the *Nikkei* Brazilian community and in Kani, Japan, the *Nikkei* Peruvian community, was "in but not of" the surrounding Japanese community. One could feel the polarization of cultures that was almost palpable between the resident Japanese community and the immigrant worker *Nikkei* population, i.e., with the not so subtle sense that "we are not the same and you are not welcome here." Inside Brazil, on the other hand, there was a definite sense of fusion between cultures where one could clearly be both Brazilian and "Japanese" at the same time, without too much sense of dissonance or contradiction. I myself felt this even as a visiting *Nikkei* when people spoke Portuguese to me and didn't even give me the second look that I often get in other contexts. Inside Peru, I felt an embedding of identities where people almost seem determined to be either "Japanese" or Peruvian or both. In other words, people came across as consciously choosing to be who they were; they were also able to clearly state reasons as to why this was true for them. Even with these examples, it can be seen that ministry outreach would not be the same for each population.

Thus, in application, for such variegated homogeneity, it would not be appropriate to generalize or use a "one-size-fits-all" approach, i.e., to think that one type of evangelism or discipleship methodology will "suit" any kind of *Nikkei* or that "if it works in Japan, it will work with 'Japanese' everywhere." As already noted above in missiological implication #1, *Nikkei* identity formation is complex and beyond simple generalizations. For individuals on a personal level and sometimes even communities, it appears that *Nikkei* identity is less defined by skin color or Japanese language proficiency, and more by the composition of one's home, upbringing and environment, educational connections and the desire one has to be/become a Japanese. So, if such factors are not carefully considered, many could "fall through the cracks" and be missed by a so-called "cookie cutter" approach in reaching these disparate populations.

Missiological implication #3: Triadic convergence
Taking into consideration the similarities and differences between both the dominant culture and the *Nikkei* sub-cultures mentioned above in missological implication #2, my research data findings agreed with Hirabayashi, Kikumura-Yano, and Hirabayashi on the value of relational

ties that comprise a "triadic convergence." The idea of "triadic", or a group of three, comes from the writing of *Nikkei* identity scholars looking at *Nikkei* populations in a global context. I also sensed this positive tension, as I did my fieldwork. This same term of "triadic convergence" applies to the *dekasegi* since *dekasegi* are not an ethnicity per se but *Nikkei* from different places who have become migrant workers, usually in Japan.

"Triadic" speaks of "interactive relationships between the home nation, Japan and *Nikkei* community formation."[20] Like the legs on a tripod, these three facets together are necessary for explaining and dealing with a globalized, hybrid identity like the *dekasegi*, or even the *Nikkei* in Brazil or Peru.

1. Home nation: in our case, this is Brazil or Peru or even Japan in some instances.

2. Japan: important to this is how one's concept and perceived relationship to the nation and people of Japan impacts one's life. "Japan" as a part of the convergence refers to the "big picture" part of the diagram in missiological implication #1, where one's conception and relationship to Japan is a key element in forging identity, practice and behavior in general for both individuals and communities.

3. *Nikkei* community formation: this is about how the *Nikkei* in that context perceive of themselves as regards to their Japanese "connection" within their home nation. We have already discussed this at length above.

I encountered a specific example of this kind of triadic convergence in Brazil simply because one time I happened to be visiting near that occasion on the local calendar. Traditionally, the *Bon Odori* or "Festival of the Dead" as it is often called is celebrated by Japanese in Japan during the summer months, usually August. The festival is often held for three or more days and includes civic holidays, cemetery visits and memorial celebrations as well as festivities and customs, such as *Toro Nagashi*, a traditional sending off of lit paper lanterns down rivers in Japan during *Obon*, as this festival is also called. However, in both North America and Brazil, the dates will often shift depending on the local calendar. In Brazil, for example, I discovered that the *Obon* festival is normally held during the first week of November. When I asked if this was intentionally done to coincide with the Day of the Dead in South American Catholic

---

20 Hirabayashi, Kikumura-Yano, and Hirabayashi, 338.

tradition, I was told yes.[21] Called *"Finados"* in Portuguese but synced with *Obon*, this time period is when *Nikkei* in Brazil follow the custom of their home nation yet incorporates the tradition of Japan as local Japanese Brazilians work to build *Nikkei* community formation, a practice that both sets them apart yet also allows them to participate in the local context of their home nation. This is triadic convergence.

Missiological approach: To reach various populations of *Nikkei* in a globalized world, using a triadic approach is a needed framework. We must consider the home nation, its relationship to Japan, and how the resident *Nikkei* community forms its identity as we minister to these groups. The older geographically-based, static, local context approach is inadequate to explain or deal with these and other *Nikkei* and *dekasegi* experiences.

Missological implication #4:
The effects of Dekasegi *movement should not be ignored*

In Peru, anecdotally, it is estimated that half of the entire *Nikkei* Peruvian population had been *dekasegi* in Japan for varying lengths of time. In Japan, Brazilian immigrants, most of whom are *Nikkei*, are a sizeable and influential population. The global recession that started in 2008 caused many *dekasegi* to return to their home nation from Japan, or left them stranded in Japan without a job or a future. However, even though the enormity and pace of this *dekasegi* movement from more than a decade ago has waned, missiologically speaking, opportunities for sharing the gospel with, through and in these migrant populations in any of the three countries remain ripe. What does this mean in application for mission?

First, a vision for training these *dekasegi* is strongly evidenced among professional Christian workers on both sides of the ocean. In Brazil, for example, intentional, organized efforts are taking place to specifically reach returnees from abroad because it has been found that *Nikkei* may sometimes come to Christ more easily abroad (though usually in a Portuguese language context). This can be attributed to the fact that those who leave their homeland are often more open-minded than those who remain, simply by nature of the fact that they have left their homes for regions beyond. Thus, receiving the gospel is only one of many "new" experiences that migrant workers encounter. Because of this reality, some churches in Brazil send missionaries to Japan, both

---

21 Please see the article in the *Nichi Bei* online periodical, "The Transformation of Obon in Brazil": https://www.nichibei.org/2010/06/the-transformation-of-obon-in-brazil/.

to minister to unreached Japanese but also to establish Portuguese-speaking congregations there. In 2012, it was estimated by a coalition of evangelical Brazilian pastors in Japan that there were between 200–300 Portuguese-speaking churches in Japan comprised both of *Nikkei* and Brazilians of all ethnicities. This is phenomenal since the total Christian church demographic in Japan hovers somewhere between 7,800–8,000 congregations for the entire country!

Also, some *dekasegi* who have been abroad are sometimes more open to the gospel once they return to Brazil than before they left. My respondents explained that this was because "becoming Christian"—which often meant becoming Roman Catholic—was perceived by many *Nikkei* as a betrayal of their Japanese identities and heritage so, in general, Christianity in every form was resisted by most *Nikkei* (as it is in Japan). But spiritual needs manifested overseas were met by the gospel from Christians living there. Being out of their home country actually made turning to Christ easier for many, according to my respondents.

Inside Japan itself, both Brazilian and Peruvian pastors expressed a desire to see both an expansion of their language ministry works among their own people as well as a desire to see the surrounding Japanese population reached for Christ. Two pastors I spoke with in Japan also mentioned a vision to train lay persons to lead churches so that the church could eventually function without professional clergy. This also addresses a felt need that was raised by one missionary who told me that *Nikkei* tend to feel better when a *Nikkei* church leader is over them, one who "looks like them."

On the other hand, many *Nikkei* in Peru have either lived or worked in Japan (and therefore now have connections there) or have relatives or friends who did. Similarly, because of the large, still extant Brazilian communities in Japan, with relatives and friends living there, the desire and ability to visit Japan—even if one is not a *dekasegi*—is appealing and strong to many Brazilian *Nikkei*. The question for visitors from both countries to Japan is not whether they will come but, spiritually speaking, what will be done with them when they do come? And what will be done for them or through them when they return to their own country?

Finally, whether in Japan or in their homeland, whether returning from Japan or going there for the first time, there is a viable opportunity for both a harvest of new souls and for training *Nikkei* to win *Nikkei* to Christ. As already mentioned, the prominence of the *dekasegi* in

Japan has lessened radically in 2018 from a decade ago yet their influence remains—since many have stayed as families and are still working in Japan as they continually seek to integrate into the larger Japanese context. In a different but similar way, *dekasegi* who return from Japan suffer from some of the same adjustment and adaptation issues experienced by military, diplomatic or missionary personnel in America who return from abroad. Thus, on both sides of the Pacific, the people and the influence of the *dekasegi* movement remain an issue to be engaged with missiologically. There are still many unanswered questions and untapped potential.

Missiological implication #5:
Language, culture, and other means can be tools to win **Nikkei** *to Christ* **(but not necessarily the Japanese language!)**

The heart language of the majority of *Nikkei* I met in both Brazil and Peru was NOT the Japanese language. Therefore, evangelism and training should be primarily conducted in the heart language of *Nikkei* (whether in Portuguese or Spanish), and only in Japanese and sometimes even in English as a support language or as a venue for evangelism, when necessary. Learning English as a second language was quite popular in Lima when I was there. On the other hand, *Nikkei* in Sao Paolo and other Brazilian locales seemed very interested in improving their Japanese facilities. Thus, language classes specific to such interests and contexts could become another form of outreach.

Having said this, it must also be noted that the ability to speak Japanese at varying levels, still remains a staunch vested interest for *Nikkei* communities in Brazil and Peru. Inside Japan, speaking Japanese is almost a requirement for survival for *dekasegi* communities there; it is not uncommon for *dekasegi* children in Japan, raised in the Japanese school system and fluent in the language, to become de facto interpreters and interlocutors for their parents to the larger surrounding of a Japanese-speaking community. Japanese language acquisition is difficult for many Latin Japanese so teaching the Japanese language to native Portuguese or Spanish speakers could itself be an outreach tool among *Nikkei* in Japan.

On the other hand, *Nikkei* in South America seems to cling sometimes to the Japanese language as a tool to form or protect their identity as being "special" Brazilians or Peruvians. Thus, teaching Japanese classes or, better, using Japanese biblical language to teach grammatical patterns and vocabulary for everyday use (much as TESOL classes are used for evangelism in the US and abroad) would be appealing to many Latin *Nikkei* who "like" the Japanese language or want to keep up with it for manga (comic book) reading or to learn new conversational vocabulary.

Missiological approach: The heart language of the majority of the *Nikkei* I met was either Portuguese or Spanish; many spoke better English as a second language than speaking Japanese. But Japanese as a language remains a tool, a venue, for reaching *Nikkei* everywhere for Christ.

Some Final Thoughts

My research raised many questions that weren't answered. Much more research and active outreach among *dekasegi* communities in Japan as well as toward returnee *Nikkei* in their home contexts of Brazil and Peru needs to be conducted. As previously noted, there are consonant 'touchpoints' between Brazilian and Peruvian *Nikkei* regarding their identities. Such topics would include shared and similar experiences under World War II, generational changes in language and culture, and racially-charged impressions from the local culture. Because of the influence and experience of migration, the effects of globalization are deeply engrained into the *Nikkei* psyche, whether in Brazil or Peru, and should not be ignored. Identity regarding *Nikkei* is fluid and changing, defying conventional wisdom because there is no singular categorization for *Nikkei* "ethnicity." Hybrid identification may be the answer here but further research will need to be conducted since Brazilian and Peruvian *Nikkei* seem to view themselves as both the same and different from their local setting at the same time. For individuals personally, their *Nikkei* identity is less defined by skin color or Japanese language proficiency, and more by home upbringing/environment, educational connections and the desire to be a "Japanese." *Nikkei* in both countries remain a largely unreached people group. Utilizing existing Japan-Brazil or Japan-Peru relationships must be considered, because of immigration and identity issues, especially the reciprocal (on both sides of the ocean) training of lay Christians for evangelism, church planting and training in leadership and multiplication. Strategies for reaching *Nikkei* should be considered from the basis of a variegated perspective rather than from a 'cookie-cutter' approach. Finally, since we live in a globalized, migratory world—

especially as this relates to *Nikkei* traveling to and from Japan—we must seek to strategize with this in mind, not merely looking at a local context or even countrywide. As a focus of evangelism, training and church planting, *Nikkei* are globalized sojourners. Those of us who seek to reach them must expand the horizons of our own mindsets, methodologies and practices, as we pray and plan to reach *Nikkei* everywhere for the gospel of our Lord Jesus Christ.

BIBLIOGRAPHY

Adachi, Nobuko. *Japanese and* Nikkei *At Home and Abroad: Negotiating Identities in a Global World.* Amherst, NY: Cambria, 2010.

Hirabayashi, Lane, Akemi Kikumura-Yano and James Hirabayashi. *New Worlds, New Lives: Globalization and People of Japanese Descent in the Americas and from Latin America in Japan.* Stanford, CA : Stanford University, 2002.

Kuhn, Thomas S. *The Structure of Scientific Revolutions.* Chicago: University of Chicago, 1962.

Romanucci-Ross, Lola, and George DeVos. eds. *Ethnic Identity: Creation, Conflict and Accommodation.* Walnut Creek, CA : Alta Mira, 1995.

Rynkiewich, Michael A. *The World in My Parish: Rethinking the Standard Missiological Model.* Missiology 30, no. 3: 301–21, 2002.

Werbner, Pnina, and Tariq Modood. *Debating Cultural Hybridity: Multi-Cultural Identities and the Politics of Anti-Racism.* Ebook ed. London: Zed, 2005.

About the Author

GARY FUJINO is professor of Diaspora Studies for Missional University. He served as a missionary church planter to the Japanese diasporas with the International Mission Board of the Southern Baptist Convention. Gary co-edited and co-authored the EMS 20 Monograph, Reaching the City: Reflections on Urban Mission for the 21st Century. *He has published on cross-cultural identity and mission in EMQ, IJFM , and other publications. He currently resides in the Chicago area.*

CHAPTER 11 | Sam George

Coconut Generation, Hybridity, and Hybrid Missions

I n this chapter, I want to briefly introduce you to the world of Americanized Asian Indians. For me, this enquiry began in the late 1990s when I was studying at the Princeton Theological Seminary and was serving as a youth pastor of an Asian Indian immigrant (*Mar Thoma*) church in Philadelphia. It forced me to reflect on my own upbringing as a child of immigrants from Kerala, India, and about the second-generation young people I was ministering to, who were born and raised by Kerala immigrants and settled in the USA. It resulted in the writing of a popular book titled *Understanding the Coconut Generation*.[1] Later in the chapter, I expand the conversation to a theoretical framework on hybridity and liminality and close with two biblical characters to elucidate how the mission of God naturally flows out of hybridized individuals through cultural diffusion and translations.

---

1 Sam George, *Understanding the Coconut Generation: Ministry to the Americanized Asian Indians* (Mall Publishers, Niles, IL. 2006). See www.CoconutGeneration.com.

The Coconut Generation

Coconut is a metaphor for Indian Americans or Westernized Asian Indians. They are the second and third generation of Indian immigrants who were born and/or raised in the West. Like a coconut fruit, these Westernized Indians are "brown on the outside and white on the inside." The colors brown and white signifies two sides of hybridized Indian Americans and is analogous to metaphors like Oreo and Banana for children of other ethnic immigrants to the West. This term is popularly used to describe emerging generations of brown Indians in Caucasian white cultures. It denotes the two sides of the emerging generation, with life like a complex diametrically opposing fact lived in reality where neither narratives alone is sufficient to fully describe themselves. The brown side of coconuts embraces family/community, structure/order, emotional restraint, and respect for authority, while the white side prefers autonomy, individuality, expressiveness, and creativity. These are essentially opposed sets of values and coconuts live daily through this predicament by bringing the Eastern and Western worlds together into a new hybridized self. Coconuts are also referred to as ABCD (American Born Confused *Desis*), referring to a state of confused identity prevalent among the second generation, which, however, has been reclaimed by the second generation when they came of age as American Born Confident *Desis*. Other metaphors of Westernized Asian Indians include *Chai, Masala*, and Chicken *Tikka*.

The ontological reality of coconuts involves navigating across landmines of two or more cultures continually and stockpiling many trophies of battle scars of diasporic displacements. For immigrants, the struggle is often geographic dislocation and survival in a foreign place, while for their progenies it is cultural and psychological disruptions. Why do I look like one way, but feel another way that is entirely different? The divergence between the nuances of ancestral culture, though never fixed but continually evolving, and the unconscious assimilation into host culture leaves children of immigrants with a convoluted stalemate. They exhibit an intense longing for belonging while not fully fitting in any of the worlds before them. Their miseries are multiplied on account of suffering from the Western notion of guilt of wrongdoings while being subjected to Asian shaming behaviors. They exist in the precarious margins of societal groups and often fall through many fissures found between them. They are generally misunderstood by others and frequently required to demonstrate their cultural competency concurrently in multiple worlds. The notions of identity confusion and caught in-between cultures can feel like you are stuck in the middle, being neither here nor there, and being on both shores at once.

The Palestinian American Edward Said's description is true of hybrid coconuts, "...the pathos of summer and winter as much as the potential of spring are nearby but unobtainable. Exile is life led outside of habitual order; nomadic decentered contrapuntal... no sooner does one get accustomed to it than its unsettling force erupts anew."[2] The coconut generation is more westernized than we realize and more Indian than they would like to admit it. They show shades of brownness and whiteness woven together in this generation and not narrowly describe them monochromatically. They need to be continually aware of their world at any given point in time and become adept at interpreting one world to the other in order to make sense of their liminal transcultural existence. All expressions and meanings are reinterpreted afresh as they move across cultural lines, as those boundaries are blurred in their unique subculture and duality of personhood. Hybrids suffer from a perpetual cultural jetlag, a sense of disorientation of being in one place while feeling they are somewhere else, as they daily traverse between different worlds many times. Any untimely act or word can have disastrous long-term consequences from which it is nearly impossible to recover from. When these different worlds collide, the tectonic plates of diverse worldviews and customs, it sends giant tsunami waves on the shores of the coconut psyche and life. If they find nothing or no one to hang on to when these tremors occur, many are swept away in the receding waves and drown in the depths of confusions of hybridity. Hall believed that "Diaspora identities are those which are constantly producing and reproducing themselves anew, through transformation and difference."[3]

Those who believed that 'the East and West shall never meet' were completely mistaken. While a myriad of paradoxes paralyzes the immigrant generation, their descendants thrive amidst the chaos and perfectly upholds these discordant dilemmas. They fit in effortlessly everywhere and nowhere in particular. They are both insiders as well as outsiders at the same time. Their roots lie in uprootedness and in multiple

2 Edward Said, "The Mind of Winter," *Harpers* (September 1984), 51.

3 Stuart Hall, "Cultural Identity and Diaspora" in *Identity: Community, Culture and Difference*, J. Rutherford. Ed. London: Lawrence and Wishart (1990): 222-37.

locales, while their allegiance remains beyond cultures and geographies. By the time their subculture is defined, this generation morphs into a disparate entity altogether. Those who amalgamate multiple modes of thinking and functioning have a distinct advantage over those who do exclusively in unilateral terms and ensues in multifarious polyphonic sensibilities. They extract cues from manifold diverse contexts and synergize them for an appropriate response, without weighing one over the other or subjugating any one of those realities. This generation is mixed up into one potent concoction such that without every piece of all of its components, it will lack its intoxicating power. It seeks deeper for truth by keenly listening with their eyes and intently pursuing authentic relationships that will transform their lives inside out. In order to evangelize and disciple this generation, both parents and church leaders have to take every facet of their complex being seriously and refrain from forcing them into molds of yesteryears born out of solitary cultural charter.

The Coconut Generation does not live in 'either-or' world but in 'both-and' world. The divergent worlds, which were totally incompatible with each other in the past, have beautifully coalesced together in creative convergence with the new generation. They become adept at circumnavigating through the hybridized terrains and acquire essential life skill of intercultural competency which enables them to thrive in the complex contemporary world and facilitates the transference of realities from one world to another. The fusion of the East and the West springs forth new imaginative vitality and this creative creolization along the cultural borderlands is subversive to master codes, current statutes, and dominant ideologies. By de-centering norms and reordering sequences, it creates many new strategic inflection points through narrative transformation, re-accentuations of traditions and interrogating prevailing systems. As a result, new rituals are invented, new meaning are given to practices and new levels of devotion to ultimate questions of life and eternity are established. Parenting and ministering to this generation continue to puzzle and remain an exorbitant challenge to immigrant generation as well as immigrant church leaders, while promises are just beginning to be realized.

Theoretical Framework on Hybridity

A growing body of literature on diaspora on account of globalization, transnational migration and de-territorialization, has critiqued and deconstructed discourses on rootedness and hegemonic views of identity, culture and religion. Purity and pollution was the defining order of the ancient world and mixing up any kind were derided such that many religious and civil laws had the strictest stipulation forbidding any form of interaction with people unlike themselves. The social hierarchy was invented and prohibitions with a severe penalty were established to restrict interactions only within certain categories. The miscegenation laws were legislated and racially mixed people were shunned and marginalized. The polluted ones have to undergo cumbersome cleansing rituals to be reinstated into the social order or suffer from ostracization. The elaborate customs and rigid boundary walls were erected by the social, economic, political and religious elites to keep the other as other while pursuing self-interest at all cost. In postcolonial discourse, the subaltern margins contest hegemonic power structures of the center and hybridity disrupts the exclusive prerogative of a select few by contaminating the boundaries of inquiry and grafting new knowledge from various disciplines, including that of subjugated knowledge of subaltern groups. Consequently, hybridity is defined not by essence or purity, but by the recognition of a necessary fluidity, heterogeneity, and diversity on a continuous basis.

In a seminal essay, "How Newness Enters the World," Indian postcolonial theorist Homi Bhabha shifted the limelight from the binary of the colonizer and the colonized to the liminal spaces in-between. The vantage point of liminality, he elaborated using architectural simile like stairwell as a pathway between upper and lower levels of a house and literary conception of blasphemy, which is "not merely as misrepresentation of sacred by secular", but as a moment when "the content of cultural tradition is being overwhelmed or alienated in the act of translation."[4] The emerging culture that develops in the new soil of the third space is alike and different from its parent cultures. Hybrids are not only double voiced and double accented but is also double languaged; in it there are two individual consciousness, two voices, two accents as there are doubling of socio-linguistic consciousness, two epochs … that come together… they are pregnant with potential for new worldviews, with new 'internal forms' for perceiving the world in words."[5] Hybridity is essentially interdisciplinary in nature and showcases

---

4 Homi Bhabha, *The Location of Culture* (London: Routledge, 1994), 225.

5 Ibid., "Culture's In-Between" in *Questions of Cultural Identity* by Stuart Hall and Paul de Gay, (London: Sage, 1996), 58.

futility of knowledge within any particular domain. It democratizes knowledge by letting discordant views of multiple worlds to participate in the production of new knowledge and grasp new realities.

With their duality of personhood and intercultural sensibility, hybrids develop a natural translation capacity by which they decipher both world inputs to each other and trying to make sense of their interstitial existence. Every sensory impulse goes through translator mechanism in the head and heart of hybrids which are converted into intelligible and appropriate responses to the new world. As long as both worlds are somewhat compatible and meaningful correlations can be made between them, they can survive and situations are manageable. Any failure to do so can result in stressful times and end up in depression. Over prolonged periods of such intricate translation processing, hybrids develop a sense of multiple belonging and adept at thriving in multiple contexts. In other words, they become like chameleons, continually adapting to their new contexts naturally and almost effortlessly. If not, they stand exposed, vulnerable and pay a dear price, sometimes with their very lives, in the interstitial crevices of their marginal existence.

The language of religious purity in the Old Testament must be read in the context of diasporic Hebrews and as a "means of emphasizing social identity and nonconformity to the world."[6] When immigrants feel uprooted and isolated in a foreign land, and faced with a strong pressure to conform to alien standards, it instinctively falls back on familiar culture and primary ties of kinship network to reaffirm its individuality in the face of threats of extinction and to maintain some form of normalcy amidst unforeseeable and stressful contingencies. Displacement brings about disruptions in sociocultural realms where assimilation into the dominant cultures and intermarriage is seen as social and economic upward mobility and in order to rid themselves of disadvantaged minority status. The social sanctions against mixed marriages in religious texts and cultures sometimes conflict with equally strong values of romantic and democratic idealism which results in boundary negotiations, violations of group solidarity and reconceptualization of identity, community, and mission of the displaced.

On account of increased human mobility and interconnectivity between people all over the world, there is unprecedented levels of interaction between people and intermingling of cultures, leading to

---

6 Daniel L. Smith-Christopher, *A Biblical Theology of Exile* (Minneapolis: Fortress, 2002), 162.

formation of ever greater fluidity in cultures. The growing hybridization will challenge prevailing notions of identity, community and mission, while the diasporic narratives of the Bible, such as expulsion, exodus, exile, dispersion etc., and theological and anthropological resources have much to contribute in missiological reimagination on account of hybridity. In developing a theology of race, Jennings locates the root error in the forcible subjugation, dispossession, and removal of non-European peoples from their homelands where displacement inflicted on them an incalculable loss of identity that is fundamentally tied to the land. The point he stresses is that "Christian theology and segregationalist mentalities" are firmly entrenched within "a style of imagining social reality" that is "diseased . . . in the kind of community imagined—its scope, character, and materiality. . . . [These] thwart the formation of Christian community beyond the strictures of nation, language, and peoples."[7]

At their core, hybrids exhibit a duality of personhood—two natures, two tendencies and two personas, fused together into one new kind of person who is able to switch between multiple spheres easily. Some may see this as abnormal multiple personality or cultural schizophrenia, but others view this as a double consciousness. Theologians have described Jesus as a *mulatto*, a hybrid between divinity and humanity[8] or showcased Jesus as a *mestizo* as a son of Galilee's mixed and marginalized society, who enters the great city of Jerusalem in order to challenge its wealth, to confront the racial arrogance of the culturally pure elites.[9] The construction of new Christological vision of Jesus as tragic *mulatto* and marginalized *mestizo*, confronts the contrived delusions and violence of racial purity, wealth and power dynamics, which emerges from the mixedness of flesh and spirit as well as geographical and sociocultural blending in the person of Jesus and offers a new hopeful model for identity, community and mission for today's hybrids in our contemporary world of much chaos, pain and confusion.

Latin American scholars have helped us to understand mixed-ness using the concept of *mestizaje*, which helps communities to draw

---

7 Willie James Jennings, *The Christian Imagination: Theology and Origins of Race* (New Haven: Yale University, 2011), 233.

8 Brian Bantum, *Redeeming Mulatto: A Theology of Race and Christian Hybridity* (Waco, TX: Baylor University, 2010).

9 Virgilio P. Elizando, *Galillean Journey: The Mexican American Promise* (Maryknoll, NY: Orbis, 1983).

equally from its diverse cultural inheritances. The *mestizo* (of mixed blood) "affirms both identities received while offering something new to both."[10] They are uniquely qualified to question the arrogant claims to purity made by some states and races. Since they have no abiding city on earth, *mestizo* loyalty lies neither to race or a nation, but the New Jerusalem, the eternal city of God. Alvarez uses the *mestizaje* concept to develop a theology of immigration by highlighting identity and otherness of the context of undocumented immigrants by mirroring the imminent and transcendent God in Pentecostal praxis.[11] Such a viewpoint is disruptive to traditional social, economic and racial hierarchies. It transcends historical and sociocultural sentiments to knit together a global multiethnic Kingdom vision (Rev 7:9) for a society where there is no Jew or Greek, no slave or free, no male or female (Gal 3:28). It is without domination or inherent privileges. This is a potent theology for a de-racinated and hybridized people in an ever-globalizing world, who define their identities not by roots of race, but by routes of diasporic displacement and incoherent sense of mixedness who are constantly on the move.

Moses and Paul: God's Mission through Hybrids

In this final section, I want to reflect on two hybrid characters of the Bible, one each from the Old Testament and the New Testament, namely Moses and Paul. Moses was a fourth generation Hebrew on his fathers' side and third generation on his mothers' side, who was born and raised in Egypt and struggled between being a Hebrew and Egyptian. Moses was born at a time when Israelites were perceived as a threat because of their large numbers and there was a national edict to kill all baby boys in the land. Family gave him up to the Nile and he was "drawn out" of the river to be adopted into the royal family. He was well trained for leadership in the greatest empire of his times with the largest economy and advanced learning and military. On account of his Hebraic roots, he had compassion for the kinsmen who were brutally mistreated. In an attempt to help them, he becomes a murderer and was rejected by his own people. Fearing the wrath of the emperor, he ran away to a faraway desert land to work for as a shepherd of a foreign priest and married his

---

10 Virgilio P. Elizondo, Ed. *The Future is Mestizo* (Boulder, CO: University Press of Colorado, 2000), 84.

11 Daniel O. Alvarez, *Mestizaje and Hibridez: Latin@ Identity in Pneumatological Perspective* (Cleveland, TN: CPT, 2016).

daughter. While tending his father-in-law's flock, Moses has a profound life-altering encounter with God who identifies and calls him to a new mission. God used every facet of his life for the unique mission of his life to be the deliverer and to lead the children of Israel out of their bondage in Egypt into the Promised Land.

Likewise, the Apostle Paul was a diaspora Jew who grew up in Tarsus, probably a second or third generation Jew in the province of Cilicia in the southeastern region of Asia Minor. He was trained under the best Hebrew scholar of his times, Gamaliel in Jerusalem and was well-learned in Hebrew Scriptures. He was an ardent Pharisee and unmatched in his zeal to persecute Jesus' followers. He was a Hellenized Jew well-versed in Greek literature and philosophies. He was born a Roman citizen with distinct privilege and prestige in the Romanized world. However, his encounter with the risen Jesus Christ on his way to Damascus changed everything—his identity, meaning and mission in life. His Jewish heritage and learning, his diasporic upbringing as well as prized citizenship, he later counted as "loss" in order that he may know Christ. Again, God took advantage of every facet of his life for the advancement of the gospel in the world.

Moses and Paul had a very strategic influence on the Hebrew and Christian communities respectively, primarily on account of their hybridity. Moses remains the most influential leader for the Israelites in the Old Testament and Paul is the most influential leader in the early days of the Christian church in the New Testament. God used the Egyptian background of Moses to secure freedom for the enslaved Jews and lead them to the Promised Land, while God used the Greek background of Paul for the expansion of the gospel to the Gentiles. God used both of them to write sizable parts of the Old and New Testaments respectively. The turning points in their lives in spite of their unique background and exceptional abilities was their dramatic encounter with God (Ex 3, Acts 9), which completely re-oriented each of their calling and mission in life. Both not only had to overcome the liminality of hybrid selves but also effectively used their multiple cultural bearings for the advance of their missions. Their socio-cultural plurality requires a strong theologically compelling center to which all diversities can be held together, a core that remains faithful and true, who radically reorients our view of self and our mission in the world. Due to cultural diffusion that occurs naturally in hybrids and their concomitant existence in multiple worlds, they become proficient translators who can help to negotiate boundaries by repairing identities and narrative reconstruction. The liminal creativity helps to "engage in critical historiography that condemn the sins of the ancestors" while forging new fidelity and faithful community because "to be diaspora people is to be people on mission."[12]

Conclusion

I close this chapter with a quote from Saint Mother Teresa of the Sisters of Charity in Kolkata, India. I had the privilege of meeting her several times and came across this quote in one of her personal journals when I visited her office in the mid-1990s. After wrestling about her identity and calling in life over many years of missionary work among the poorest of the poor in India, she claimed, "By blood and origin, I am an Albanian. By citizenship I am Indian. I am a Catholic nun. As to my calling, I belong to the whole world. As to my heart, I belong entirely to Jesus." It beckons and challenges us to establish the very core of our identity and our notion of ultimate allegiance beyond the place of birth or current habitation, ethnicity or citizenship, and vocations. We could add other identities like qualifications, credentials, titles, brands and status markers. However, our identities built upon a deeper sense of life calling and heart allegiance will not only liberate us from common trappings of psycho, social, cultural and ideological notions of identification, but endow with faith filled fidelity to a vision for life that is deeply meaningful and enduring.

On account of substantial gains in human mobility and interconnectivity, our world will witness unprecedented levels of interaction between people and blending of cultures everywhere leading to a surge in hybridizations in the coming decades. The diaspora communities must realize the perils and promises of the hybrid generations by providing compassionate care and transformative guidance to help them discern God's mission in the world. The redemptive purposes of cultural liminality of hybrids can be realized only in and through a transformative encounter with the ultimate hybrid of all times, Jesus Christ, who bridged the chasm of heaven and earth, such that all hybrid find their eternal destiny in the finished work of God and life-fulfilling mission in the world.

---

12 Smith-Christopher, 200.

BIBLIOGRAPHY

Alvarez, Daniel O. *Mestizaje and Hibridez: Latin@ Identity in Pneumatological Perspective*. Cleveland, TN: CPT, 2016.

Bantum, Brian. *Redeeming Mulatto: A Theology of Race and Christian Hybridity*. Waco, TX: Baylor University, 2010.

Bhabha, Homi. "Culture's In-Between" in *Questions of Cultural Identity* by Stuart Hall and Paul de Gay. London: Sage, 1996.

———. *The Location of Culture*. London: Routledge, 1994.

Elizando, Virgilio P. *Galillean Journey: The Mexican American Promise*. Maryknoll, NY: Orbis, 1983.

Elizondo, Virgilio P., ed. *The Future is Mestizo*. Boulder, CO: University Press of Colorado, 2000.

George, Sam. *Understanding the Coconut Generation: Ministry to the Americanized Asian Indians*. Mall Publishers, Niles, IL, 2006.

Jennings, Willie James. *The Christian Imagination: Theology and Origins of Race*. New Haven: Yale University, 2011.

Said, Edward. "The Mind of Winter." *Harpers* (September 1984): 51.

Smith-Christopher. Daniel L. *A Biblical Theology of Exile*. Minneapolis: Fortress, 2002.

 ## ABOUT THE AUTHOR

SAM GEORGE is the Lausanne Movement's Catalyst for Diasporas. He is also the Executive Director of Parivar International and author of Understanding the Coconut Generation.

CHAPTER 12 | Kamal Weerakoon

Hybridity and Identity Development of Second-Generation Diaspora

How might Christians of a migrant background, especially those of later generations who are conscious of their culturally pluralised identity, live well as Christians today? How might first-generation immigrant Christians faithfully transmit the Christian gospel to later generations, and seek to form Christian identity in them? This chapter brings missiological literature on contextualization into dialogue with secular literature on cultural hybridity. It will argue that drawing upon modes of Christian faithfulness from both our native and adoptive homes, without being uncritically bound to either of them, and an attention to our status as culturally pluralised hybrids, opens new opportunities to apply the Protestant principle of constant reformation according to the Word of God, which in turn shapes robust Christian faithfulness in the next generation. Examples of both effective and ineffective discipleship will be provided from interviews conducted for my doctoral research.

First-generation Traditions: Respect without Replication

The need for, indeed inevitability of, contextualization is well accepted within missiological literature. The gospel is universally relevant, not by being abstracted from the concrete realities of the cultures and societies of this world, but precisely by being expressed in and through the languages, attitudes, perspectives, relationships, etc. which constitute the cultures and societies of this world.[1] Deep contextualization creates traditions that endure because they are effective in bringing people to Christ, and shaping Christian identity in them. They represent the forms of corporate worship and individual and communal life which have shaped the Christian identity of first-generation migrants, and which these migrants therefore seek to replicate in their new homes. Unless and until proven otherwise, we should consider first-generation immigrant Christian traditions as expressions of contextualized theologies which have endured precisely because they were effective in shaping Godly Christian identity—back home.

But in this question of home lies the intergenerational issue, for "home" is located differently between the generations. A shift in geographic, therefore ethno-cultural (and temporal) location means we cannot assume that the forms of Christian faithfulness which shaped Godliness in our previous home will effectively shape Godliness in our new home. A new context requires (re)new(ed) contextualization.

This does not denigrate the impressive pedigree of first-generation traditions. But it does locate those traditions within our previous home, thereby creating space for, and requiring renewed effort towards, discovering and constructing forms of individual and corporate life and worship which properly respond to our new home—the new context wherein we seek to be Christian.

---

1 See, inter alia, Stephen B. Bevans, *Essays in Contextual Theology, Theology and Mission in World Christianity* (Boston: Brill, 2018); Stephen B. Bevans, *Models of Contextual Theology*, revised & expanded ed., Faith and Cultures Series (Maryknoll, NY: Orbis, 2002); Matthew Cook, *Local Theology for the Global Church: Principles for an Evangelical Approach to Contextualization* (Pasadena, CA: World Evangelical Alliance Theological Commission, 2010); Rose Dowsett, *Global Mission: Reflections and Case Studies in Contextualization for the Whole Church* (Pasadena, CA: William Carey Library, 2011); Jeffrey P. Greenman and Gene L. Green, *Global Theology in Evangelical Perspective: Exploring the Contextual Nature of Theology and Mission* (Downers Grove, Ill.: IVP Academic, 2012); Dale T. Irvin, Peter C. Phan, and Stephen B. Bevans, *Christian Mission, Contextual Theology, Prophetic Dialogue: Essays in Honor of Stephen B. Bevans, SVD*, The American Society of Missiology no .57 (Maryknoll, NY: Orbis, 2018); Paul Duane Matheny, *Contextual Theology: The Drama of Our Times* (Eugene, OR.: Pickwick, 2011); A. Scott Moreau, *Contextualization in World Missions: Mapping and Assessing Evangelical Models* (Grand Rapids, MI: Kregel, 2012); A. Scott Moreau, *Contextualizing the Faith: A Holistic Approach* (Grand Rapids, MI: Baker, 2018); Gailyn Van Rheenen, *Contextualization and Syncretism: Navigating Cultural Currents, Evangelical Missiological Society Series* (Pasadena, CA: William Carey Library, 2006); Christopher J. H. Wright, *The Mission of God: Unlocking the Bible's Grand Narrative* (Nottingham: IVP, 2006); Jackson Wu, *One Gospel for All Nations: A Practical Approach to Biblical Contextualization* (Pasadena, CA: William Carey Library, 2015).

This is where contemporary social research into cultural hybridity can be useful. Recent hybridity research has examined the processes of hybridisation—the methods, means, and manoeuvres that individual diasporans utilize as they bring together the apparently disparate elements of their past and present to construct their individualized narrative. It focuses on the agency of the culturally hybridized diasporan in their autonomous self-construction of their autobiographical self[2] via the creative synthesis of the ways-of-life they have inherited from their different "homes." For our purposes, it is useful to note that these ways-of-life endure, and are located deep enough in the consciousness of a people-group to form their tacit, taken-for-granted "culture," is prima facie evidence of the suitability of those ways-of-life to that particular place and society. Traditions are, by their nature as traditions, durable—they only endure long enough to become "traditional" if they bear ways-of-life that "work" for the people who identify with that tradition.[3]

To respect inherited tradition is different from uncritically replicating it. Lack of attention to the need for tradition to be reformed to suit the hybridized Christian's new context will probably subvert Christian identity. Uncritical replication of Christian ways-of-life drawn from the native land binds Christian identity too tightly to native identity and increases the risk that the second generation, as they make a new way of life in their new home, will dismiss Christianity as foreign and therefore irrelevant.

This is illustrated by one of my Indian-background research subjects. The way she recounted her childhood experiences of Christian life and worship indicated that she experienced them to be alien, irrelevant, and

---

2 The atheistic, humanistic assumptions which underlie most secular cultural hybridity and hybridization research leads the literature to valorise individualistic autonomy and self-expression as the ultimate good for human being. This will be critiqued below.

3 See, inter alia, Homi K. Bhabha, *The Location of Culture* (London & New York: Routledge, 2004, 1994); Vanessa Guignery, "Introduction: Hybridity: Why It Still Matters," in *Hybridity: Forms and Figures in Literature and the Visual Arts*, ed. Vanessa Guignery, Catherine Pesso-Miquel, and Francois Specq (Newcastle: Cambridge Scholars, 2011); Marwan M. Kraidy, *Hybridity, or the Cultural Logic of Globalization* (Philadelphia: Temple University, 2005); Jan Nederveen Pieterse, *Ethnicities and Global Multiculture: Pants for an Octopus* (Lanham: Rowman & Littlefield, 2007); Jan Nederveen Pieterse, *Globalization and Culture: Global Melange* (Lanham & Oxford: Rowman & Littlefield, 2004); Keri E. Iyall Smith, "Hybrid Identities: Theoretical Examinations," in *Hybrid Identities: Theoretical and Empirical Examinations*, ed. Keri E. Iyall Smith & Patricia Levy (Leiden: Brill, 2008); Gayatri Chakravorty Spivak, "Can the Subaltern Speak?," in *Marxism and the Interpretation of Culture*, ed. Cary Nelson and Lawrence Grossberg (Basingstoke: Macmillan Education, 1988).

'oppressive' in the sense of contradicting her well-being.[4] Her parents enforced quite a strict gender role upon her, which emphasized the preservation of her sexual chastity: "no sleep-overs, don't hang out with boys … very [much] like how it was in India".[5] This also demonstrates they operated according to a collectivist mindset, because this preservation of a daughter's chastity is a public virtue amongst the Indian community, which enhances both the family's honour and the daughter's status as a potential future bride. She said her parents took her to church "forcibly"[6]—not meaning literal physical violence, but against her will—which indicates her parents operated according to a relatively high power distance. That church conducted its services in an Indian language which was, to her, foreign: "I don't know what I'm doing here"; "the language is different"; "I didn't enjoy it, I didn't like it".[7] The use of English-language Sunday school materials sourced from India, and a 'didactic' form of teaching which emphasized rote memorisation, reinforced this alien irrelevance—she acknowledged the materials and teaching style may be "great for the Indian kids that are growing up there, because they … can relate to" it, but they did not engage the "Aussie kids here",[8] by which she meant second-generation diasporans like herself. According to this research subject, this tight connection between Christianity and Indian identity prevented her Sunday school from effectively shaping Christian identity in her: "if you ask me what I learned from Sunday School, I genuinely can't remember anything that I learned."[9]

---

4 Cultures have been noted as differing along various axis. The following six have become well-established: (1) the degree to which the person exhibits a collectivist or individualist mindset, and the nature of how and where that collectivism or individualism manifests; (2) expectations concerning degrees of power distance; (3) expected gender roles; (4) expectations concerning whether and how social status is ascribed or achieved; (5) the nature of politeness; and (6) the operation of 'face' and 'shame'—the accrual, and loss, of personal and public dignity: John Corbett, "Discourse and Intercultural Communication," in *Bloomsbury Companion to Discourse Analysis*, ed. Ken Hyland and Brian Paltridge (London & New York: Bloomsbury, 2013), 310.

5 Research Subject MBSJN, Transcript of Interview 1, 19 March 2018, lines 200-01.

6 Ibid, lines 324-26 and 329.

7 Ibid.

8 Ibid, lines 376-77.

9 Ibid, lines 382-83.

Future-Generation Christians: Agency without Autonomy

Scripture respects the agency of children—their ability to reflect on and internalize patterns of teaching and ways of life. The fact that the book of Proverbs calls on the son to hear and obey the father's voice implies the possibility of callous, disobedient ignorance. The Apostle Paul dignifies children by addressing them directly and by instructing fathers not to exasperate them but instead train them in Godliness (Eph 6:1-4). Personal agents are individuated, not necessarily individualistic, in recognizing both the opportunity, and the responsibility, of exercising personal discretion and choice in the conduct of their life.

Robert Bellah has observed how the Western social concept of individual well-being has shifted from locating it in a person's contribution to society to locating it in their expression of their desires and preferences—"expressive individualism."[10] Christian authors have commented on the atheistic, narcissistic, hedonistic assumptions which underlie this view of the self, and on how it systematically contradicts and undermines traditional Christian belief and lifestyle.[11] For our purposes, it is sufficient to note that the kind of personal agency the Bible affirms is nothing like the kind of rebellious, self-indulgent autonomy which characterizes contemporary Western society. One of Paul's favourite metaphors for Christian identity is that of a slave.[12] To be Christian is to accept radical heteronomy—to be ruled by someone else—because we have surrendered ourselves to Christ as our Master.

---

10 Robert N. Bellah, *Habits of the Heart: Individualism and Commitment in American Life: Updated Edition with a New Introduction* (Berkeley: University of California Press, 1996), 333-35.

11 See, e.g., discussingmarriage.org, "Expressive Individualism vs. Christian Discipleship: Is our highest duty to the self, or to God?", Discussing Marriage website, no date, https://discussingmarriage.org/expressive-individualism-vs-christian-discipleship; Jaquelle Crowe, "How Youth Like Me Learn Expressive Individualism", *The Gospel Coalition* website, 4 Jan 2017, https://www.thegospelcoalition.org/article/how-youth-like-me-learn-expressive-individualism; David Qaoud, "The False Gospel of Expressive Individualism", *Gospel Relevance website*, http://gospelrelevance.com/2018/05/28/expressive-individualism; David S. Schrock, "The Air That We Breathe: Expressive Individualism, I, and Me", Via Emmaus, https://davidschrock.com/2017/01/23/the-air-that-we-breathe-expressive-individualism-i-and-me; Trevin Wax, "Expressive Individualism: What Is It?" *The Gospel Coalition*, https://www.thegospelcoalition.org/blogs/trevin-wax/expressive-individualism-what-is-it.

12 On which, see Murray J. Harris' magisterial *Slave of Christ: A New Testament Metaphor for Total Devotion to Christ*, New Studies in Biblical Theology (Downers Grove, Ill.: IVP/Apollos, 2001).

Our previous review of contextualization demonstrated how the precise shape of faithfulness differs from location to location. The challenge for both first and later-generation Christian migrants is to see this reformation of their heritage not as a "Western" act of independent, self-assertive rebellion which insults their native people and homeland by disavowing their roots, but as an attempt to be properly faithful to Christ in their new home, their new context.

By inhabiting the "interstices,"[13] the gaps, between cultures, culturally hybridized diasporans have an enhanced ability, not to abstract themselves from their cultures and stand "above" them with an "objective" birds-eye view, but to inhabit both simultaneously and therefore see ourselves through the eyes of the other. Sociologists have used the term "double consciousness" to describe this ability to see oneself from multiple perspectives.[14] Double consciousness makes diasporans "sensitive to the [cultural] currents around them," therefore able to "spot 'what is missing' in [various] societies".[15] This is akin to Derrida's insight into the nature and responsibility of 'inheritance'. The next generation, by their character as the next generation, cannot mimic the patterns of life of a previous generation, because they are not their ancestors; they are their ancestors' heirs. Therefore,

> *the presumed unity [of any inheritance], if there is one, can consist only in the injunction to reaffirm by choosing. 'One must' means one must filter,*

13 Theologians have used the term 'liminality' to describe the diasporan experience of hybridization—e.g., liminality "is a space where a person is freed up from the usual ways of thinking and acting and is therefore open to radically new ideas" whereby they "can become acutely aware of the problems of the existing structure" and thereby be motivated "to reform the existing social structure": Sang Hyun Lee, *From a Liminal Place: An Asian American Theology* (Minneapolis: Fortress, 2010): kindle locations 295-99. I prefer to metaphorise diasporan hybridization as 'interstitial'. An 'interstice' is a crack, a small gap between otherwise uniform places. Hybridized diasporans exist in these cracks between cultures. That interstitial existence may lead to liminality which motivates reform—or they can just fall through the crack and be lost.

14 The term was coined in 1903 by African-American journalist W.E.B. Du Bois in *The Souls of Black Folk: Essays and Sketches* (Chicago: A. C. McClurg, 1903), 8. Du Bois meant the term to describe a detrimental experience of self-objectification, where one internalizes the negative evaluation of oneself by another—specifically, in his case, the perspective of "white" Americans that the Negro is a "servant" who is an object of derogatory attitudes such as amusement, contempt or pity. However, the term has come to be used in a positive sense to denote a cultural hybrid's ability to simultaneously inhabit multiple sub-identities, so as to view and evaluate one activity from multiple perspectives: Judith R. Blau and Eric S. Brown, "Dubois and Diasporic Identity: The Veil and the Unveiling Project," in *Hybrid Identities: Theoretical and Empirical Examinations*, ed. Keri E. Iyall Smith and Patricia Levy (Leiden: Brill, 2008).

15 Robin Cohen, *Global Diasporas: An Introduction*, 2nd ed. (London: Routledge, 2008), 148.

sift, criticize, one must sort out several different possibles [sic] that inhabit the same injunction.[16]

And that act of choosing the "best" combination affirms the agency and dignity of the heir, precisely in the heir's act of honouring the ancestors by reworking their inheritance into a new, creative form intended to advance human flourishing. The challenge for Christian migrants is to work out forms of Christian life best suited to their new location as culturally hybridized Christians—an endeavour which can only be adequately carried out through thoughtful and prayerful attention to holy Scripture as the transculturally and transgenerationally authoritative word of God.

Diasporans associate in various ways and to varying degrees, with (at least) three people-groups: their native homeland and people/s; their new homeland and its people/s; and co-diasporans worldwide. They thereby inherit, again in various ways and to varying degrees, the traditions from the "ancestors" of these three "homes."

Culturally hybridized diasporans may prioritize ways-of-life drawn from their native land, if they are convinced that their native ways-of-life are, at least in this aspect of life, better express Christian faithfulness than the ways-of-life of their new home. First-generation Christians need not be ashamed to suggest, and later-generation Christians need to consider (not uncritically accept—but be willing to consider) that "traditional" forms of Christian belief and behaviour from their "native" land may, at least in some aspects, be superior to "novel," "Western'" beliefs and behaviours.

The experiences of co-diasporans are another source into the process of hybridized identity construction. The experience of having to construct a pluralised autobiography creates fellowship with those who share a similar experience, possibly including diasporans from a different native ethnicity. One of my Sri Lankan-background research subjects recounted his joy at meeting, at high school, young people of Indian, Chinese, and Korean background who were "just like" him.[17] They had a similar history to him—"most of them were born overseas, [but] the majority of their life was here"—and similar experience of family life: "their parents were pushing them in the exact same way",

---

16 Jacques Derrida, *Specters of Marx: The State of the Debt, the Work of Mourning and the New International* (London: Routledge, 2006), 18.

17 Research Subject MBSJR, Transcript of Interview 1, 27 Feb 2018, line 111.

towards "success, and … getting good … stable jobs, and … good mark[s]".[18] This person's pan-Asian diasporan identification has persisted to adulthood: "even now to this day … my good friends are all from those kinds of backgrounds".[19]

This possibility of pan-diasporan identification may help us engage with the phenomenon of the "silent exodus" from immigrant-background churches.[20] Todd observes that "US studies indicate that from 75 to 90% or more of second generation Chinese and Asian young adults leave their churches".[21] However, Park's analysis of a large-scale 2012 Pew survey of Asian American Christians showed that approximately two-thirds of Asian Americans "who grew up Protestant were still Protestant at the time they were surveyed".[22] So the exodus is not so much from the faith as from immigrant-background churches. Cha further notes that while some members of the silent exodus "are joining pan-Asian American churches or predominantly white mega churches", others are forming new "English-speaking Asian ethnic congregations that are independent from their ethnic immigrant churches".[23] These new churches seek to develop their own distinctive congregational identity and mission, selectively appropriating certain theological and cultural resources from Asian immigrant churches as well as from the broader ecclesial community in a way that attempts to hold "on to their unique second-generation Asian American congregational identities" while simultaneously welcoming "those who come from other ethic/racial backgrounds, thus gradually expanding the group boundary and incrementally reshaping their group identity".[24] Similarly, Kurien reports that the second-generation Indian-background Christian youth she interviewed "[e]mphasize[d]

---

18 Ibid., lines 111-15.

19 Ibid., lines 119-20.

20 First documented, and the term invented, by Helen Lee in her "Silent Exodus: Can the East Asian Church in America Reverse the Flight of Its Next Generation?," *Christianity Today*, 1996, 50-53.

21 Matthew R. S. Todd, *English Ministry Crisis in Chinese Canadian Churches: Toward the Retention of English-Speaking Adults from Chinese Canadian Churches through Associated Parallel Independent English Congregational Models* (Eugene, OR: Wipf & Stock, 2015), kindle locations 285-89.

22 Jerry Z. Park, "Keeping (and Losing) Faith, the Asian American Way," http://www.asian-nation.org/headlines/2014/05/keeping-losing-faith-asian-american-way.

23 Peter T. Cha, "Pastoral and Missional Reflections of Asian North American Congregational Experiences," *Common Ground Journal* 12, no. 1 (2015), 61, http://www.commongroundjournal.org.

24 Ibid., 61-62.

that heaven is going to be multicultural", therefore did "not see a [racially] mixed church as a compromise" but as a "theological mandate rooted in the Bible".[25] Further research will hopefully document how these mixed-race later-generational churches, as an aspect of their Christian faithfulness, express inter-racial harmony in the face of an increasingly fragmented and nationalistic world, and thus provide an embodied apologia for the gospel itself.

The third source for hybridized diasporan Christian identity is the traditions of life and worship of the migrant's new home. Just as first-generation Christian traditions deserve respect for shaping Christian identity in the native home, the traditions of the new home deserve respect as seeking to express contextualized theologies which seek to advance Christian faithfulness in the new home. Again, this respect is not uncritical. "Western'" church culture and tradition needs critical reformation as much as majority-world culture does. But we must ask, at least at first, questions like: why do Western churches operate in this manner? Why do Western Christians live in this way? What scriptural truths are they seeking to express? What generally accepted Western cultural values are they contradicting, and why?

The experience of my Indian-background female research subject shows how the thoughtful utilization of "Western" ministry practices can facilitate a personal appropriation of Christian identity. In contrast to Sunday School, her youth group used a "constructive" form of education, of a "decentralized" and "conversation[al]" character[26] which decreased the power distance between leaders and youth through delegating authority and responsibility to the youth. She "loved" the fact that "all the Bible readings and any prayers would be done by a youth member", and that the monthly Bible studies were "run purely by the youth members" without the church priest—whose absence she interpreted positively, as an act of trust in the youth leaders.[27] She found it "really exciting" when the youth group engaged topics of immediate relevance to the youth, like "homosexuality", "sex before marriage",

---

25 Prema Kurien, "Decoupling Religion and Ethnicity: Second-Generation Indian American Christians," *Qualitative Sociology* 35 (2012), 457. For an astute and encouraging introduction to this theological mandate, see M. Sydney Park, "Theology of the Household of God: Identity and Function of Christ's Body in Ephesians," in *Honoring the Generations: Learning with Asian North American Congregations*, ed. M. Sydney Park, Soong-Chan Rah, and Al Tizon (Valley Forge, PA: Judson, 2012).

26 Research Subject MBSJN, Interview 1, line 382.

27 Ibid., lines 397-400.

"depression", and "mental health", "because that's what's happening in society right now".[28]

The participatory form of the youth ministry, which respected and encouraged individual agency, seems to have been effective in shaping Christian identity in ways that the strictly 'traditional' form of the Sunday School did not. This research subject is now in her mid-twenties, employed in a professional career in a prestigious workplace, involved in various forms of church leadership, and professes a thoroughly missional Christian self-identity:

> For me being a Christian is every element of my life … whether it's waking up in the morning, going to work, … understanding the word, going to church … [and] also spreading the word to those who need to hear it.[29]

Conclusion: Constantly Reforming According to the Word of God

The Christian gospel, and Christian Scriptures as the word and words of the one true creator and redeemer God, are trans-temporally and trans-culturally relevant. This relevance is expressed not by abstraction from time and place, but in and through faithful Christian life in the particular time and place God has providentially located us. Culturally hybridized diasporan Christians have the honour of inheriting varied traditions of Christian faithfulness, and the responsibility of reforming them, according to the scriptural gospel, so as to continue Christian faithfulness in their generation and beyond.

BIBLIOGRAPHY

Bellah, Robert N. *Habits of the Heart: Individualism and Commitment in American Life: Updated Edition with a New Introduction*. Berkeley: University of California Press, 1996

Bevans, Stephen B. *Models of Contextual Theology*, revised and expanded ed. Faith and Cultures Series. Maryknoll, NY: Orbis, 2002

———. *Essays in Contextual Theology, Theology and Mission in World Christianity*. Boston: Brill, 2018

Bhabha, Homi K. *The Location of Culture*. London & New York: Routledge, 2004, 1994

Brown, Judith R., and Eric S. Blau, "Dubois and Diasporic Identity: The Veil and the Unveiling Project" in *Hybrid Identities: Theoretical and Empirical Examinations*, edited by Keri E. Iyall Smith and Patricia Levy. Leiden: Brill, 2008

---

28 Ibid., lines 334-38 and 343-45.

29 Ibid., lines 334-39.

Cha, Peter T. "Pastoral and Missional Reflections of Asian North American Congregational Experiences" *Common Ground Journal* 12, no. 1 (2015): 60–66 .

Cohen, Robin. *Global Diasporas: An Introduction*, 2nd ed. London: Routledge, 2008.

Cook, Matthew. *Local Theology for the Global Church: Principles for an Evangelical Approach to Contextualization*. Pasadena, CA: World Evangelical Alliance Theological Commission, 2010.

Corbett, John. "Discourse and Intercultural Communication," pages 306–20 in *Bloomsbury Companion to Discourse Analysis*, edited by Ken Hyland and Brian Paltridge. London & New York: Bloomsbury, 2013.

Derrida, Jacques. *Specters of Marx: The State of the Debt, the Work of Mourning and the New International*. London: Routledge, 2006.

Dowsett, Rose. *Global Mission: Reflections and Case Studies in Contextualization for the Whole Church*. Pasadena, CA: William Carey Library, 2011.

Du Bois, W. E. B. *The Souls of Black Folk: Essays and Sketches*. Chicago: A. C. McClurg, 1903.

Greenman, Jeffrey P., and Gene L. Green. *Global Theology in Evangelical Perspective: Exploring the Contextual Nature of Theology and Mission*. Downers Grove, Ill: IVP Academic, 2012.

Guignery, Vanessa. "Introduction: Hybridity: Why It Still Matters", pages 1–8 in *Hybridity: Forms and Figures in Literature and the Visual Arts*, edited by Vanessa Guignery, Catherine Pesso-Miquel, and Francois Specq. Newcastle: Cambridge Scholars, 2011.

Harris, Murray J. *Slave of Christ: A New Testament Metaphor for Total Devotion to Christ, New Studies in Biblical Theology*. Downers Grove, Ill: IVP/Apollos, 2001.

Irvin, Dale T., Peter C. Phan, and Stephen B. Bevans. *Christian Mission, Contextual Theology, Prophetic Dialogue: Essays in Honor of Stephen B. Bevans, SVD*. The American Society of Missiology no 57. Maryknoll, NY: Orbis, 2018.

Kraidy, Marwan M. *Hybridity, or the Cultural Logic of Globalization*. Philadelphia: Temple University. 2005.

Kurien, Prema. "Decoupling Religion and Ethnicity: Second-Generation Indian American Christians" *Qualitative Sociology* 35 (2012): 447–68.

Lee, Helen,. "Silent Exodus: Can the East Asian Church in America Reverse the Flight of Its Next Generation?" *Christianity Today* 40 no. 12 (1996): 50–53.

Lee, Sang Hyun. *From a Liminal Place: An Asian American Theology*. Minneapolis: Fortress, 2010.

Matheny, Paul Duane. *Contextual Theology: The Drama of Our Times*. Eugene, OR: Pickwick, 2011.

Moreau, A. Scott. *Contextualization in World Missions: Mapping and Assessing Evangelical Models*. Grand Rapids, MI: Kregel, 2012.

———. *Contextualizing the Faith: A Holistic Approach*. Grand Rapids, MI: Baker, 2018.

Nederveen Pieterse, Jan. *Globalization and Culture: Global Melange*. Lanham & Oxford: Rowman & Littlefield, 2004.

———. *Ethnicities and Global Multiculture: Pants for an Octopus*. Lanham: Rowman & Littlefield, 2007.

Park, M. Sydney. "Theology of the Household of God: Identity and Function of Christ's Body in Ephesians" in *Honoring the Generations: Learning with Asian North American Congregations*, edited by M. Sydney Park, Soong-Chan Rah, and Al Tizon. Valley Forge, PA: Judson, 2012.

Smith, Keri E. Iyall. "Hybrid Identities: Theoretical Examinations," pages 3–11 in *Hybrid Identities: Theoretical and Empirical Examinations*, edited by Keri E. Iyall Smith & Patricia Levy. Leiden: Brill, 2008.

Spivak, Gayatri Chakravorty. "Can the Subaltern Speak?" pages 271–313 in *Marxism and the Interpretation of Culture*, edited by Cary Nelson, and Lawrence Grossberg. Basingstoke: Macmillan Education, 1988.

Todd, Matthew R. S., *English Ministry Crisis in Chinese Canadian Churches: Toward the Retention of English-Speaking Adults from Chinese Canadian Churches through Associated Parallel Independent English Congregational Models*, Eugene, OR: Wipf & Stock, 2015

Van Rheenen, Gailyn. *Contextualization and Syncretism: Navigating Cultural Currents*. Evangelical Missiological Society Series. Pasadena, CA: William Carey Library, 2006.

Wright, Christopher J. H. *The Mission of God: Unlocking the Bible's Grand Narrative*. Nottingham: IVP, 2006.

Wu, Jackson.*One Gospel for All Nations: A Practical Approach to Biblical Contextualization*. Pasadena, CA: William Carey Library, 2015.

RESEARCH INTERVIEWS

Research Subject MBSJN, Transcript of interview 1 conducted on 19 March 2018 by Kamal Weerakoon.

Research Subject MBSJR, Transcript of interview 1 conducted on 27 February 2018 by Kamal Weerakoon.

WEBSITES ACCESSED

discussingmarriage.org, "Expressive Individualism vs. Christian Discipleship: Is our Highest Duty to the Self, or to God?" *Discussing Marriage.* https://discussingmarriage.org/expressive-individualism-vs-christian-discipleship.

Crowe, Jaquelle. "How Youth Like Me Learn Expressive Individualism." *The Gospel Coalition.* https://www.thegospelcoalition.org/article/how-youth-like-me-learn-expressive-individualism.

Park, Jerry Z. "Keeping (and Losing) Faith, the Asian American Way." http://www.asian-nation.org/headlines/2014/05/keeping-losing-faith-asian-american-way.

Qaoud, David. "The False Gospel of Expressive Individualism." *Gospel Relevance.* http://gospelrelevance.com/2018/05/28/expressive-individualism.

Schrock, David S. "The Air That We Breathe: Expressive Individualism, I, and Me." *Via Emmaus.* https://davidschrock.com/2017/01/23/the-air-that-we-breathe-expressive-individualism-i-and-me .

Wax, Trevin. "Expressive Individualism: What Is It?" *The Gospel Coalition.* https://www.thegospelcoalition.org/blogs/trevin-wax/expressive-individualism-what-is-it.

ABOUT THE AUTHOR

KAMAL WEERAKOON *is a minister of the Presbyterian Church of Australia; an associate staff worker, Australian Fellowship of Evangelical Students (AFES); and a PhD candidate, Morling Theological College/Australian College of Theology.*

CHAPTER 13 | Leiton & Lisa Espineli Chinn

Bi-National Mixed Marriages: Contributions and Challenges Affecting Ministry Among the Diaspora Academic Community

Our background covers nearly forty years of service together in the *Missio Dei* of diaspora ministry among international students. We are diaspora ministry practitioners in a bi-national hybrid marriage blending our Filipino and American nationalities and cultures. Our mission context is not the world of academia, research, or teaching missions. However we felt welcomed to present a paper for the Hybridity, Diaspora, and Missio Dei: Exploring New Horizons Consultation, which included in its invitation "practitioners...who are engaged in ministry among diaspora people groups." We chose to limit the design of our paper to align with this consultation's subtheme of Exploring New Horizons with a singular emphasis and exploration of the contributions a bi-national marriage may provide in ministry among international students and their academic community.

Methodology and Approach

The approach of this paper is to utilize heuristic learning, that is, gaining insights that may be applied to international student ministry, through reflection of the personal experiences of spouses in the context and crucible of a bi-national marriage. Our approach is not to summarize or draw from existing research on our very narrow topic, which is non-existent, but to discover and explore a new field of personal reflections and perspectives from a survey of international student ministry (ISM) staff practitioners who have a bi-national marriage and family. The survey was sent in the Spring of 2018 to thirty-eight couples, with an assurance that both their personal identity and nationality would remain anonymous to garner a better response. The responses of fifty-two spouses in bi-national marriages representing twenty-two nations (see end note), who are serving in six countries, are presented as an initial and preliminary self-evaluation assessment that could stimulate a more expanded and in-depth research regarding this fascinating topic. The summarized survey results could be of particular interest and encouragement to ISM staff of campus ministries, churches, mission agencies, and their volunteer co-workers, who also have a bi-national marriage and family.

What do hybrid-nationality marriages offer and contribute to ISM? Answers to the survey questions yielded nearly 32,000 words, or ten times the allotted word limitation of this paper. The responses are not meant to be quantitatively analyzed, but to be considered as helpful insights and perspectives of ISM practitioners. Repetitive themes, along with supportive quotes, will be highlighted as enriched qualities and contributions for ISM that flow from a bi-national marriage.

Primary Contribution:
Identification, Empathy, Mutuality and Relatability

In various ways, whether ethnic or geographic backgrounds or common cross-cultural experiences, the subject of commonality between the bi-national ISM staff couple and international students, surfaced as a primary added-value that the hybrid marriage offered to the relationship and facilitated the bonding process.

Jesus set the example of what it means to love across cultures, differences, and distance. He became a man to communicate in ways that we can understand. His incarnation powerfully connects Him with His audience and thus becomes the prime model for those who are called to cross cultures and countries for the sake of the Gospel. Like Jesus identifying with us, what points of contact and commonality do spouses of a bi-national marriage have with international students that easily serve as identity bridges? When international students say, "You are one of us" and spouses in bi-national marriages declare, "I know how you feel," there is an almost instant rapport that happens between them.

In Their Own Words

... Internationals can relate to us because we are not North Americans living in North America and because we are living a cross-cultural life just as they do... students quickly develop trust that I really get their situation.

... It was encouraging for the couples that we met to have friends who are in the same boat.

... The moment my international friends learn that I am also an international, they have the sense of belonging. We can relate, it is like they found an insider.

... Having a direct personal identification with others experiencing cross-cultural relationships, and the dynamics associated with adjusting to another culture.

... We tend to find wider acceptance across the broad categories of culture; I fit into Asian contexts and my Asian wife into Western. It's like being a cultural translator and we can mediate the gap for others. So it is a bit of a bridge-building marriage.

... Internationals are attracted to us because we are a bi-national couple. They open up their hearts to us, and seek our advice. Our marriage also helps us build bridges a little easier. I can help be a bridge between my African husband and my North American culture while ministering in North America. We can be a bridge together between internationals and the North American church, speaking to issues on each side because we have worked to understand each side and represent each side well.

... Students have referred to me as "one of them".

... When either of us is speaking to students or doing training, we seem to have added credibility because people trust that we have 'walked in each other's shoes' and so can speak for each other's culture. So Asian students trust my European husband's teaching because they feel he relates well to Asian culture, while European volunteers and staff know that I generally understand how European people 'tick' and thus can help explain the cultural questions that puzzle them.

... I think our transnational marriage makes us approachable. Students are comfortable around my African husband because he's been in their shoes and they're intrigued that he chose to stay in North America and marry a North American.

... My wife is sensitive to the needs and feelings of internationals because she was one herself. She has also her instant rapport with internationals because she was one that enriched our ministry a lot. And when we

moved to her European country, it was the reverse. I was the foreigner who empathized and identified with the international students.

... One of us is usually the foreigner, that is a hardship but also a blessing for the International Student Ministry.

... Students feel safe speaking to us, knowing my wife is North American who can help them understand being in North America, but who also loves internationals enough to marry one from Africa that opens doors for her. They also feel like I have much to offer them because I have lived in North America and have married a North American.

... Hybrid (bi-national) families and bi-racial children have always been a good initial point of contact.

... Being an international and having bi-national kids often helps us to build trust with students.

... When internationals see us, they seem to respond well with our initial interaction with them because they see a Caucasian and an Asian couple being interested to meet them. Being an international myself has opened doors for me to have international students have an instant "you can relate to me more because you have been in my place before" feelings. I sense a faster "building of trust" stage that may not have happened as quickly if the couple are both native-North American.

Other contributions gleaned from survey responses

The following additional examples are "added-values" and "ministry advantages" emerging from the unique learning environment of a bi-national marriage and family that enhances their cross-cultural ministry with international students:

1. **How have you grown through marriage with a spouse from another country?** Often cited growth areas that are advantages in relating with international students include:

   a. Gaining awareness of personal blind-spots, biases and ethnocentrism for one's own culture, and a limited world-view. This confession was repeatedly shared. Inherent in bi-national marriages are a much higher level and variety of cross-cultural interactions that may significantly improve the personal awareness of one's own biases. Such awareness is a ministry advantage that can reduce errors, blunders, and embarrassment compared to someone who might be personally and culturally clueless about their own limited view of the world.

... I feel extremely enriched as a person because I married someone from a different country. I have had to face my biases and work through them in a way I never would have otherwise. I have learned more about myself, and my own culture by marrying cross-culturally. I have been educated on the ins and outs of being from a developing country like my husband is from. I never would have intimately known some of the struggles and challenges (students) and families face.

... Being married to my husband of a different culture and color unveiled my hidden biases. It stirred up debris of my own judgmental heart that I never knew I had.

... I recognized some of the downsides of individuality, which is a high value in North America.

... I learned to subjugate a natural tendency towards ethnocentrism and accept another culture as equally valid and valuable, while realizing that neither are perfect.

... My wife being from a different culture helped me see things from different perspectives that I hadn't considered.

... It's easy to stereotype people from other countries, until they become family. Specifically, because I'm also in relationship with the extended family, I have been forced to understand cultural differences instead of discarding them as strange.

b. Respect and appreciation for another culture (a foundational posture in missions)

... I have learned to see people in the broader context of their culture. I have grown to be more curious and learn about my husband's history and family life. Instead of jumping to conclusions, I have learned to first ask questions and learn his context and why he does things the way he does. I have learned to celebrate our differences.

... It helped me experience what it is to love and respect people who have a radically different perspective on some issues.

... I have learned in her culture the relationship is more valued and it's important to lift each other up when in public and not to criticize.

... Learning more specifically about Asian culture through my marriage has directly impacted my understanding of Asian students.

... My Asian husband is another set of eyes on the world - we have multilateral vision (Asian, European, North American); we can become all things to all people, and are bridge builders between East and West. He has taught me a lot about extended family: its beauty and importance.

... Learned that it's not healthy to mentor and counsel exclusively from a Western perspective because every culture has something to offer, and when it comes to marriage the statistics show that the Global South (South America, Africa, & Asia) has a lot to offer, but they are seldom invited to the table for discussion.

... I have grown to be more independent and confident (in my culture, often women are told to rely more on their husband).

... My life has two halves: the 'potato eating years' and the 'rice eating years'!

... In many ways, the perspectives from European culture (and the European church) have been very good for me, driven home by actually being married into the culture.

... I grew up with very different views about how much productivity and money we need to have a satisfying life. Now I can sit back and relax with a cup of coffee and do absolutely nothing every now and then without feeling guilty for my lack of productivity.

... I now have a second "home" culture with values that I understand and can defend.

c. **Practice in communicating across cultures, resulting in better understanding of the contrasts between Non-Western and Western cultures, mutuality in learning cross-cultural differences and how to navigate them, and handling conflict resolution. Bi-national marriages equip spouses with needed skills in communicating cross-culturally that include observing, listening, asking questions, and negotiating, all of which are valuable assets in ISM.**

... A bi-national marriage presents opportunities to grow and gain from the differences it inherently brings, on a continuous, 24/7 basis.

... My husband has also translated the things I observe about his culture and helped me understand the "why" behind what I see and experience.

... I have learned to listen better and try to understand my husband's point of view and how he deals with life's issues.

... We have gotten better at asking clearer questions so we can understand each other better. Sometimes the same words can have totally different meanings.

... Certain aspects of your culture that you take for granted are new to your spouse. And so frequent questions and answers are important so we understand each better and also enjoy each other's reactions, responses, and company.

d. Growth in attitudinal transformation from pride to humility, teachability, vulnerability, flexibility, adaptability, and patience

... I have learned to share life deeply across a cultural divide, without retreating into my 'comfort zone' when it suits me. Whenever we argued early in our married life, I would retreat to the 'self-sacrificial Asian wife' mode of "being quiet and enduring in silence". I have learned to be more vocal and demonstrative, both about my love and appreciation within our family and beyond, as well as my opinions and feelings in general. I was brought up in a typical Asian family where communication is subtle, layered and nuanced, physical affection like hugs were rare, and expressions of love came in the form of food or words of concern, rather than a simple "I love you"

... On relationships and the dynamics associated with adjusting to another culture, I have learned important lessons of harmony and the need to set aside personal preferences and freedom to honor those around me, especially my elders.

... I'm thankful that a culturally heterogenous marriage potentially affords an expanded and richer perspective in life and interpersonal dynamics than a homogenous marriage...if one is humble and teachable enough to accept the gift of the differences a bi-national union provides.

2. **What challenges and complexities have you experienced related to your bi-national marriage?** Successfully navigating through the stresses, challenges, and complexities of a cross-cultural bi-national marriage can be valuable lessons to share with international students. Some of the repeated challenges include:

a. family responsibilities (such as child-rearing) and extended family expectations

... Raising children with two different cultural backgrounds and upbringing is also a challenge. We have different expectations for the children and deal with discipline differently.

... Our parents are very different in how they view parenting. Her parents can be pushy sometimes, in how they tell us we should raise our son. Indirect communication can also be interesting sometimes (there are unspoken expectations that are not always easy to understand).

... As an egalitarian North American, I needed to humble myself and give-up my value of 'equal status' between people, and learn to genuinely accept (rather than tolerate) the honorific-system of the Asian culture. I had to learn and accept the reality that I married into an extended family and its complexities. Even though we live in North America and therefore in the environment of the Majority North American Culture that cherishes 'individual rights', I 'became' an Asian in the context of the extended family I married in to, where I was the Minority culturally.

b. living in a distant foreign land of the spouse

... Being there for family, especially aging parents is tricky - we can't be near both sets of parents. Norms for how to relate to the wider family, how much is expected and what it takes out of us—all these need to be negotiated. Living in Europe can sometimes feel a bit lonely for me, but living in Asia will probably feel very intrusive to my European husband. Balancing my spouse's needs against my parents is quite hard from an Asian perspective.

... Another complexity is the distance factor. No matter where we are in the world, one of us will never be close to family. While I think, we as a couple are fine with this, I do know that both sets of parents would love us to be near by.

... Deciding where to live in the world. Financial strain of traveling around the world just to see family. Also as we grow as a family it means little vacation time is spent as just us, since we take all our vacation to visit family.

c. conflict resolution

... Coming from a direct and indirect culture—how we choose (or not choose!) a conflict resolution style in resolving conflicts, reading between the lines for the direct person is not an inherent skill, nor receiving direct feedback can be separated from being personally "attacked" (issue vs person) for the indirect person.

... In my upbringing, harmony held such a high value that it often trumped clear communication which affected relationships, or at times undermine someone's freedom to be themselves.

... Shame vs guilt have influenced our marriage.

... Making joint decisions by two people from different cultures requires compromise and time to understand the other perspective. This sometimes leads to conflict.

... My wife's model was that everybody had something to say on everything and could give advice even when not asked for. And we would follow the advice of the most experienced on a particular topic or on the consensus. For my side, I grew up giving advice only if asked for it and not asking much advice. Problems were often solved, by paying quickly some professionals who could get us sorted out. It was therefore hard for me to get rid of an individual view of problem solving.

d. cultural differences, including ethnic/racial issues

... The main challenge I had to deal with was that European culture is more direct.

... In Asia, hospitality is very important, and one of the ways for people to show their hospitality is asking guests to keep eating and drinking (alcohol). When we visited my country, my husband didn't really like it when he said "no" to my parents or my relative offering food/drink, they still keep offering and asking him to try.

... Having a bi-national marriage doubles the normal stress of marriage, because you always have to be aware of cultural differences and be ready to process and accept them. The main culprit is the lack of awareness of how tenacious the underlying cultural values can be. We were idealists before we decided to get married. We thought we would learn from each other and assimilate to each other's cultures. We later found out how hard it would be to accept, to adjust to, to yield to, to adapt to, to respect each other's values and tastes. We thought our commonalities (faith, calling and goals in ministry, and our love for internationals) were strong enough to override these challenges, but they were not as strong as we had hoped.

... Cross-cultural marriage allows me to see the challenges of leadership and how white North Americans tend to get promoted into positions easier than minorities and internationals. My husband has been a ministry leader for quite a few years and still, some people do not take him seriously.

... It's a challenge in my own culture, seeing how my wife can so easily be overlooked and underestimated, just because of her race and cultural reserve.

3. **What are some lessons learned from it (complexities/ challenges of bi-national marriage) that you could share in ministry?** Examples cited include:

... Occasionally, we share our cross-cultural differences in talks/Bible studies to make a point of application e.g. sharing stories of my wife's Buddhist grandmother offering sacrifices for protection against evil spirits.

... All our cultural blunders, misunderstandings and discoveries make good stories over dinner.

... Able to discern foreigners with where they are at and not expecting them to be someone they are not simply because of my cultural bias.

... If they say or do something you find hurtful, offensive, etc., don't rush to judgment. Consider the very real possibility that the problem is rooted in cultural differences or language problems.

4. **What are some ways your hybrid bi-national marriage and family have already been used in your ministry among the international academic community?**

   ... Our bi-national marriage....
   - *demonstrates that, in Christ, we truly belong to one another irrespective of normal cultural and racial divide.*

   - *disarms the students a little bit. Part of this might be because it is not 'two white westerners ministering to the rest of the world'.*

   - *speaks about reconciliation in Christ amidst the wounds of European and African colonization.*

   - *is a transnational bicultural home, so we offer hospitality as part of our ministry in a way which is uniquely a combination of Asian and European culture, with other cultural influences thrown in. We have been told by students that hybrid transnational marriages provide a picture of how through the Gospel, all are equal before the cross, and that our marriage and family life provide an example of that.*

   ... Students are often curious about how we raise our children, make decisions, resolve conflict, or show honor to our family, and are comfortable asking those questions, giving us many opportunities to share.

   - *helps me understand pressures and perspectives of internationals. For several years, I was oblivious to the stress of immigration and visa status. Now I regularly have conversations with students making important decisions and struggling with ethics relating to their status. It helps me realize that this is a huge area of discipleship that many ISM workers are not addressing or helping students walk through.*

- *turned out to be the major factor in our success in relating with internationals as they were curious about how we live, with me being from the Middle East. Muslims were especially curious about how I relate to my Western wife and some commented that it was life-changing for them.*

... We already integrate lessons from our bi-national marriage in our ministry, using many of these lessons to help international students to adapt to life in Europe, while at the same time helping ISM staff and volunteers to be aware of some of the inherent inequalities in how we treat people, even in subtle ways. This has helped our staff to understand what international students experience.

... Almost everything we have been through can be integrated into ministry. From how we dealt with our parents' disapproval of us as a couple to working through challenges/complexities regarding unique backgrounds, there are always applications to helping university students who are also dealing with relationship issues. As a couple, we may be able to help another bi-cultural couple think through things ahead of marriage that they may not have otherwise.

... Being married to an international husband in North America, gives me insight and insider perspective into ministry. Students often share with us negative feedback about ministry that they would rarely share with a ministry leader. Having this perspective and insight helps me see the mistakes we've made in ministry and ways we could change it to be more effective.

... In planning events or working with our teams, our different cultural backgrounds help us to better understand others from the same culture and explain cultural differences to each other. We also help each other see blindspots and biases. Both of us have felt like outsiders in each others homelands and this opens our eyes to what international students experience.

... I am a dark skinned African and married to white North American. For some international students it was shocking to see people from different cultures being married to each other. Our marriage gave us the opportunity to tell them that Jesus is universal to all cultures.

... Students feel safe speaking to us, knowing my wife is North American who can help them understand North America, but also loves internationals enough to marry one from Africa that opens doors for her. They also feel like I have much to offer them because I have lived in NA and have married a North American.

... I've used my wife's and my different reactions to shame (like when our kids misbehave) to illustrate shame from the Bible.

... Our bi-national experiences could be used as a topic for sharing in a program; I always have ready illustrations for cross-cultural misunderstandings and differences.

... Personally as a white Christian male there is a lot of baggage in the eyes of some students. Ministering as an 'international marriage' helps break down that barrier in some ways.

... Hospitality is huge in International Student Ministry. I see the blending of our two cultures as contributing well to discerning effective ways of extending hospitality to a broadly diverse group.

Conclusion

Bi-national marriages offer a variety of advantageous contributions towards ministry among international students. We hope that those in bi-national marriages doing international student ministry, whether as ministry staff or volunteers, will be encouraged and also reflect on the benefits of their hybrid marriage.

In a globalized world more and more bi-national hybrid marriages are likely to occur. We present these reflections to those who may be considering a ministry among the global international student diaspora.

End Note

Home countries of respondents include India, Kazakhstan, Cameroon, Lebanon, Kenya, Slovakia, Romania, Northern Ireland, Austria, Netherlands, England, Thailand, Australia, China, Malaysia, Germany, Singapore, United States, Philippines, Canada, France, and Madagascar; plus those of 2 TCKs (Third Culture Kids).

ABOUT THE AUTHORS

LEITON CHINN has been mobilizing the church for international student ministry since 1977, including serving as the Lausanne Catalyst for ISM from 2007–2017 and as president of the Association of Christians Ministering Among Internationals from 1999–2008. He has authored chapters on ISM for mission books: Global Diasporas and Mission; Scattered and Gathered: A Global Compendium of Diaspora Missiology; *and* Globalization and Mission.

LISA ESPINELI CHINN is a former graduate international student from the Philippines in the United States. She served with both InterVarsity Philippines and InterVarsity USA. She was the national director of the International Student Ministry of InterVarsity/USA for fourteen years and has pioneered and published in the area of international student reentry. She is currently a leadership mentor with InterVarsity/USA, a cross-cultural trainer, mission consultant, and conference speaker.

CHAPTER 14 | Miriam Adeney

Helping Hybrid Children Shine: What the Global Church Can Do

Research indicates both benefits and detriments when children are raised transnationally. Many such children demonstrate an excellent educational grounding, broadly cosmopolitan worldview, creative problem-solving, and confident interaction with all kinds of people. At the same time, it is not uncommon for bicultural children to exhibit depression, reduced affect, an emphasis on adapting rather than belonging, and sometimes increased prejudice. Similarly, returning to the home country may temporarily reduce a child's sense of wellbeing and induce stress and grief over the loss of treasured people and places, ignorance of customary practices and terms, and confusion over worldview and identity.

Children in the Field is a compilation of essays written by a dozen anthropologists who took their children to other cultures.[1] These scholars came from wealthier settings than some migrants, but the issues their children struggled with span the economic spectrum. How much to expect children to adapt to their new context was a key concern for these scholars. On one side were "those who are most committed to bridging the terrible division between the haves and the have-nots, who feel

---

1 Joan Cassell, ed., *Children in the Field: Anthropological Experiences* (Philadelphia: Temple University), 1987.

that protecting their children from the rigors other children are forced to endure is an act of moral cowardice." On the other side were those who wondered "what right parents have to subject their children to dangers and discomfort in the pursuit of the parents' preoccupation?"[2] Such questions frequently face parents who take their children abroad.

Consider Jennifer (12), Sarah (10), and Nathanael (8), who lived in a Brazilian slum where their mother did research on the admittedly traumatizing subject of infant mortality. Their father "attempted to provide a more familiar and less threatening round of daily activities for the children—marketing, Portuguese lessons, organized games and sports with neighborhood children," and visiting with friendly families. They also had pets and family weekends at the beach twice a month.

All the children found slum life hard. However, Jennifer picked up the language easily, and discovered that she liked helping out at the clinic where her mother did research. Nathanael got caught up in playing street soccer. But Sarah suffered. A series of events heightened the pain. First, their pet chickens died. Next, they attended a cockfight. (After that, the children refused to eat chicken for the rest of their stay in Brazil.) Finally, Sarah came upon a group of boys stoning a puppy to death. She took to her bed with a high fever. When her depression did not lift, the family decided that Sarah and her dad should return early to the US.

Sarah balked. She was afraid to go back to America now, she said, "because everything was changed...What if now I might even hate the US and all its fat, selfish people?" Her mother comments:

> She was expressing a fear of loss of social identity and of the confusion that accompanies this. Then angrily she accused me of taking away everything that meant anything to her: her home, her friends, even her country. She said that I was changed, too, because I was always "defending" the Brazilians even when they were "bad" or wrong about things...and condoning behaviors that I would never for a moment accept at home. I had perhaps succeeded as an ethnographer, but I had failed miserably as a mother. From that point on I at least tried to collude with Sarah in making moral judgments and evaluations that were more consistent with her level of cognitive development and more in keeping with our usual household and family values. It helped considerably.[3]

2 Ibid., 262–63.

3 Nancy, Schleper-Hughes, "A Children's Diary in the Strict Sense of the Term: Managing Culture-Shocked Children in the Field," *Children in the Field* ed. Joan Cassell (Philadelphia PA: Temple University), 198, 229.

Such awkward, perplexing and sometimes unanswerable questions will arise when children live in two cultures. While adults can understand the difference between deep and surface adaptation, and can behave appropriately in different cultures within that framework, children cannot switch standards so easily. They are struggling with an emerging sense of self. They live in the present. Reality is what surrounds them now. They cannot stand outside and suspend judgment.

Christian parents will be inclined to bond with local people because God loves all people. Nevertheless, bewildering cultural differences will arise. What is the right way to plan our time? To expend money and to account for it? To exercise authority? To express initiative? To settle quarrels? What is proper etiquette? Sanitation? Material standard of living? What are the important social relationships? When people move to a new land, they will inevitably face dilemmas like these.

Beyond culture differences are power differences. These may loom large. In the Arabian Gulf, for example, local citizens often look down on laborers from poorer countries. Migrants have fewer rights and opportunities. They cannot retire in the countries where they work, and their children have no future there. Often the children will not be allowed into local schools. When power inequalities seem particularly unfair, parents may need to place their family story in the long tradition of the suffering Servant and his followers described in Hebrews 11, with the sure knowledge that in God's time we shall overcome.

What Parents Can Do: Recommendations For Life On The Road

Children are gifts from God. They are treasures. It is their parents' privilege to model the loving Father as they help their children flourish. Parents will sacrifice time and attention to listen to their children, and will intervene to protect them (Eph 6:4; Matt 7:11; Deut 6:6–9; 1 Tim 5:8). Other Christians in the migrant community can help nurture these children too.

Theology of culture

Before developing practical strategies, it is important to think through a simple theology of culture. As noted above, children will raise awkward questions about culturally-patterned behaviors. "Why can't I ride my bike down the street just because I'm a girl? Why are they always late? Why do they pinch my cheek and then smile?" A theology of culture can help us work through such questions.

We can teach that all people are created by God, and all people are sinners. Cultures reflect this tension, because cultures are made by people over time. Therefor all cultures will include patterns of wisdom and beauty and truth, and at the same time all cultures will contain patterns of exploitation.

Different cultures may be strong and weak in different areas. Some cultures may be more efficient. In others, people may be more generous. Some may be more orderly. Others may be more vivacious. Some cultures have lower death rates. Without creating overall stereotypes, such variables can be discussed.

We love the country where we were born, because it is the land of our forefathers and foremothers. We love the new land because it is the home of friends with whom we are passing irreplaceable years now. Certainly God loves both cultures.

Sometimes we will adapt our behavior motivated by courtesy, because the issue at hand is simply one of politeness. At other times the issue is one of conviction, and we must stand firm. We can draw these distinctions for our children. In the best situations, we will consult local Christians to see how they interpret what seem to us to be matters of conviction. Then we may learn new facts that will cause us to alter our views.

It is important not to lose our roots nor to diminish the value of others' roots. *In Being Latino in Christ: Finding Wholeness in your Ethnic Identity*, Orlando Crespo describes his friend Daniel, who "did everything within his power to stay far away from his family. He did not want to deal with his Dominican father, because deep down he knew he would have to face the good and the bad of his culture and identity."[4]

Only after Daniel became a pastor and moved out of New York City did he realize how important it was to come to terms with his Latino heritage and his family of origin. Several years later he moved back to NYC and deliberately chose a pastoral position near where his relatives lived. He did this in order to explore his identity as a Dominican man. *"This has been a valuable and important part of Daniel's journey toward self-understanding, especially as he has had to confront issues of machismo,"* says Crespo. *"It has not been an easy journey but it has been fruitful, as he has opened his heart to his family and reconciled with his father."*

---

4 Orlando Crespo, *Being Latino in Christ: Finding Wholeness in your Ethnic Identity* (Downers Grove IL: IVP), 138.

While it is important not to lose our roots, there are times when our culture must take second place. In the early twentieth century, many decades after they had migrated from Germany to Canada, some Mennonites made an unsettling discovery: their churches were filling up with nominal Christians who used church as a social center, cultivating their cultural roots more than their relationship with God. To avoid spiritual stagnation, some of these German-Canadians decided to send their children to Prairie Bible Institute and other English-speaking schools. When they did this, the next generation lost the German language. Many also lost strong convictions about pacifism, which was a value the people had treasured for centuries. But they recovered evangelistic zeal, and considered the trade worth the cost. According to historian Frank Epp, they also gained—

> The use of the English language in preaching, four-part singing, Sunday schools, mission programs, budgets, evangelistic revivals, use of pianos, cathedral-style churches, personal conversions, private enterprise, independent congregations, and above all better organization, with non-ordained members in church councils and constitutions curbing the power of bishops.[5]

These German Canadians were willing to pay with their ethnicity in order to keep their faith alive in the next generation.

Cultures also will clash when children return to their home country. Inevitably they will experience some confusion. That cannot be avoided. Living in two cultures costs the psyche something. Here, too, a simple theology of culture can be useful.

Referring back to that theology, parents can show their children the strategies they use to cope with new cultural adjustments, and can help the children find some that fit their own personalities. For example:

1. Take time to maintain your physical, emotional, and spiritual health.
2. Escape now and then through creative hobbies.
3. Accept yourself and your emotions.
4. Forgive yourself and others.
5. Enjoy learning.
6. Find out how local people enjoy life, and do the same.
7. Keep a journal.
8. Cultivate a sense of humor.

5 Frank Epp, "The Mennonite Experience in Canada," *Religion and Ethnicity*, Harold Coward and Leslie Kawamura, eds. (Calgary: Calgary Institute for the Humanities and Wilfred Laurier University, 1978), 27.

9. Sing, and surround yourself with music.
10. Read some good books.
11. Accept loneliness when it comes, and allow your prayer life to deepen.

Schooling

Education has received extensive attention in the literature on expatriate children. It is a major reason why missionary families return home. Depending on the parents' situation and the country's policies, the family may need to consider international or missionary schools; local private or local public schools; boarding or day schools; home schooling or internet classrooms; or some combination. To add complexity, different siblings may blossom in different school settings. Language also must be considered. Recognized K–12 Filipino and Indian schools have been established in a few Middle East countries. The issue of schooling overseas is discussed in detail in *Encountering Missionary Life and Work: Preparing for Intercultural Ministry* by Tom Steffen and Lois McKinney Douglas.[6]

Social media

There has been a revolution in global family communication patterns since the development of social media. Consider Donna, a Filipina care-home worker in Cambridge, England.[7] Every evening at about 10 p.m. she webcams her husband and two sons, ages 10 and 12. They are eating breakfast. Donna always has loved the breakfast hour, and now because of social media she can still be present. Through the camera she admires her sons' school uniforms, and gives them advice on their homework.

When that call is finished, Donna webcams her mother who looks after her eight-month-old daughter. How did Baby sleep? What will she eat? Donna sings songs to Baby and plays peek-a-boo with her.

The next morning, Donna's first action is to read the texts that her sons have sent. She made them promise that they would text her every day, and sends them money to do that.

Next, she will call her husband and her mother to ask how their day has gone, and maybe webcam them again. Later, during her break from work, she will call her husband again just to say Kumusta? (How are you?)

---

6 Tom, Steffan, and Lois McKinney Douglas, *Encountering Missionary Life and Work: Preparing for Intercultural Ministry* (Grand Rapids MI: Baker, 2006), 27–94.

7 Mirca Madianou, and Daniel Miller, *Migration and New Media: Transnational Families and Polymedia* (Routledge: New York, 2012), 69.

Finally, when all her relatives gather at her mother's house for the family meal on weekends, Donna will webcam her mother and talk to many of her kin. They in turn will leave the camera on for hours, sometimes as long as eight consecutive hours, so that she can be part of their lives.

Meanwhile, Donna "owns" her own café in the Facebook social networking game "Café World." She has made one of her sons her virtual employee, and they interact daily through this online game.

How this contrasts with the old days when a lonely mother waited for letters that rarely came! This media involvement is not cheap, but many overseas parents consider it a priority.

Children, however, are divided on whether they like this much communication. Approximately 50 percent of the children surveyed value it greatly, whereas the other 50 percent found it annoying.

The rise of social media present other challenges for childrearing. Pornography is one issue. Another is the temptation to spend too much time on media and not enough time in face-to-face relationships.

Family time together

"What can we do for family fun?" asks one Asian couple in the Middle East. The mother is a nurse, and the dad is an office administrator. They have three early teen children. "Where can we take our kids during the holidays? We go to the desert and take photos with camels. But there is not the natural or cultural variety that we would have back home. The kids ask, 'Why can't we live a normal life? Ride bikes? Have a backyard?'"

Parents overseas must develop fun times, teach their children skills, and cultivate their personal gifts. The best approach will cover a range of activities, such as

- Large muscle activities—sports, games, hikes
- Fine muscle activities—arts and crafts, blocks, Legos, clay, all kinds of paper creations
- Imagination—book stories, made-up stories, dress-up dramas, play with dolls, small figures, cars
- Music and poetry—from pot-and-pan bands to creating music CDs and videos
- Physical projects—cooking, carpentry, paper-mache, pet care, plant care

- Social skills—peer friendships, a welcoming attitude to newcomers, intergenerational relationships

- Spiritual and ethical discernment

A migrant family is uniquely placed to explore culture, language, and contemporary church history. Parents and children should encourage each other in these areas, and appreciate each other's discoveries. Regarding church history, after learning a little about the background of the gospel in that country, family members should be alert to happenings in the local and national church. Enterprising children may even want to write new "chapters" of local church history as they see and hear it developing.

More important than all these skills and learnings, however, is just having fun and living life together—loving, laughing, and praying together.

Separated children

If living abroad is a big part of a family's or community's life, even those who stay home may be shaped by the experience. *Transborder Lives: Indigenous Oaxacans in Mexico, California, and Oregon* by Lynn Stephen traces three generations of Mixtec Oaxacans—non-Spanish speakers—who move regularly from southern Mexico to Woodburn, Oregon. So many have traveled so often that even those Mixtecs who have not made this journey feel that they know certain places along the route. For these people, "hometown" exists in more than one space. They live "multi-sited" lives.

The effect of travel impacts children who are left behind with relatives. Although several suggestions below will apply to them, the observations are focused primarily on children who return to the home country while their parents remain abroad.

"Re-entry shock" can be as severe as the original "culture shock", even for mature adults. Familiar places have changed. Friends have moved on. The returnee also has changed. He or she looks at "home" through new eyes. For the young person who has spent a lot of his life in another country, the stress may be great. How can this experience be made positive?

Community makes a tremendous difference. If the young person is returning to genuinely loving and capable relatives or friends or church, this will be a great asset. Parents should make every effort to ensure this.

While basking in the love of relatives and friends, the returnee also will want to spend time with others who have lived overseas. They will share a broader, more cosmopolitan worldview. It will be a relief to socialize with people who don't require explanations for what the returnee is thinking and feeling. Church networks should provide places where such people can hang out together.

If parents are still working overseas, they can keep in touch regularly with their returned children through social media. One family shares communion over Skype every week, with bread and wine ready at each end of the line so they can eat and drink together at the same time.

Before children travel home, parents should prepare them for extra stress. Together they can discuss coping strategies. Parents also can help their young people plan words to talk about their time overseas, and think of ways to use their experience to serve in the church and community back home.

The truth is that we can never completely go home again if we make deep friendships overseas. There will be some pain. That is the price we pay for loving and being loved in more than one place. Some adults who grew up overseas regret that they never were encouraged to mourn their losses when they came home. One said, "Our parents are proud of our independence and cite how 'well-adjusted' we are…(but) in fact that very toughness is the only protection a missionary kid can make for the intense pain of separation."[8]

Lament is a valid biblical activity. The alternative is numbness when the pain is great. Lament lets us feel authentically. The Japanese have a phrase—*mono no aware*—about the pain that we feel when we see something beautiful. We know that we cannot keep the beauty, and we ache. Spanning cultures is like that. The experience is too big for us. Subtly it nudges us to long for heaven.

A community of pilgrims

Calvin College has sponsored year-long think tanks that focus on specific topics and result in books. One year the topic was "youth and music." The book that emerged was Dancing in the Dark: Youth, Popular Culture and the Electronic Media.[9] While the research explored various

---

8 Brian Hill, "The Educational Needs of the Children of Expatriates," *Missiology* 14, no. 3 (1986): 332.

9 Quentin James Schultze, *Dancing in the Dark: Youth, Popular Culture and the Electronic Media* (Grand Rapids MI: Eerdmans, 1991).

genres of popular music from a Christian perspective, an unexpected finding emerged: the music a young person listens to is less important than their intergenerational friendships for their spiritual, social, and emotional development.

Friendships with older adults shape us profoundly. Parents are key, but children also need to know grown-up Christians with different personalities, gifts, and perspectives. Such variety helps them envision how they, too, might fit in the church.

Sociologist Christian Smith, (co-authored with Melinda Lundquist Denton) in his award-winning book *"Soul Searching: The Religious and Spiritual Lives of American Teenagers "*, emphasizes similarly that adult-child relationships are key to faith formation. It is essential for churches to encourage intergenerational projects and activities, and for parents to connect their children with godly adults spanning racial, economic, gender, and age lines. Social media cannot replace ongoing casual face-to-face talks.

Parents' modeling matters, too, of course! In *Growing Up in Christ: A Guide for Families With Adolescents*, Eugene H. Peterson writes, *"The task of the parent…is not directly to confront the problems of the young and find the best solutions for them. It is to confront life, and Christ in life, and deal with that. A parent's main job is not to be a parent but to be a person."*[10]

Alta Barge Shenk, a Mennonite missionary mother in rural Africa, modeled this for her children. After her death, they said, *"As adults it was clear to us that mother was on a journey…We were astonished at the joyousness and contemporaneity of her faith. Although our parents had buried themselves in the backwoods, she was modern, understanding, sympathetic, and perceptive of the issues that we confronted in our university experiences, or in city ghettos, or in modern suburban culture… She was walking with God in response to the call of Jesus Christ."*[11]

We are a company of pilgrims. Many stories vie for central place in our children's lives. When my sons were small, they liked to play super-heroes. One day Dan asked me, *"Why can't Jesus be Superman? Why didn't he just shoot the bad guys who were nailing him to the cross?"* Children like Dan sense that we are in a battle. They need to be shown

---

10 Eugene H. Peterson, *Growing Up in Christ: A Guide for Families With Adolescents* (1976), 15.

11 Elaine Sommers Rich, *Mennonite Women: A Story of God's Faithfulness 1883–1983* (Scottdale, PA: Herald, 1983), 146.

what our battle is. They need to see a spectrum of Christian adults who are part of a powerful movement, pilgrims journeying together toward the kingdom of God. From Abraham to Esther to the New Testament's scattered believers, to various odd individuals of our own acquaintance, God's people often have lived outside their homelands while moving in a common direction. Children need to see that story take on hands and feet through the people they know.

What the Church Can Do: Recommendations for Making a Difference

A family is not necessarily parents and children settled in one place. Moves uproot millions. This is our reality in the twenty-first century. So churches must adapt their teaching and services to bless mobile families as well as established ones. Below are a few suggestions. Some can be carried out by local congregations. Others would benefit from an international network to provide structure and coherence and economies of scale.

1. Create teaching resources for diaspora families

Christian teaching materials, applying the Bible to specific diaspora issues, should be produced and made accessible in print or online for diverse groups, such as parents, youth, children, and pastors and leaders.

Youth enjoy phone-friendly and online-friendly media, though the media they prefer change continually. For example, Facebook and websites are no longer so popular. Social media are preferred, where participants can exchange comments rapidly. Many youth and young adults would rather write their own opinions than read others' (although they may not take time to support their opinions with much substance). Youth also like creating their own videos and posting them online.

Given such media preferences, how can youth be nurtured to grow deeper in their knowledge of Scripture and life with God? Trained peer and adult mentors can enter their media platforms, and sequentially raise questions and make comments with biblical-theological significance. Some youth may be open to extremely brief daily biblical reflections through tweets or WhatsApp on topics like sports, beauty, jealousy, self-esteem, loneliness, career choice, sexual attraction, peer pressure, pornography, charitable services, justice, honesty, respect, forgiveness, etc. If carefully planned, pithy and cumulative biblical teaching can occur in this way.

Identity is one topic that is crucial for diaspora youth. Through occasional longer biblical lessons, this can be explored, with a frank statement of problems, positive stories of young adults who have pushed through the difficulties to productive life roles, and lists of strategies and resources and agencies. Another key topic is how media can be addictive for teens, and how to talk back to media and not be enslaved by it. Useful general resources are: *Losing Face and Finding Grace: 12 Bible Studies for Asian-Americans* by Tom Lin, and *Understanding the Coconut Generation* by Sam George. An attractive and meaty online resource is *The Bible Project*, which teaches the whole Bible narrative in a youth-friendly way.

Online degree programs' combinations of activities offer intriguing models. These programs do more than transmit information. They supplement that with regular interactive online gatherings, and annual or semiannual face-to-face gatherings. Participants identify strongly with such programs, with fellow participants, and with the information learned. It appears that young people learn better when they have the opportunity to speak up, write, create, and participate in events.

Beyond youth, parents appreciate curricular guides for Bible study groups, mothers' groups, general adult study groups, etc. Devotional guides tailored to migrant families would be a blessing. Children would enjoy a Christian E-magazine with comics, interactive exercises, and directions for activities. Pastors and leaders need preaching notes on marriage and parenting, with applications for the boggling problems they face as they counsel families living overseas.

Whether online or printed, these materials should be in the migrants' languages: Filipino, Tamil, Spanish, Portuguese, Korean, Chinese, and/ or Arabic. While English-language resources may serve as models, the materials themselves should be originally written, with culturally-specific issues and illustrations. Translation apps can jumpstart the indigenous language versions, with further writing and editorial fine-tuning to follow.

To begin developing a resource, the Diaspora Task Force Children's Committee can:

(1) Choose a topic (2) Conduct extensive brainstorming on what specific issues face diaspora people in this area (3) Decide on a media distribution plan, whether print, online, audio, or a combination (4) Gather sample curricula or books relevant to this segment of people (pastors, parents, youth, etc.) and investigate whether there are models online.

2. *Collate and create teaching resources for established churches*

In almost every congregation, some family members are thinking about working abroad. Others are already overseas. Meanwhile, others are coming back home. As well, newcomers are moving into the community. Faced with this mobility, a series of classes about the challenges of cultural adaptation, set in theological context, may be useful. Local children as well as adults need to learn how and why culture entry is hard for newcomers. In turn, immigrant children might benefit from a pamphlet or online interaction describing local lifeways. Then the church can plan steps to help diaspora families transition easier.

The class on culture adaptation should have a frank session on family economics. Many migrants move for financial reasons. Yet the resulting stresses on the family may be huge. Moving has hidden costs. Therefore one pastor in Dubai advises prospective migrants, "Don't come if you can possibly stay home." Can the church help such people find ways to make more money right where they are? If some church members model simplicity with contentment, can they be interviewed? There are no easy answers, but the church can foster biblically-framed discussions, as well as connecting members with practical strategies and structures and kingdom community collaboration.

Children left behind with relatives while their parents work overseas constitute a special challenge. Could churches form strong peer groups of left-behind children, each headed by a trained and caring pair of adults? A partial model is found in Ugandan church-based households for orphans headed by widows and surrounded by the whole believing community. Camps for left-behind children also would be valuable.

3. *Research to help children on the move*

Research on Diaspora Families. What do migrant Christian families need in order to flourish? What are the big problems? What are some solutions? What are some illustrative stories?

Research on Re-Entry Issues. What is needed when migrant children come back to the home country? What might churches do to help meet these needs?

Research on Teaching Resources. What Christian materials contextualized to diaspora families' issues are available for various age groups in various languages and media?

Local Bible school and seminary students should be encouraged to write MA theses in this area. If necessary, the Lausanne Diaspora Task

Force can offer a little training and guidance. At least one researcher should interview selected wise parents on the field. Findings from various theses should be consolidated and made available globally.

4. Logistics: Finding money, finding writers

To help pay for research and publications, grants can be sought. As projects are envisioned, Christians who have gifts in procuring resources should be brought into the team.

On a broader scale, a campaign might challenge local churches. When churches allocate funds for their own children's and youth activities, they might be challenged to give five per cent—or even two per cent—to a fund for diaspora Christians' children's programs.

In regard to writers, some of the best writers for the resources described above may be mothers and fathers and youth already living overseas. They know the issues and the dramas first hand. At least they could provide cases and illustrations. These potential authors could be found through writers' contests, and nurtured through writing mentors. There is a lot of creative potential lying latent in the diaspora.

Bridge-Builders of the Future

We all need roots. We cannot be citizens of everywhere. But we can connect to multiple places. People with such connections will be the bridge-builders of the future. What movement spans cultures, races, genders, rich and poor, illiterates and PhD holders? The church of Jesus Christ. Yet not all Christians are equally qualified to connect. In the globally-networked world of the future, the leaders will not be the mono-cultural Christians. The natural bridge-builders will be the liminal, hyphenated, polycentric, multi-lingual Christians—the children who are on the move today. For them we pray—

Now may the radical justice of God the Father,
The liberating forgiveness of God the Son,
And the revolutionary transforming presence of God the Holy Spirit
So blow through your lives
That you may go forth into this broken world
And fight the Lamb's war
Knowing that the risen King has already won
The victory over injustice, violence, and death.
Hallelujah. Amen.[12]

---

12 Sider (1979), 101.

BIBLIOGRAPHY

Adams, Leah, and Anna Kirova, eds. *Global Migration and Education: Schools, Children, and Families*. Mahwah, NJ: Lawrence Erlbaum Associates, 2007.

Adeney, Miriam. *A Time for Risking: Priorities for Women*. Downers Grove IL: IVP, 1987.

———"Colorful Initiatives: North American Diasporas in Mission," *Missiology* 39 (1), January 2011, 5–23.

———"Is God Colorblind or Colorful?: Gospel, Globalization, and Ethnicity," *Perspectives on the World Christian Movement Reader*, ed. Ralph Winter and Steven Hawthorne. Pasadena CA: William Carey Library, 2009.

Aguilar, F. et.al. *Maalwang Buhay: Family, Overseas Migration, and Cultures in Relatedness in Barangay Paraiso*. Manila: Ateneo de Manila University, 2009.

Bell, Linda. *Hidden: Immigrants' Legacies of Growing Up Abroad*. Notre Dame IN: Cross Cultural, 1997.

Bikos, L. H. et.al. "A Consensual Qualitative Investigation into the Repatriation Experiences of Young Adult Missionary Kids," *Mental Health, Religion, and Culture* 12 (7), 2009, 735–54.

Caouette, Therese. *Small Dreams Beyond Reach: The Lives of Migrant Children and Youth Along the Borders of China, Myanmar, and Thailand*. Save the Children, UK.

Cassell, Joan, ed. *Children in the Field: Anthropological Experiences*. Philadelphia PA: Temple University, 1987.

Crespo, Orlando. *Being Latino in Christ: Finding wholeness in your Ethnic Identity*. Downers Grove IL: IVP, 2003.

Eakin, Kay. "You Can't Go Home Again," *Strangers at Home*, Carolyn Smith, ed. NY: Alethia Publications, 1996.

Epp, Frank. "The Mennonite Experience in Canada," *Religion and Ethnicity*, Harold Coward and Leslie Kawamura, eds. Calgary: Calgary Institute for the Humanities and Wilfred Laurier University, 1978.

George, Sam. *Understanding the Coconut Generation*. Niles IL: Mall Publishing, 2006.

Hill, Brian. "The Educational Needs of the Children of Expatriates," *Missiology* 14, no. 3 (1986).

Joaquin, Nick. *Portrait of the Artist as Filipino*. Manila: Alberto S. Florentino Publisher, 1966.

Leo, P. *Nurturing Our Children's Resilience*, Dec. 15,2003, http://connectionparenting.com/parenting_articles/resilience.html.

Lin, Tom. *Losing Face and Finding Grace*. Downers Grove: IVP, 1996.

Madianou, Mirca, and Daniel Miller. *Migration and New Media: Transnational Families and Polymedia*. Routledge: New York, 2012.

Parrenas, R. *Children of Global Migration: Transnational Families and Gendered Woes*. Palo Alto CA: Stanford University, 2001.

Peterson, Eugene H. *Growing Up in Christ: A Guide for Families With Adolescents.* 1976, 15.

Pollock, David, Ruth Van Reken, Michael Pollock. *Third Culture Kids: Growing Up Among Worlds*, 3rd ed. Yarmouth, Maine: Intercultural, 2017.

Reyes, M. *Migration and Filipino Children Left Behind: A Literature Review.* Manila: UNICEF, 2008.

Rich, Elaine Sommers. *Mennonite Women: A Story of God's Faithfulness 1883–1983.* Scottdale PA: Herald, 1983.

Schleper-Hughes, Nancy. "A Children's Diary in the Strict Sense of the Term: Managing Culture-Shocked Children in the Field," *Children in the Field* ed. Joan Cassell. Philadelphia PA: Temple University, 1987.

Schultze, Quentin James. *Dancing in the Dark: Youth, Popular Culture and the Electronic Media.* Grand Rapids MI: Eerdmans, 1991.

Smith, Christian, and Melinda Lundquist Denton. *Soul Searching: The Religious and Spiritual Lives of American Teenagers.* Oxford: Oxford University, 2005.

Steffen, Tom, and Lois McKinney Douglas. *Encountering Missionary Life and Work: Preparing for Intercultural Ministry.* Grand Rapids MI: Baker, 2006.

Stephen, Lynn. *Transborder Lives: Indigenous Oaxacans in Mexico, California, and Oregon.* Eugene OR: University of Oregon, 2007.

Van Reken, Ruth. *Third Culture Kids—Raising Children in a Cross-Cultural World and Making the Most of the Journey.* Paper presented at the Supportive Parents and Resource Conferences, Singapore, 2001.

Woodley, Randy. *Mixed Blood, Not Mixed Up: Finding God-Given Identity in a Multicultural World.* Hayden AL: Healing the Land, 2004.

Wolf, D. "Family Secrets: Transnational Struggles Amongst Children of Filipino Immigrants," *Sociological Perspectives* 40 (3), 1997, 457–82.

ABOUT THE AUTHOR

MIRIAM ADENEY, PhD, is a professor, anthropologist, missiologist, and journalist at Seattle Pacific University. Among her books are Kingdom Without Borders: The Untold Story of Global Christianity, Daughters of Islam: Building Bridges with Muslim Women, God's Foreign Policy: Practical Ways to Help the World's Poor, *and* Wealth, Women and God. *Miriam has been president of the American Society of Missiology, recipient of the Lifetime Achievement award from Christians for Biblical Equality, board member for* Christianity Today, *and staff member and Publications Secretary for the Philippine InterVarsity Christian Fellowship.*

CHAPTER 15 | Godfrey Harold

Hybridity: A Witness in South Africa

The land in pre-colonial South Africa was never owned by the Dutch but belonged to the indigenous people, something the Dutch settlers could never understand. "Forgetfulness by definition is never creative; nor is it instructive. The one, who forgets to come back, has forgotten the home where he came from and where he or she is going."[1] Forgetfulness closes down both the past and present. It is, therefore, crucial that a history of people displacement in South Africa be undertaken to give context and meaning to the article under discussion.

This first displacement of the South African indigenous people came only eight years after the Cape of Good Hope was colonized by Jan van Riebeek in 1652 when he planted a hedge of bitter almond across Cape pasturelands through which the indigenous black herdsmen were not permitted to cross.

The displacement of people was further enhanced by the 1913 Native Land Act that prohibited black ownership in all but 7 percent of South Africa's landmass. These so-called "reserves," increased to 13 percent of the country in 1936, that would later provide the basis for

---

1 E. Wiesel "Longing for Home" in The Longing Home, ed. L.S. Rouner (Indiana: University of Notre Dame, 1996), 19.

the "homeland" system through the Bantu Authorities Act, Act no. 68 of 1951 which was abolished in 1993. Meanwhile, white farmers were given land and obtained additional support in the form of massive subsidies for the production and marketing of their crops from the past government.

Those 300 years of racial oppression were consolidated and expanded by the National Party control in 1948. The government further advanced the security of the white minority by demanding that race-based measures be institutionalized as a comprehensive apartheid system of laws designed to achieve racial separation in every aspect of South African life. The Group Areas Act, Act 41 of 1950 provided for the designation of residential areas along racial lines, and barred blacks from owning property in urban areas. The Promotion of Bantu Self-Government Act, Act 46 of 1959 allowed the creation of independent homelands, the law stated that blacks with ethnic ties to cease being South Africans. This was the most significant displacement of people ever recorded in history.

While the social condition of apartheid allowed the church to flourish, this growth was only experienced within the strict racial context in which the church found herself. Due to this past social system, the local churches in South Africa today are predominantly homogeneous and mono-cultural.

How then must the church respond to this continuation of segregative worship that stands in dark contrast to the changes that are happening in the rest of South Africa? The workplace, school and public spaces reflect the hybridity of the new South Africa. The church, however, still maintains this legacy of apartheid in forms of segregated worship. Thus, the church become the last bastion of a dehumanizing system, called apartheid. How then does the South African Church break itself from this legacy to bring about the redemption of sociality, as a means of restoring communion? Hauerwas[2] claims that the "church does not have a social ethic it is a social ethic" This then is not merely a description of the church, instead what is offered by the church is a normative account of human relationships within communities. This will be discussed in the next section.

---

2 S. Hauerwas, *The Peaceable Kingdom: A Primer Christian Ethic* (Indiana: University of Notre Dame, 1993), 99.

Definition

Hybridity in its most basic definition refers to a mixture, in the South African context mixture of races, more specifically in the community of faith concerning Evangelical Ecclesiology.

The Expression of the Church as a Hybrid Community in South Africa

The expression of the church in South Africa must be undergirded by our understanding of the Scripture that calls us to love one another. Kant[3] put it very clearly:

> *For love as an inclination, cannot be commanded. However, kindness done from duty, also when no inclination impels it, and even when it is opposed by a natural and unconquerable aversion, is practical love, not pathological love. It resides in the will and not in feeling, in the principle action and not in tender sympathy; and it alone can be commanded.*

However, this love has its first expression in the action of Jesus on the cross. This action that has its birth in the *missio Dei* finds expression through the actions or praxis of the Church in faithful communion with the God, who acts. Root[4] states that in *participatio Christi* the Church participates in God through Jesus Christ. It affirms our cooperation with the divine life that our life is hidden with Christ in God. Thus, God's being is given in God's acts—God's act is the revealing of the Godself for the sake of ministry.[5] When the church engages ministry as the body of Christ, it reflects the being of God as a "moved" being—a compassionate Being and a Social Being. God moves towards humanity in the shape of ministry, as an invitation to take action and share in another's being. This act of God is seen in reconciliation. Therefore, Root (2014:94) argues that ministry as the act of God is the event of the God's being coming to humanity. This takes shape in the Christ action what Root[6] terms the *Christopraxis* of the Church. When the church expresses compassion, it expresses the God Being. The expression of this hybrid community is thus one of engagement: in the internal (spiritual) and

---

3 I. Kant, *Ground Work for Metaphysics of Morals,* transl. M. Gregor and J Timmermann (UK: Cambridge University, 2012), 15.

4 A. Root, *Christopraxis* (Minneapolis: Fortress, 2014), 81.

5 K. Barth, *Church Dogmatic* iii/2: *The Doctrine of Creation*, tran. G. W. Bromiley and R. J. Ehrlich (Edinburgh: T &T Clark, 1961), 85.

6 Root, *Christopraxis*, 2014.

external (socio-political) through prophetic[7] engagements by speaking to institutional structures that keep people separated and by acting out through creative compassionate acts that demonstrate love at its fullest. Reuther[8] states:

> The theology of prophetic critique locates God and the spokespersons for God on the side of those victimized or despised by the so called social and political elites. The Word of God comes as a critique of these elites, calling them to reform their ways in order to be faithful to divine justice.

Frame[9] makes this clear by stating, "For the Christian life is not only a matter of following rules of morality but a dynamic experience: living in a fallen world, in fellowship with the living God". One of the tests of the authenticity of the church's claim to transcendence or to be counter-cultural is its capacity to represent in its congregation a "socially heterogeneous" people.[10] This is a community that reflects Jesus Christ as the One who breaks down barriers that separate people. It is an integrated community which undergirds hybridity.

Reconciliatory

The fundamental message of the church is one of reconciliation. McNeil[11] states "reconciliation is an ongoing spiritual process involving forgiveness, repentance and justice that restores broken relationships and systems to reflect God's original intention for all creation to flourish." The church becomes prophetic when it creates and sustains a reconciled and reconciling community. Thus, the task of the prophetic ministry of the church is to nurture and nourish an alternative consciousness to the dominant culture around us[12]. Reconciliation with God must be demonstrated by genuine reconciliation within the church and by continuing the ministry

---

7   By prophetic I mean, "a theology that is socially critical and world transformative, that is, one that explicitly relates the Word of God to the social and political context within which it is proclaimed" See J. W. de Gruchy, *Liberating Reformed Theology* (1990), 19.

8   R.R. Reuther "Religion in Society: Sacred Canopy vs. Prophetic Critique, in *The future of Liberation Theology. Essays in Honor of Gustavo Gutierrez*, eds. M.H. Ellis and O Maduro (New York: Orbis Books, 1989), 173.

9   J. Frame, *The Christian Life* (New Jersey: Pand R Publishers,2008), xxv.

10 J. Cone, *Speaking the Truth* (Grand Rapids: Eerdmans, 1986), 119.

11 B. S. Mc Neil *Road Map to Reconciliation* (Illinois: IVP, 2015), 22.

12 W. Bruggeman cited in McNeil, 2015.

of reconciliation to the world. Volf[13] calls this a Pauline concept of social reconciliation. Such a community of reconciliation is then alternative in South Africa because it is in active tension with the surrounding context and culture of separateness. As South Africa can be still characterised as socially and racially separated, the Church should structure herself to become an alternative conscience and counter-cultural or what Barth refers to as a "foreign community". In the place of justice and righteousness, normal society brandished violence and oppression- and call it justice. Bonhoeffer[14] encapsulated this function of the Church well:

> The church is the place where the witness is given to the foundation of all reality in Jesus Christ. The church is the place where it is proclaimed and taken seriously that God has reconciled the world to himself in Christ. The space of the church is not there in order to fight for territory, but precisely to testify to the world that it is still the world, namely the world that is loved and reconciled by God.

While the church pursues justice and reconciliation, it defines its mandate in biblical terms and thus rejects all forms of violence, manipulation, and injustice. Liberation then is not a mere political movement and power struggle. The reconciliatory message of the church is to preach the good news about the peace Christ brings, reconciling man to God, man to man, and harmony with God's creation. This is what Conradie[15] calls cosmic reconciliation. Reconciliation is thus with God, with the Church and with those who have been sinned against. How then is reconciliation to be enacted? Thus, the hybrid church community must be agents of spiritual and racial reconciliation. Reconciliation that is more than mere words, a reconciliation that demands action. Vellem[16] underscores that if justice becomes subservient to reconciliation then, reconciliation is cognitive, something that aborts the true reconciliation. He[17] states that what is needed is the discovery of reconciliation through experience. It is through restitution

---

13 M. Volf "The Social Meaning of Reconciliation in *Transformation* 16 no. 1 (1999): 7–12.

14 D. Bonhoeffer "Ethics" in, *Dietrich Bonhoeffer* Vol.6 , trans R. Krauss, R. West, and D. W. Stott (Minneapolis: Fortress, 2005), 63.

15 E. Conradie, *Reconciliation: A Guiding Vision for South Africa* (Stellenbosch: Sun, 2013), 27.

16 V. Wellem, "Rediscovering Reconciliation: A response to the Call for Reconciliation in *Reconciliation: A Guiding Vision for South Africa*, ed. E. Conradie (Stellenbosch: Sun, 2013),111.

17 Ibid.

that I believe this is possible. In a previous article that I co-authored with Alexander, we state "that when the church fully understands the impact of decades of separateness has on the masses and the degradation it has caused, by making human beings non-persons requires a practical engagement" or what Vellem[18] terms "logic of experiential clarity regarding reconciliation". If reconciliation is to be realized, then restitution has to be made. This is where Evangelicals can challenge the government to speed up its programme of Land Reform and where certain racial groups in South Africa benefited unethically from the 1913 Land Act, reconciliation requires that restitution is made to those who suffered under an evil system. Restitution is perhaps the most human part of the reconciliation process, and restitution requires that we give up something, which brings us to a better understanding of the suffering that apartheid caused to the majority. When the church as the community of God's people leads this process, it does so from a "place" of compassion.

Compassion

In Exodus 33, Moses requests YAHWEH to show his glory; that request was denied because no man can see God and live. God did reveal to Moses, who He is, a loving and compassionate God. The church is thus called to reveal the character of God demonstrated through her acts of compassion and love. This, therefore, requires that a definition of compassion be explored and applied to the South African context. The Church in South Africa can become what all other communities aspire to be, a loving, caring and compassionate community. Davies[19] states that compassion calls for the radical decentering of self, and putting at risk, in the free re-enactment of the dispossessed condition of those who suffer. Compassion, I believe begins with the recognition of the other as created in the image of God, it is because of this understanding that the self assumes the burden of the other. It is here Davies (2001:17) argues that in recognizing the veiled presence of God's image in the other that we come to understand our identity. Nouwen, McNeil and Morrison[20] state that the word compassion means to "suffer with". Compassion, therefore, requires one to enter into spaces where one identifies with the weak, vulnerable and powerless. Compassion means

---

18 Vellem, "Rediscovering Reconciliation: A Response to the Call for Reconciliation," 109.

19 O. Davies, *The Theology of Compassion* (Grand Rapids: Eerdmans, 2001),17.

20 Henry Nouwen, D. P. McNeil and D. A. Moriison, *Compassion* (USA: Image, 1982), 3–4.

full immersion in the condition of being human. Therefore, compassion is not "simple pity" but finds it is the purest expression unfolding in the incarnation of God. God's compassion becomes our compassion. This principle of self-denying or "kenotic love"[21] touches all levels of human experience and tries to make social harmony a possibility. This radical manifestation calls then for the reflection of personhood. Thus, the church as the alternative community seeks to see the image of God in all persons in the society. This call for a radical shift, from theology to ministry, Stone[22] elaborates that "ministry has a three-fold character: it is a response to grace, a participation in grace, and an offering of grace." Through the ministry of the church, the work of restoration of the image of God in us is extended to the rest of the world. This calls for a very intentional entrance into the suffering of the other and labor on behalf of their liberation. The Church as an alternative community reflects their knowing of God in two ways, namely theologically and practically. I believe the latter is a stronger demonstration of our love for God. Brown[23] states this very clearly.

> This notion is so strange to us that 'knowing God' is a matter of deed rather than word, that one could affirm God without saying God's name or deny God while God's name is on our lips is not so strange to the Bible.

This is seen most clearly in Matthew 25:31–46 that distinguishes knowing God and knowing about God. James (2:19) qualify this statement even further by mocking those who claim to have faith but who fail to take care of the marginalised in society. *"You believe that God is one. You do well; the demons also believe and shudder."* Mere knowledge of God cannot replace living faith…living a compassionate life. Thus, the Church as an alternative community is called to action.

This action to compassion is brought into focus, by asking the question, what is it to be created in the image of God (*Imago Dei*)? This "image" is given by God and is central to human dignity because the central theological issue in human dignity is the merciful, compassionate God. This understanding compels the church as an alternative community to be confrontative and transformative. To speak to institutional and economic barriers that keep people

---

21 Davies, *The Theology of Compassion* 21.

22 B. Stone. *Compassionate Ministry: A Theological Foundation* (New York: Maryknoll, 1996), 43.

23 R. M. Brown, *Unexpected News: Reading the Bible with Third World Eyes* (Philadelphia: Westminster Press, 1984), 69.

separated. Evangelicals must assume the responsibility to see people as children of God, created in His image rather than being dictated to see people through the socio-economic and political policies of the land. The Evangelical churches in South Africa must become places where people who were once stripped of their humanity and dignity find hope and restoration of being human again.

When the church shows compassion, it demonstrates the heart of God and is concerned with sharing God's love in words and deed. It becomes an alternative community.

Another aspect of the South African context that assaults the "image of God" and human dignity is racism. Grant[24] writes:

> Politically, racism disenfranchises; socially it ostracizes; culturally it degrades and robs the people of those characteristics that make them individuals; religiously it brainwashes and indoctrinates so that the oppressed people believe not only that it is impossible for God to like them or for them to have the image God, but that God ordains racist oppression.

The Church as a hybrid community must speak out against these issues that blur the image of God in persons by creating a community of faith where these differences do not impede fellowship and love one for another. When governed by this vision, the Church will have adequate theological resources to resist the temptation to become accomplices in racial and socio-economic segregation.[25] Thus, through the acts of compassion, the church becomes agents of reconciliation, where human flourishing takes place. St. Augustine On the Trinity writes, "God is the only source to be found any good thing, but especially by those which make a man good and those which will make him happy; only from him do they come into a man and attaches themselves to a man."[26] Human beings truly flourish in this alternative community, when love is demonstrated by God becoming the center of our lives. A human being as with all created things ought to be loved. However, the only way to properly love is to love people in God.[27]

---

24 J. Grant, "Poverty, Womanist and the Ministry of the Church in Cambridge Companion To Christian Ethic" in *Standing with the Poor*, ed. P. P. Parker (Cleveland: Pilgrims, 1992), 49.

25 Volf, "Social Meaning of Transformation," 19.

26 Augustine, *On the Trinity* ,http://newadvent.org/fathers/130113.html.

27 M. Volf, *A Public Faith: How Followers of Christ Serve the Common Good* (Grand Rapids: Brazos Press, 2011), 58.

Love

The good news of the Bible is that the "kingdom of heaven has come near (Matt 10:7) and fundamentally through the incarnation of Jesus Christ (Luke 17:21). Therefore, the message of the gospel is "a spontaneous love that forgives sins and serves others."[28] This love is beyond calculation and payment (Matt 10:8). Thus, Jesus calls his followers to follow his example, to love God unconditionally, love your neighbour as oneself (Mark 12:29–31). This is the fundamental aspect of prophetic utterances and compassion. Therefore, within Christian thought, God is love and loves unconditionally. Thus, a relational community, the triune God provides a model for human love. The life and practice of the church in response to God's love are summarised adequately in Mark 12:29–31. Hence the term "living in love" is not something a community can achieve by their efforts and in their strength, but something that happens to them in faith, from God. This decisive element in this life in love is therefore always to allow ourselves to be loved by God. By being loved by God, the church understands what it means to reflect the reality of God, to demonstrate the reality in all we do. This means we perceive through the lens of God's love[29]. Brunner[30] argues that this unique love is only manifested to those in faith through Jesus Christ. Therefore, the expression of love that has its genesis in God through Jesus Christ is portrayed by the action of the Church.

Conclusion

Before his ascension, Jesus instructed his followers to continue his teaching to the entire world (Matt. 28:19). This prophetic engagement continues through the Church, the visible manifestation, the body of Christ (1 Cor. 12:12). As a follower of Jesus, this prophetic task continues by responding to challenges today. The reason the Church can make a difference in the world is because of Christ, who made the difference by becoming man and fulfilling the just requirements of God in reconciling man to God. This act of love, compassion, and reconciliation is demonstrated through the life of Christ, the Head of the Church, who left us an example to follow, empowered by the Holy Spirit, who leads us into all truth. The Evangelical Church, therefore, has no excuse but

---

28 T. P. Jackson, "The Gospel and Christian Ethics" in *The Cambridge Companion to Ethics*, ed. R. Gill (Cambridge: Cambridge, 2001), 44.

29 M. Labberton, *The Dangerous Act of Loving your Neighbor* (Ill: IVP, 2010), 175.

30 E. Brunner, *The Divine Imperative* (New York: Macmillan, 1937).

to become hybrid by engaging, inviting and loving our friends and neighbours to develop an authentic community of faith that reflects the nation in which we are called to live and exact the true body of Christ.

BIBLIOGRAPHY

Augustine. *On the Trinity*. http://newadvent.org/fathers/130113.htm.

Barth, K. *Church Dogmatics III/2: The Doctrine of Creation*. G. W. Bromiley and T. F. Torrance (ed). Translated by G. W. Bromiley and R. J. Ehrlich. Edinburgh: T & T Clark, 1961.

Bebbington, D. W. *The Dominance of Evangelicalism*. Great Britain: IVP, 2005.

Bonhoeffer, D. "Ethics," in Clifford J. Green, *Dietrich Bonhoeffer Work* 6, R. Krauss, C. West & Stott D. W. (transl). Minneapolis: Fortress, 2005.

Brown, R. M. *Unexpected News: Reading the Bible with Third World Eyes*. Philadelphia: Westminster, 1984.

Brunner, E. *The Divine Imperative*. New York: Macmillan, 1937.

Chester, T. *Good News to the Poor*. Wheaton: Crossway, 2013.

Cochran, C. E. "Life on the Border: A Catholic Perspective" in P. C. Kemeny (ed.) *Church, State and Public Justice: Five Views*. Illinois: IVP, 2007.

Cone, J. *Speaking the Truth*. Grand Rapids: Eerdmans, 1986.

Conradie, E. (ed), *Reconciliation: A Guiding Vision for South Africa*. Stellenbosch: Sun, 2013.

Davies, O. *The Theology of Compassion*. Grand Rapids: Eerdmans, 2001

De Gruchy, J. W. *Liberating Reformed Theology*. Cape Town: David Philips/ Eerdmans, 1991.

Dykstra, C., and D. C. Bass. "A Theological Understanding of Christian Practice". In M. Volf and D. C. Bass. *Practising Theology: Beliefs and Practices in Christian Life*. Grand Rapids: Eerdmans, 2002.

Ellis M. H. and Maduro, O. (eds.) *The Future of Liberation Theology*. Essays in Honor of Gustavo Gutierrez. New York: Orbis, 1989.

Erickson, M. *Christian Theology*. Grand Rapids: Baker, 1999

Frame, J. M. *The Doctrine of the Christian Life*. New Jersey: P & R, 2008.

Gill, R. (ed). *The Cambridge Companion to Christian Ethics*. Cambridge: Cambridge, 2001.

Grant, A. and Hughes, D.A. (eds.) *Transforming the World?* United Kingdom: Apollos, 2009.

Grant, J. "Poverty, Womanist Theology and the Ministry of the Church." in *Standing with the Poor*. P P. Parker (ed.). Cleveland: Pilgrims, 1992.

Jackson, T. P. "The Gospel and Christian Ethics". In R. Gill (ed.) *The Cambridge Companion to Christian Ethics*. Cambridge: Cambridge, 2001.

Gustafson, J. *The Church as Moral Decision-Maker*. Philadelphia: Pilgrims,1970.

Harold, G., and Alexander C. "Affirmative Action as an Approach to Economic Restitution in Post-Apartheid South Africa: A Reading of Luke 19:1–10". *The South African Baptist Journal Of Theology* 24 (2015): 29–42.

Hauerwas, S. *The Peaceable Kingdom: A Primer Christian Ethic.* Norte Dame, Indiana: University of Notre Dame, 1983.

Jones, M. J. Christian *Ethics for Black Theology.* New York: Abingdon, 1974.

Kant, I. *Ground Work for Metaphysics of Morals*, trans. M. Gregor and J Timmermann. Cambridge University Press: UK, 2012.

Keller. T. *Generous Justice.* London: Hodder and Stoughton, 2010.

Kemeny, P. C., ed. *Church, State and Public Justice: Five Views.* Illinois: IVP, 2007.

Küng, H. *The Church.* Great Britain: Search, 1981.

Labberton, M. *The Dangerous Act of Loving Your Neighbor.* Illinois: IVP, 2010.

Myers, B. *Walking with the Poor: Principles and Practice of Transformational Development.* Maryknoll: Orbis, 1999.

McNeil, B. S. *Road Map to Reconciliation.* Illinois: IVP, 2015.

Nouwen, H. J. M., McNeil, D. P., and Morison D. A., *Compassion.* USA: Image, 1982.

Parker, P. P., ed. *Standing with the Poor.* Cleveland: Pilgrims, 1992.

Pillay, J. "An Exploration of the Idea of Ecodomy in Calvin's View of God and the World: Its Implications for Churches in South Africa Today", *Verbum et Ecclesia* 36, no. 3, Art. #1474 (2015): 10.

Reuther, R. R. "Religion and Society: Sacred Canopy vs. Prophetic Critique" in *The Future of Liberation Theology.* Essays in Honor of Gustavo Gutierrez. M. H. Ellis and O. Maduro (eds.), New York: Orbis, 1989.

Root, A. *Christopraxis: A Practical Theology of the Cross.* Minneapolis: Fortress, 2014.

Rouner, L. S. *The Longing Home.* Indiana: University of Notre Dame, 1996.

Saaymann, W. "Alternative Community and Antibody: A Dimension of David Bosch as Public Theologian" *Missionalia* 39, nos. 1 and 2: 5–17, 201.

Shabala, T. "Entitlement is the Key Word in Racist Thinking." http://www.rdm. co.za/business/2016/01/12/entitled-is-a-key-word-in-racist-thinking, 2016.

Sider, R. J. "The Anabaptist Perspective" in *Church, State and Public Justice: Five Views.* PC Kemeny, ed. Ill: IVP, 2007.

Stone, B. P. *Compassionate Ministry: Theological Foundations.* New York: Maryknoll,1996.

Swinton, J., and Mowat, H. *Practical Theology and Qualitative Research.* London: SCM, 2006.

Vellem, V. "Rediscovering Reconciliation: A Response to the Call for Reconciliation as a Governing Symbol in Post -1994 South Africa" in *Reconciliation: A Guiding Vision for South Africa.* E. Conradie (ed.) Stellenbosch: Sun, 2013.

Volf, M., "The Social Meaning of Reconciliation" in *Transformation* 16, no. 1 (1999): 7–12.

———. "Theology for a Way of Life." In M. Volf and D. C. Bass. *Practising Theology: Beliefs and Practices in Christian Life*. Grand Rapids: Eerdmans, 2002.

———. *A Public Faith: How Followers of Christ Serve the Common Good*. Grand Rapids: Brazos, 2011.

———, and D. C. Bass, eds. *Practising Theology: Beliefs and Practices in Christian Life*. Grand Rapids: Eerdmans, 2002.

ABOUT THE AUTHOR

GODFREY HAROLD teaches at Cape Town Baptist Seminary; is an Associate Researcher at University of Pretoria; and Distinguished Professor at BH Caroll Theological Institute, USA.

CHAPTER 16 | Uday Mark Balasundaram

Hybridity, Arts, and Mission

Diaspora environments offer creative opportunities and challenges for hybrid art-making for mission. Our focus for this paper is to take a closer look at some of the ways in which hybridity-arts nexus creates new spaces for mission. Hybrid art-making has its theological basis in the creativity of God (*creatio Dei*). It is intrinsic to and proceeds from the *creatio Dei*. Hybrid art-making for mission therefore refers to translating the creativity of God in and through art forms and processes of art-making in the world in the light of *missio Dei*. Hybrid art-making for mission therefore can be a dynamic process of translation that invites participation in the creativity of God. Hybridity resists the hegemony of aesthetics. Hybrid art-making raises questions of how we evaluate the legitimacy of global and indigenous art forms in a context where hybridity is the norm. Hybridity compels us to revisit simplistic definitions of art, and by implication invites us to recognize the legitimate place of art and artists in the mission of God.

Cultural Hybridity, Art-Making, and Mission

Conceptually, cultural hybridity, art-making, and mission are uniquely enmeshed in the creativity of God (*creatio Dei*). Here, we briefly recollect some salient features of the logic of creativity in the context of the *creatio Dei* to clarify the link between cultural hybridity, art-making, and mission.

First, in the context of *creatio Dei*, creativity refers to the larger theological backdrop for the products and processes of art-making in general. It is the ontology of participation in the creativity of God. Thereby, we may distinguish between creativity and art or art-making. Second, theological creativity in the *creatio Dei*,[1] encompasses the interactive communal nature and dynamic exchange between the individual members of the Godhead. The locus for creativity therefore is the diversity of the community of the Trinity. It follows that cultural hybridity is not merely something we encounter on the so-called "mission field" through processes of gospel enculturation. Rather, theologically, cultural hybridity may be understood as intrinsic to and proceeding from the diversity of the creativity of God. Third, the concept of cultural hybridity with theological precedent in the *creatio Dei* has particular missiological implications, not necessarily obvious in dominant renderings of *missio Dei*, significantly, that hybridity is not an end in itself; it resolves to creativity. How this happens in the context of art-making for mission we will explore in the rest of this article.

Defining Hybrid Art

Recent scholarship on the arts and mission has contributed to our understanding of how the arts impact and enhance the missionary potential of the body of Christ in a variety of ways.[2] The inter-mixing of motifs and materials and the representation of forms and philosophies is evident in the expressive social forms of art in cultures all over the world.[3] Hybridity, however, brings into focus

---

1 Most of us are familiar with the concept of *missio Dei*. The concept of *creatio Dei* is less well-known. For more on *creatio Dei* and a missiological framework for mission, which forms the basis for much of what is shared here, see Uday Balasundaram, "Creativity and Captivity: Exploring the Language of Musical Creativity for Mission," *NAIITS Journal* 11, no. 4 (2013). In the context of *creatio Dei*, "creation" is conceptualized both as a noun and a verb as compared to "mission" in the context of *missio Dei*.

2 For example, IVP's Studies in Theology & the Arts Series, https://www.ivpress.com/studies-in-theology-and-the-arts-series and the Routledge Congregational Music Studies Series. Also, The International Council of Ethnodoxologists Handbook and Manual, https://www.worldofworship.org/ethnodoxology-handbook-manual/.

3 An excellent resource addressing the overlap of Christianity and art in the South Asian context is, Anand Amaladass and Gudrun Löwner, *Christian Themes in Indian Art: From the Mogul Times till Today* (New Delhi: Manohar Publishers & Distributors, 2012). Also, recently, Gudrun Löwner, *Intercultural Dialogue in Art and Religion* (New Delhi: Manohar Publishers & Distributors, 2018).

the issue of what qualifies as "art" in the first place.[4] It is concerned with the larger complex of histories and narratives related to who is doing the qualifying and the implications thereof.[5]

Victoria Vesna, an artist and professor at UCLA's Department of Design, engaged in experimental creative research linking the worlds of technology and creativity describes hybrid art as something that is yet emerging, "resides in between, around, above and below what is generally accepted as 'culture.'" It is experimental, collaborative, and many times not regarded as "art" since hybridity "does not subscribe the usual, established categories and definitions." It is "art in process" and is constantly changing, evading rigid definition.[6]

Vesna's definition broadly captures the notion of hybrid art that pertains to our approach in this paper—hybridity as intermixing. Here, however, we are not so interested in hybrid art per se, but in the processes of hybrid art-making for mission that compel the Church to think creative: look for knowledge in the unfamiliar, and be creative: embrace diversity, without which there can be no true creativity for the building up of community in Christ with others.

---

4 In general, art refers to "a diverse range of human activities in creating visual, auditory or performing artifacts, expressing the author's imaginative or technical skill, intended to be appreciated for their beauty or emotional power," https://en.wikipedia.org/wiki/Art (accessed June 9, 2018). Anthropologically, art includes varied meaning-making processes, products, communicative dimension, transformational potential, and a capacity for technical skill that may not be shared equally by all. See Gary Ferraro, *Cultural Anthropology: An Applied Perspective*. Fifth Edition. Belmont, CA: Thomson Learning, 2004), 359ff.

5 For me, growing up, art pertained primarily to the visual or so-called fine arts. Music was often in its own category. On the one hand, for example, we have the "church's disregard" for the arts, the subversive potential of artists as threat to society, and the perception of the "art world's hostility to religious belief." See Cameron Anderson, *The Faithful Artist: A Vision for Evangelicalism and the Arts* (IVP Academic, 2016), 3-4. On the other hand, the deep significance of art in primal and tribal cultures and the status accorded to artists who embody a creative spirituality e.g., in the light of the "sonic theology" of the classical music traditions in India. See Guy Beck, *Sonic Theology: Hinduism and Sacred Sound* (Columbia, South Carolina, 1993). Also, in the context of neoliberal agenda, Simon Frith, "The Discourse of World Music," in *Western Music and Its Others: Difference, Representation, and Appropriation in Music*, ed. Georgina Born and David Hesmondhalgh (Los Angeles, CA: University of California Press), 309. Hybridity is an overarching idea that refers to the discourses of World Music as an "ideological category" that caricatures inclusivity while being in reality "systematically exclusive."

6 Victoria Vesna, "What is Hybrid Art?" *Arts Electronica Blog*, 2015, 2, https://www.aec.at/aeblog/en/2015/03/24/was-ist-hybrid-art/.

Hybridity, Art-Making, and Diaspora New Spaces

Why is it even significant that we introduce the variable of hybridity mixed into "arts and mission"? Here are some pertinent ways in which hybridity is helpful to reimagine the integration of art-making and mission for ministry. First, in post-colonial nomenclature, hybridity resists the hegemony of aesthetics.[7] The concept of aesthetics as a "new science of sensory cognition"[8] is a relatively recent development typically associated with Western aesthetic formalism.[9] The idea of an objective aesthetic assessment of an artwork according to a pre-established criteria can be antithetical to the process of determining the fundamental worth or legitimacy of an art work derived from the feelings associated with the process of art-making or its ongoing and unfolding social significance in a given context. Hybridity as intermixing is often suspect especially in the light of the hegemony of dominant aesthetic cultures.

In my research among diaspora musicians I had the opportunity to connect with J. B., a Naga-Indian living in the diversity of diaspora in New York. While growing up in India, J. B. realized that he had developed a prejudice against a particular local language-speaking people group in the context of his worship community. The dominant aesthetic framework in his home church in India favored music styled and influenced by the West. Yet, it was in the diversity of diaspora in New York that he overcame the barrier of his prejudice and opened himself up to embrace his innate hybridity to where he now writes and performs in ethnic-influenced fusion styles of music that he had in a passive sense learned to ignore. His story of overcoming cultural barriers through music in diaspora is captured in these words:

---

7 The ambivalence and ambiguity of hybrid processes resist commodification and homogeneity. See, Homi K. Bhabha, *The Location of Culture* (New York: Routledge, 1994 [2004].

8 Alejandro García-Rivera, *The Community of the Beautiful: A Theological Aesthetics* (Collegeville, MN: Liturgical), 9.

9 See Clifford Geertz, "Art as a Cultural System," *Modern Language Notes* (Baltimore/ Md./USA: The Johns Hopkins), 91 no. 6 (1976): 1473-1499, http://hypergeertz.jku. at/GeertzTexts/Art_Cultural.htm (accessed December 8, 2018). Also, modern art abstraction in India may be understood as a reaction to the "academic realism" of certain foreign art traditions. National Gallery of Modern Art, http://ngmaindia.gov. in/sh-academic.asp. The influence of British art schools in the nineteenth century promoted the development of "fine" arts, emphasizing naturalistic representation of objects as they appear versus conceptual art that represented ideas.

"When that barrier was crossed and I started learning Hindi music and playing it even on the guitar, obviously I had to change the way I play the guitar too. I am still learning, that was a whole different area of learning and enjoyment. Before, I was out of it. I was being a critic and looking down on it. But now, I am playing and leading these songs, and singing these songs, I don't know how to describe it."[10]

Hybridity therefore raises issues concerning how we evaluate the legitimacy of global and indigenous art forms in a context where hybridity is the norm, such as in the diasporic imagination of creatives such as JB.

Second, the concept of hybridity compels us to revisit simplistic definitions of art, and by implication invites us to the rightful "place" of art in the mission of God. It raises the issue of "where" is art rather than "what" is art. Art is often a suspect in cultures that privilege what is perceived as non-art, such as words (e.g., logocentrism), as somehow more authentic for the articulation of knowledge and truth than art.[11] The default association of literate forms with scientific rational cognition and artistic/oral forms with the so-called non or supra-rational cognitive is evidence of a dichotomized worldview that inhibits the adaptation and adoption of multiple learning behaviors for disseminating Christian truth, preferring homogeneity and traditionalism to diversity and risking experimentation.

For example, a church in the global North had the opportunity to host several refugees from a particular South Asian ethnic background. The prevalence of dance and singing as a preferred way of learning and community formation for the refugee community was evident. However, such oral preference clashed with the perception of what the rightful place of art and especially dance was in the host church culture. Over a period of time many of those initially received from the refugee

---

10 Interview with J. B., a musician living and practicing a music ministry amongst the diaspora communities based in New York. For more, see Uday Balasundaram, "Creativity and Captivity: Exploring the Process of Musical Creativity amongst Indigenous Cosmopolitan Musicians (ICMs) for Mission" (PhD Dissertation, Asbury Theological Seminary, Wilmore, KY, 2014), 175, ProQuest Dissertations & Theses Global.

11 Elsewhere I have referred to this as the epistemological captivity of creativity. The epistemological captivity of creativity is evident when there is undue emphasis on scientific "fact" versus the "ambiguity" of hybrid creative processes. The epistemological captivity, among other things, refers to the illegitimate shift of the canonical heritage of the Church into the "arena of becoming a criterion of truth." William J. Abraham, *Canon and Criterion in Christian Theology: From the Fathers to Feminism* (Oxford University, 2002).

community into the host community left the church. Eventually many reverted to their previous Hindu belief system. The idea of the rightful place of art is significant since it draws us out of the homely silos of aesthetic constructions and into the new "unhomely" globalizing proximations of diasporic creative consciousness.

Third, hybridity brings to the fore the real (theological) potential that all true art-making is essentially and ultimately a hybridizing process. In order to better understand the connection between art-making and hybridity, we recollect our earlier proposition, first, that hybridity is theologically anchored in the diversity of God and, second, diversity is a core dynamic of the creativity of God. When it comes to the idea of cultural hybridity therefore diversity is not merely optional or something to be tolerated. Rather, in the context of the *creatio Dei*, diversity is something that needs to be prioritized and even sought after, without which there can be no true creativity.

What might the prioritization of diversity mean for the diasporic reconfiguration of cultures and boundaries through processes of art-making for mission? To illustrate, J. S., a South Asian Indian comes from a Hindu background. He responded to an open invitation on "meetup.com" to be part of a guitar orchestra that I had initiated on the premises of a local church in Orlando, FL, USA as a way to connect with and learn from other musicians in the local diaspora. It so happened that J. S. invited a few of us from the guitar orchestra to perform at the Diwali celebration being hosted at the local Hindu temple that he attended not far from where we met. We obliged with the rendition of a Bollywood classic song that he led along with a Hindi rendition of a popular Christian song on the theme of Jesus as Light of the World. The response was overwhelmingly well received. We were invited to return. Several from the temple were interested to learn more about our church and some even inquired regarding a possible visit. In retrospect I am grateful to the church that allowed for the hosting of the space for the guitar orchestra. The "new space" created at one end resulted in a "new space" created at the other end in the Hindu temple. This set the stage for further interactions and a friendship with JS that we enjoy and cherish as a family to this day.

Fourth, as a corollary to the last point, the concept of cultural hybridity itself is expanded in the light of the creativity of God whereby, as indicated earlier, hybridity resolves to creativity. Subsequently we may understand cultural hybridity as the spatial-temporal analogue to creativity (theological) and, in the light of its theological potential, as briefly indicated in the narrative above, cultural hybridity can be a breeding ground for vital spontaneous combustive community in Christ.

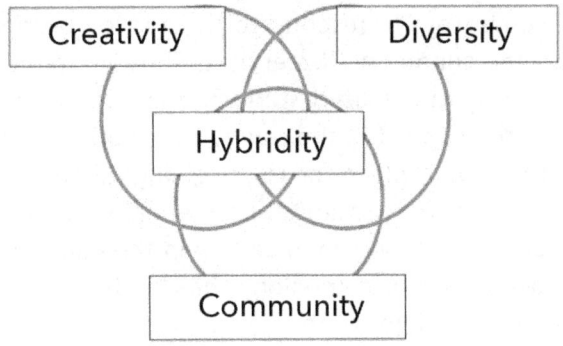

Figure 1: Theological hybridity at the intersection of core dynamics of creatio Dei

Hybrid Art-Making and Identity

Cultural hybridity is not new to Christian art-making practices in the West nor in India.[12] Historically, however, many Christian South Asians in India and in diaspora are reluctant or hesitant to take up Indian classical systems of art given the innate link between Hindu religion and art in India. A family I know struggled with a decision to enroll their daughter in *Bharatanatyam*[13] dance classes offered at the local Hindu temple in a city in the US. The idea of enrolling their daughter in the dance classes was problematic since it included telling stories through dance that had Hindu religious significance. Further, as part of their repertoire, participants' year-end performance included performing in the temple in the context of idol worship. Should the Indian couple participate in

---

12 See Anand Amaldass S. J., and Gudrun Löwner, *Christian Themes in Indian Art,* 2012. Also, Jutta Vinzent, "In Search of Hybridity: Inculturation, Interculturation and Transculturation in Contemporary Religious Art in Britain," *Exchange* 39, no. 1 (2010): 29–48. doi:10.1163/016627410X12559405201117.

13 Bharatanatyam is a classical Indian dance with theoretical foundations in the ancient Sanskrit text Natyashastra. For more, see "Bharatanatyam" in *https:// en.wikipedia.org/wiki/Bharatanatyam*. Along with other classical dance forms of India, apart from offering a way to sustain Indianness in a transnational context, Bharatanatyam is part of a contemporary Indian dance repertoire that resonates among South Asian diaspora as a form of devotion. See Katrak, Ketu H., "Innovations in Contemporary Indian Dance: From Religious and Mythological Roots in Classical Bharatanatyam." *Religion Compass* 7 (2). doi:10.1111/rec3.12030.

Hindu religious-cultural art-making? The answer is beyond the scope of this paper.[14] However, for now the issue is enough for an initial response to the dilemma of diasporic participation in transnational social-religious art-making processes, in this case Hinduism. In such a scenario, could hybrid art-making allow for a place for experimentation and dialogue?

Here are some ways to respond to the above question. First, art-making within the context of Westernized Christian traditions in India promoted a compartmentalized spiritual and cultural experience of Christianity.[15] In the context of the *creatio Dei*, hybrid art-making holds potential to serve as a place for re-imagining creative identity and purpose in the light of the proximity and overlap of cultural boundaries in transcultural environments in India and in the context of diaspora. Second, the lack of a robust theology that helps to locate the artist and artistic practice in light of the creativity of God from a missional perspective (i.e., hybrid yet not necessarily syncretistic[16]) is evident in the low view of creative arts exponents as ministers of God by other so-called more legitimate offices, such as "pastor" in the context of the institutional church, in comparison to their Hindu counterparts.[17] When it comes to the context of art-making and artists in the Indian or South Asian diaspora scenario, first, hybrid art-making in the context of Christianity needs to account for the rich sonic theology of Vedic

---

14 For a discussion on the response to the appropriation of *Bharatanatyam* as a way of inculturation by "Catholic Christians" see Michelle Voss Roberts, "'Who Is My Good Neighbor?': Classical Indian Dance in the Prophetic Work of the Church." *Exchange* 41, no. 2 (2012): 103–19. doi:10.1163/157254312X638337. Voss responds to three issues, the association of *Bharatanatyam* with Hindu religious culture, the embodiment of divinity and its gender-specific depiction and association, and the more pertinent issue of the dance form being appropriated by Christianity for its own agenda.

15 While in recent years there have been several instances of indigenous hybrid Christian music making, the dominant expression for English-speaking Christian gatherings in urban India is the "K-Love" repertoire. Popular local Christian expressions tend to be translations of Western hymn tunes and contemporary Christian music (CCM).

16 Syncretistic need not necessarily imply uncritical adoption or adaptation of cultural forms in mission. See Shaw, R Daniel. "Beyond Syncretism: A Dynamic Approach to Hybridity," *International Bulletin of Mission Research* 42, no. 1 (January 2018): 6–19.

17 In general, both Western and Indian traditions affirm music as a pathway to the spiritual. However, the development of Christian theology and practice in the light of neo-Platonic and post-Enlightenment traditions have stunted the development of a vibrant theology of creativity for Christianity, preferring rational cognitive intellectual forms as more legitimate conveyors of truth and knowledge to theology in terms of sound and movement. See earlier footnote10 on "epistemological captivity."

classical Hindu religious cultural traditions. Third, the undue emphasis on theology in lyrics in the context of logocentrism[18] is antithetical to theological aesthetics in terms of body movement, *jugalbandi* (extended improvisational dialogue between instrumentalists and/or vocalists most often without words except for syllabification), and emotional quotient.[19] Hybrid art-making can fill this gap.

Hybrid Art-Making and Implications for Mission

The failure to recognize hybrid art-making processes in general as a legitimate or authentic vehicle for embodying truth and knowledge undermines the effectiveness of the church when it comes to embracing the fullness of its creative and thereby missional potential. How can the Church become more intentional in creating new spaces for the nurture of artisans involved in hybrid art-making as an interface with the world?

First, when it comes to creating new spaces in global diaspora environments what Jyoti Sahi says is pertinent and takes courage to implement. According to Jyoti Sahi, Indian aesthetics has a distinct offering to make "in a world plagued by the speculative divisions made in Greek philosophy between truth, goodness and beauty."[20] Hybrid art-making when encouraged by the church can offer a unitive vision, concerned with living values ... Art serves as a process, through which layer by layer man attempts to strip off the various masks, or cosmetic coverings, that hide him from himself. Atmanam viddhi, the Indian equivalent of the Greek "know thyself" is at once an exploration into the unconscious psyche and the Divine Brahman. It is the process of knowing oneself by ceasing to assume the role of the 'persona'.

---

18 Music captures and reveals experiences that cannot ever be put into words or syllogisms. We do not dispute the place of lyrics in the construction of meaning in music. Yet, words need not necessarily be the primary yardstick for the effectiveness of music as a system of knowledge. For Jacques Derrida, "logocentrism" emphasizes the privileged place of words in the context of Westernization. See Jacques Derrida, Margins of Philosophy (Brighton, Sussex: The University of Chicago Press, 1984).

19 Guy L. Beck, "The Magic of Hindu Music: Exploring the religious, historical and social forces that shaped Hindu music and now propel it into the future," *Hinduism Today* (October 2007), 20. Classical forms of Indian music, both instrumental and vocal, are considered to be of divine origin and are closely identified with the Hindu deities; the instruments of the gods symbolize Nada Brahman—"the sacred, primeval, eternal sound, represented by the syllable Om, which generates the universe... [and] symbolizes Brahman, the Supreme Absolute." Time and space do not allow for a discussion of rasa or Indian aesthetics.

20 Jyoti Sahi, *The Child and the Serpent: Reflections on Popular Indian Symbols*, Asian Trading Corporation, Bangalore, 1980[1994], 22.

This is likewise the final object of art.[21] Churches therefore should strive to develop a robust theology of creativity of God for mission in order to legitimize the role of hybrid art-making as well as guide its aesthetic development for contextually relevant practice.

Second, given the theological bond between creative being and creative activity in the light of the *creatio Dei*, it follows that a devaluation of creative expression amounts to a devaluation of the creator. The "epistemological captivity" of creativity results in a spiritual alienation, both within the conscience of creative practitioners and in the efficient application of their ecclesial calling in the context of the ministry of the Church. Such "captivity" is detrimental for mission, in particular for the self-understanding and practice of creative arts practitioners for whom a strong theological foundation can help them to see how their creative contributions are not just about "arts and entertainment." Rather, art-making is a way of participating in the creativity of God and thereby offers a critical pathway for inviting others to participate in the creativity of God.

Third, according to Poka Laenui (2000), the process of decolonization consists of rediscovery and recovery of one's own voice and identity. Second, it is a process of lamenting, identifying with the stories of the other. There is no dearth of stories of the rejection and marginalization of artists when they experiment with "tradition." In extreme situations cultural art-making as a legitimate pathway to the divine has been in the context of ecclesiological praxis with roots in modern foundationalism and colonialism. A third factor of the decolonizing process is dreaming—imagining alternate ways of doing research by way of invoking indigenous knowledge systems; in this case, hybrid creativity.[22] As we explore hybrid art-making as a creative process of rediscovery, lamentation, and dreaming here is a relevant anecdote from my experience. Upon returning to India from theological studies abroad I excitedly went to a local record label and shared with the producer my dream of a music ministry. To my utter dismay however he responded in the following way, roughly recollected here: "But why, especially when we can get Vineyard and Hillsong here…18–20 songs for Rs.200. Who is going to [want to] buy your music?"

The narrative above demonstrates how the neoliberal "aesthetic"— as long as it sells—shapes the agenda for what is permissible and what

---

21 Ibid., 22-3.

22 Poka Laenui, "Processes of Decolonization," in M. Battiste, ed., *Reclaiming Indigenous Voice and Vision*, 150–60. Toronto: UBC Press. See also, Chilisa (2012).

may not be so. In the above scenario the neoliberal agenda legitimizes dominant Westernized forms of Christian musical expression at the cost of indigenous agency. In the context of neoliberal "assimilation" strategies, however, hybrid art-making processes help to articulate the difference between the authentic and inauthentic,[23] helping to oppose neoliberal impulses in transnational space. A concern is raised that the encounter with global neoliberal agendas unduly puts what is locally produced (technologies and related processes) in competition with state-of-the-art global technologies. And this is true in reality. On the other hand, however, hybrid art-making could stimulate creatives to take their local contexts more seriously. It calls them to pay close attention to indigenous sources, local nuances, and explore how such might apply in terms of differentiating themselves from mainstream categories despite neoliberal impulses. Hybrid art-making could possibly help local artists to learn to appreciate the unique contributions from their own local creative cultures to the ministry of the local church. In doing so hybrid art-making platforms can help negotiate what qualifies as "heart-music" for a given context.

Pure Hybridity

In addition to reshaping mission practice, hybrid art-making for mission invites us to think of theological hybridity in a fresh way. Pure or theological hybridity, as differentiated from hybridity borne out of colonial contact, may be described as a process of distinguishing oneself from another primarily as an act of communality, and not primarily resistance[24] as a postcolonial response. Outside of a theological context the idea of pure or "original purity" prior to intermixing may be

---

23 Richard Middleton, "Musical Belongings: Western Music and Its Low-Other," in *Western Music and Its Others: Difference, Representation, and Appropriation in Music*, eds. Georgina Born and David Hesmondhalgh, 59–85 (Los Angeles, CA: University of California Press, 2000), 59–62. See also, Simon Frith, *Performing Rites: On the Value of Popular Music* (Cambridge, MA: Harvard University Press, 1996), 307; and, Jo Haynes, "World Music and the Search for Difference," *Ethnicities 5*, (3, 2005): 365–385. Also, in Balasundaram 2014.

24 Pure hybridity here is to be distinguished from perspectives on hybridity that tend to define it primarily in terms of resistance to "partisans" of ethnic purity or racial supremacy, or those who demand a supreme aesthetic, or those who deny hybridity its social, cultural, and political roots. See Vanessa Guignery et al, 1. Hybridity: Forms and Figures in Literature and the Visual Arts, 3–4. Newcastle upon Tyne, U.K.: Cambridge Scholars Publishing (2012), http://ezproxy.asburyseminary.edu/login?url=http://search.ebscohost.com/login.aspx?direct=true&db=nlebk&AN=524470&site=eds-live.

less common.[25] But art-making-as-hybridizing-process can draw participants toward pure or theological hybridity. As such, therefore, hybridity may not primarily be conceived as a response to colonialism; it is a capacity for human imagination and being that encourages healing in human relationships. It is a place for dialogue and inter-subjective formation. It is a place of possibility and potential for freedom.

By way of example, A. R. Rahman, a well-known Indian film music composer is well versed in fusing together seemingly disparate sounds (tribal, folk, urban, classical) for film. His first film, Roja, was a near instantaneous hit in Bollywood in India as well as among South Asian diaspora worldwide. Many years later in a personal conversation with me, Rahman talked about the "redemptive" nature of his music—how his music reconciles people, brings healing, and restores relationships. Rahman converted from nominal Hinduism to Islam and attributes his worldwide influence and success to Allah. For Rahman, music is about "seeing through the eyes of the heart." Rahman's remake of the National Anthem of India was endorsed by the government of India. This is significant given the backdrop of Hindu-Muslim communal conflict in the country. However, what struck me as truly significant was Rahman's recomposition of the Tagore classic, Vande Mataram, popularly known as India's National Song. The art-making process brought together people from diverse religious and cultural backgrounds in the production of the music video. Rahman's rendition of the song is not without criticism, however, Rahman's appropriation of the song sparked an ongoing discourse with regard to Indian national identity and communal consciousness of the nation.[26]

Art-Making as Hybridity Resisting Resistance

With Rahman, hybridity as art-making is something that draws participants toward the notion of pure hybridity—calling a people divided into harmony with one another. In this way hybrid art-making resists the very concept of resistance as a primary way of creative hybrid expression (identifying with self and others). The posture of hybridity resisting resistance is closely linked with freedom of expression, justice, and healing—freedom of expression because of the alignment of creative expression with creative impression: what I make is intrinsically

---

25 Ibid., 3–4. Guignery recollects Paul Gilroy, "I think there isn't any purity; there isn't any anterior purity [...] that's why I try not to use the word hybrid."

26 See "AR Rahman-CNN talk Asia-Part 2- 'Converting,'" http://www.youtube.com/watch?v=gLOB9OCj4IU.

bound up and coheres with who I am in the light of the *creatio Dei* (Gen 1:26; Eph 2:10). Here, the artist is not trying to be someone else, not copying, not creating purely under pressure of neoliberal market dynamics, even though the artist may be accused of the same by others. This is hybridity resolving to creativity.

Hybrid art-making stems not from propositional truth, but it is a process of discovery, exploration, and integration. When a child mixes together diverse elements to construct mud pancakes or twists together dried twigs to create a "decoration" there is freedom. To critique the child's imagination with an "aesthetic" that interprets the artwork in terms of a framework other than or opposed to the *creatio Dei* would be to subvert justice. In this sense, all art-making is inherently a hybridizing process, fusing intention with materials through a crafting process that eludes criticism apart from participation. What differentiates Christian hybrid art-making from that of others is that such participation is grounded in the love of God in Christ Jesus. It is the way in which such participation is welcomed and modeled that distinguishes hybrid art-making for mission from other relativized hybrid art-making processes. In this way hybrid art-making for mission emphasizes the qualitative-participative dimension of the creative process, apart from which creativity may be captive to generalized epistemologies and/or neoliberal impulses.

Developing New Spaces for Hybrid Art-Making for Mission

Hybridity in this era of digitalization draws attention to the ways hybrid art-making processes and products facilitate access to what seems to be ever-expanding online communities.[27] In a world where hybrid art-making includes loosely networked online cultures and "always on" asynchronous and synchronous learning environments, hybrid art-making for mission calls for the intentional development of cultures that promote and sustain new spaces of spiritual encounter with those who may never set foot in a physical church or even see it as critical to their spiritual life journey. Hybrid art-making internationalizes spaces for the medium itself to be the "massage," the glue that brings and holds people together in ways that foster opportunities for prophetic dialogue. Hybrid art-making in the new digital economy can empower the Church with a "unitive vision" which includes putting in place structures that validate and legitimize the roles of artists in the mission of God.

---

27 Here I am drawing from the "key words" that define a digital world. See Craig Detweiler, *iGods: How Technology Shapes Our Spiritual and Social Lives* (Baker 2011).

Second, hybrid art-making processes expose false dichotomies that restrict and prohibit the diverse expressions of the body of Christ, calling us to revisit simplistic definitions of what rightfully qualifies as art in a given context. All this can happen in the context of, for example, creative missional "new song/art" communities as hermeneutical communities of practice. Further, churches in diaspora could practice inclusion by prioritizing the creation of new art forms together with those from different ethnic and cultural backgrounds and worldviews. Hybrid art-making spaces legitimize and help in authentic retelling of our (church's) Story and inviting others to share in it by lowering our guard emphasizing creating with others prior to mission to others, preferring and seeking out the other, bearing in mind the essential diversity that forms a core component of the creativity of the Godhead.

Third, hybrid art-making raises questions regarding the Church's response to the place and role of artists as legitimate conveyers of truth and knowledge through their art as much as other more generally accepted conveyers of truth in ratio-cognitive intellectual forms such as via traditional offices of the Church. We need a substantive theology of creativity that undergirds the creative identities of artists as they build up the church for mission. Just as God called Bezalel and Oholiab and anointed them for the task of building God's dwelling place on earth (Ex 31:1–3), churches (leadership) today need to appoint and commission creatives who will equally share in the creative architecture of the Church for mission in art-full, powerful, and compelling ways for this generation and the next (Ps 102:18–22).

Fourth, the concept of hybridity as a critical part of the creative process in the *creatio Dei* clears rather than blurs the lens through which we discern the boundaries for Christian art-making and determine the rules for engaging culture. The final picture is people gathered from every nation, tribe, tongue, and language worshipping God in heaven (Rev 7:9). Hybridity does not diminish the uniqueness of our common human diversity. Exactly how we bring together our diverse best for God's creative best is a testimony to the hybrid art-making capacity of God in all cultures and peoples everywhere.

BIBLIOGRAPHY

Abraham, William J. *Canon and Criterion in Christian Theology: From the Fathers to Feminism*. Oxford University, 2002.

Amaladass, Anand and Gudrun Löwner. *Christian Themes in Indian Art: From the Mogul Times till Today*. New Delhi: Manohar Publishers & Distributors, 2012.

Anderson, Cameron. *The Faithful Artist: A Vision for Evangelicalism and the Arts*. IVP Academic, 2016.

Balasundaram Uday. *Creativity and Captivity: Exploring the Language of Musical Creativity for Mission, NAIITS Journal* 11, no 4 (2013).

Balasundaram, Uday Mark. *Creativity and Captivity: Exploring the Process of Musical Creativity Amongst Indigenous Cosmopolitan Musicians (ICMs) for Mission*. Order No. 3662598, Asbury Theological Seminary, http://search.proquest.com.ezproxy.asburyseminary.edu/docview/1675017126?accountid=8380. ProQuest Dissertations & Theses Global, 2014.

Beck, Guy L. *Sonic Theology: Hinduism and Sacred Sound*. Columbia, South Carolina: University of South Carolina, 1993.

_____. "The Magic of Hindu Music: Exploring the Religious, Historical and Social Forces that Shaped Hindu Music and Now Propel it into the Future," *Hinduism Today* (October): 2007.

Bhabha, Homi. *The Location of Culture*. New York, NY: Routledge. Kindle. 1994.

Born, Georgina and David Hesmondhalgh, eds. *Western Music and its Others: Difference, Representation, and Appropriation in Music*. Berkeley and Los Angeles, CA: University of California, 2000.

Chilisa, Bagelle. *Indigenous Research Methodologies*. Thousand Oaks, CA: SAGE, 2012.

Derrida, Jacques. *Margins of Philosophy*, trans., Alan Bass. Chicago: The University of Chicago, 1982.

Detweiler, Craig. *iGods: How Technology Shapes Our Spiritual and Social Lives*. Grand Rapids, Michigan: Brazos, 2011.

Ferraro, Gary. *Cultural Anthropology: An Applied Perspective*. Fifth Edition. Belmont, CA: Thomson Learning, 2004.

Frith, Simon. "The Discourse of World Music," in *Western Music and Its Others: Difference, Representation, and Appropriation in Music*, ed. Georgina Born and David Hesmondhalgh. Los Angeles, CA: University of California, 2000.

García-Rivera, Alejandro. *The Community of the Beautiful: A Theological Aesthetics*. Collegeville, MN: Liturgical, 1999.

Geertz, Clifford. "Art as a Cultural System" in *Modern Language Notes*. Baltimore/Md./USA: The Johns Hopkins Press 91, no. 6 (1976).

Guignery, Vanessa et al. *Hybridity : Forms and Figures in Literature and the Visual Arts*, 3–4. Newcastle upon Tyne, UK: Cambridge Scholars, 2012.

Katrak, Ketu H. "Innovations in Contemporary Indian Dance: From Religious and Mythological Roots in Classical Bharatanatyam." *Religion Compass* 7, no. 2 (2013).

Haynes, Jo. "World Music and the Search for Difference." *Ethnicities* 5, no. 3 (2015).

Laenui, Poka. *Processes of Decolonization*. In M. Battiste, ed., *Reclaiming Indigenous Voice and Vision* (Toronto: UBC, 2000), 150–60.

Löwner, Gudrun. *Intercultural Dialogue in Art and Religion*. New Delhi: Manohar Publishers & Distributors, 2018.

Middleton, Richard. "Musical Belongings: Western Music and Its Low-Other." In *Western Music and Its Others: Difference, Representation, and Appropriation in Music*. Eds., Georgina Born and David Hesmondhalgh. Berkeley and Los Angeles, CA: University of California, 2000.

Roberts, Michelle Voss. "'Who Is My Good Neighbor?': Classical Indian Dance in the Prophetic Work of the Church." *Exchange* 41, no. 2 (2012): 103–19.

Sahi, Jyoti. *The Child and the Serpent: Reflections on Popular Indian Symbols*, Asian Trading Corporation, Bangalore, 1980 [1994].

Shaw, Daniel R. "Beyond Syncretism: A Dynamic Approach to Hybridity," *International Bulletin of Mission Research* 42, no. 1 (2018).

Vesna, Victoria. "What is Hybrid Art?" *Arts Electronica Blog*. https://www.aec.at/aeblog/en/2015/03/24/was-ist-hybrid-art/. 2015.

Vinzent, Jutta. "In Search of Hybridity: Inculturation, Interculturation and Transculturation in Contemporary Religious Art in Britain." *Exchange* 39, no. 1 (2010).

ABOUT THE AUTHOR

UDAY MARK BALASUNDARAM, PhD, is Professor of Intercultural Studies at South Asia Institute for Advanced Christian Studies (SAIACS), Bangalore, India. Previously he taught as adjunct faculty at Fuller Theological Seminary, Houston, and Houston Graduate School of Theology. He is a Lausanne Arts Catalyst. Prior to serving in pastoral and worship leadership roles in India and the US, Uday worked in the Indian film and advertising music industry. Uday is founder of Estuary Cultures, "creativity inspiring diversity for community," catalyzing creative communities for social transformation and the Order of Bezalel, equipping and empowering creatives everywhere to fulfill their ultimate creative calling.

CHAPTER 17 | Peter Taehoon Lee

Toward a Third Space of Cultures: Hybridity and Multiethnic Leadership in Christian Mission

In what ways can the concept of cultural hybridity inform Christian mission today? More specifically, how does cultural hybridity relate to multi-ethnic leadership in mission? Hybridity as a concept of "mixing" and "in-betweenness" of cultures has been an important topic in post-colonial studies for over three decades.[1] Its prominence can be attributed to Homi K. Bhabha's creative work.[2] His seminal text, *The Location of Culture* may be the single most important scholarly work on cultural hybridity.[3] Bhabha contends that the most salient form of cultural innovations resides in the ambivalent, in-between space of cultures.[4] It is possible to use Bhabha's analysis of intercultural relations to develop a robust framework for missions leadership.

---

1 Jan Pieterse Nederveen, *Globalization and Culture: Global Mélange*, 3rd ed. (Lanham, MD: Rowman & Littlefield, 2015), 120. Gerald Izenberg, *Identity: The Necessity of a Modern Idea* (Philadelphia: University of Pennsylvania, 2016), 332–34.

2 Peter Burke, *Cultural Hybridity* (Cambridge, UK: Polity, 2009). Marwan M. Kraidy, *Hybridity, or the Cultural Logic of Globalization* (Philadelphia: Temple University, 2005). Pnina Werbner, "Introduction: The Dialectics of Cultural Hybridity," in *Debating Cultural Hybridity: Multi-Cultural Identities and the Politics of Anti-Racism*, edited by Pnina Werbner and Tariq Modood, 2nd ed. (London: Zed, 2015), 1–26. Robert J. C. Young, *Colonial Desire: Hybridity in Theory, Culture, and Race* (London: Routledge, 1995).

3 David Huddart, *Homi K. Bhabha* (London: Routledge, 2006).

4 Homi K. Bhabha, *The Location of Culture* (Routledge Classics ed. London, 2004).

We are currently at the forefront of exploring cultural hybridity in missiology.[5] It would be prudent to approach this new missiological thinking with caution and sound theoretical grounding. Some scholars suggest that cultural hybridity can be a powerful heuristic and analytical device that helps us learn about and interpret various cultural contexts.[6] If so, the concept of hybridity may be able to help us analyze our current rendering of multi-ethnic leadership in Christian mission. I argue that cultural hybridity concept reveals that the wide-spread model of cross-cultural leadership in mission urgently needs corrections. This chapter revisits the underlying cultural assumptions used for multi-ethnic mission leadership and teamwork. I believe that the hybridity concept will be most valuable when used as an analytical tool in re-framing existing missions paradigms.

Globalization of Missions and Hybridization

The last half century of accelerated globalization has significantly altered many societies around the globe. Local contexts that have traditionally been seen as culturally stable and homogeneous are going through rapid changes due to increasing migration of and contacts with others culturally. Jan Nederveen Pieterse argues that globalization is hybridizing all cultures at an unprecedented rate.[7] These changes have huge implications for missions leadership.

Mission "through" everywhere

First, due to international migration and emergence of diaspora communities around the world, the now-well-known story of mission "from everywhere to everywhere" has a new twist: mission is increasingly from everywhere to everywhere through everywhere. It is common for diaspora

---

5 Cultural hybridity, though not a new concept, is now beginning to be useful in mission theories. Considering how theories of cultural hybridity in mainstream academia have been significant resources in understanding globalization and multi-cultural societies, it is surprising that mission scholars are not just starting to show interest and explore them for the same goal in recent years.

6 Len Ang, "Together-In-Difference: Beyond Diaspora, Into Hybridity," *Asian Studies Review* 27, no. 2 (June 2003):149–53; Nestor García Canclini, "Introduction: Hybrid Cultures in Globalized Times," in *Hybrid Cultures: Strategies for Entering and Leaving Modernity*, translated by Bruce Campbell (Minneapolis: University of Minnesota, 2005), xxx.

7 Pieterse, *Globalization and Culture*.

Christians to be ministering to other diaspora people elsewhere. It is the "through" part—the diaspora—that requires careful examination today.[8]

Mission through diasporas may be a new pattern in a world where migratory movements and hyphenated identities are becoming more common. As Nederveen Pieterse puts it, we are all now "Moroccan girls doing Thai boxing in Amsterdam."[9] As global movements of people and intercultural contacts continue their course, cultural mixing intensifies and traditional borders and identity markers become less meaningful. Grouping people based on nationality, ethnicity, race, or culture will lose its currency while shared experiences, aspirations, and social connections beyond existing boundaries become more relevant human categories. As reshuffling of existing structures creates new "social (dis-) orders" around the world, the church faces the challenge of proclaiming the gospel in a fluid and fast-moving world with ambiguous boundaries.

Multiethnic Mission Teams and Hybridity

The second implication of globalization of missions is proliferation of culturally diverse international mission organizations.[10] Those who serve on multiethnic mission teams formed by these organizations deal with unique challenges that can be attributed to the globalizing nature of mission.[11] They are part of these large transnational organizations with worldwide presence. Even as these workers live and serve in a country,

---

8   For example, during the summer of 2017, I led a group of Korean American teens on a short-term mission trip to Western Europe. There was a teenager from Germany who joined us on this outreach. His father was a Nigerian pastoring a Russian-speaking church in Germany, and his mother a Russian-Ukrainian-Uzbek-German. When he came to visit his son, I asked him to bless and pray for my group. Then he, somewhat embarrassed, said, "It's been a long time since I prayed in English. May I pray for you in Russian?" Here he was—a Nigerian, married to a Russian-Ukrainian-Uzbek-German, praying in the Russian language for a group of Korean Americans on an outreach in the Netherlands! What is significant about this experience is that this has become a common experience around the world.

9   Pieterse, *Globalization and Culture*, 123–24.

10 For the purpose of this essay, an "international mission organization" will refer to a large independent, non-denominational Christian mission agency that has a global presence and generally carries out mission work by recruiting, resourcing, and ministering in multiple countries. It would typically have hundreds or even thousands of staff workers with various citizenships around the world. Examples include SIM, Wycliffe/SIL, Youth with a Mission (YWAM), Operation Mobilization (OM), Overseas Missionary Fellowship (OMF), WEC International, Frontiers, and Pioneers.

11 For the purpose of this essay, "multiethnic mission team" will loosely refer to a missionary team composed of members who come from two or more countries and/or cultures.

they maintain social ties within their sending country. While they make cultural adjustments to their ministry context, they also adapt to their multi-ethnic team's complex cultural dynamics. By default, they become a sort of religious transnational migrants who live at intersections of multiple cultural flows. In these settings and for these people, the cultural hybridity concept is not only useful, but also necessary.

Utilizing cultural hybridity as an analytical lens for multi-ethnic mission teams can help us focus on processual realities rather than fixed traits of cultural groups. It highlights the mobile and fluid nature of cross-cultural workers, who come from diverse ethnic backgrounds. It may shed light on the global cultural flows observed by Arjun Appadurai.[12] We can look at cultural practices embedded in people's everyday experiences through the lens of cultural hybridity and discover how cultural trends and behavioral patterns of people are being shaped. Applying the hybridity concept can help us learn how cultural changes occur in people and their implications for multiethnic communities. Members of these communities can become better grounded to live out "togetherness-in-difference," which is a crucial facet of contemporary living.[13]

Cultural Hybridity as a Multi-Ethnic Leadership Framework

When thinking of ways to apply theories of cultural hybridity toward developing an appropriate framework of multi-ethnic mission leadership, I observe three interrelated themes that should demand our special attention—a Third Space perspective by Homi K. Bhabha, theology of marginality by Jung Young Lee, and global concepts of culture by Robert J. Schreiter.

A third space for multiethnic leadership

Homi K. Bhabha, the most prominent among theorists of cultural hybridity, develops the notion of a Third Space. A Third Space represents "the space across and between boundaries."[14] Bhabha hints that this is where "culture" is located and the most salient form of cultural production takes place.[15]

---

12 *Modernity at Large*; "Globalization and the Research Imagination"; Appadurai describes contemporary global cultural flows as ethnoscapes (people), finanscapes (capital), mediascapes (images), technoscapes (technology), and ideoscapes (ideologies).

13 Ang, "Together-In-Difference."

14 Jan Pieterse Nederveen, "Hybridity, So What?," The Anti-Hybridity Backlash and the Riddles of Recognition," *Theory, Culture & Society* 18, no. 2/3 (April 2001): 239

15 Pieterse, *Globalization and Culture.*

Describing realities of intercultural contacts, he explains, "[I]t is the 'inter'— the cutting edge of translation and negotiation, the in-between space— that carries the burden of the meaning of culture."[16] He calls it "that alien territory" in which there is both a risk of further friction and a potential for overcoming cultural conflicts. In discussions of Third Space, Bhabha also uses terms such as liminality, interstice, and in-between-ness.[17]

The Third Space concept highlights some of the core characteristics of cultural hybridity. Hybridity problematizes borders.[18] It blurs boundaries that are historically and culturally constructed in people's consciousness.[19] Cultural identity is not so deterministic; no one stays the same through time and places. Seeing the world through the lens of hybridity makes it possible for us to see people as going through continual changes as they incorporate new cultural elements. In globalizing missionary communities, this is an important perspective to maintain. Although we may come from different parts of the world, as we acknowledge our historical and "complicated entanglement" with one another, we can more readily commit to living out "togetherness-in-difference."[20] It means that we embrace ongoing changes in and around us. Viewed in this way, stereotypes and ethnic lines that divide us are reduced or even entirely removed. One's culture or nationality no longer matters so much. When a multi-ethnic mission team enters a liminal space between cultures, common missional commitments and shared experiences take on far more importance than one's ethnicity or race. Then the multi-ethnic team is the Third Space in which a marvelous new culture is created; the visions of Revelation 7 and Isaiah 60 are, at least in part, fulfilled. This is the kind of multi-ethnic paradigm needed for missionary leadership today.

Theories of cultural hybridity are ultimately theories of change. They show how people in various cultures accept, reject, adopt, alter, and/or blend various cultural elements they encounter in intercultural contacts. Robert J. Schreiter, a Roman Catholic mission scholar and

---

16 Bhabha, *The Location of Culture*, 56.

17 Jonathan Rutherford, "The Third Space: Interview with Homi Bhabha," in *Identity: Community, Culture, Difference*, edited by Jonathan Rutherford (London: Lawrence & Wishart 1990), 211.

18 Pieterse, "Hybridity, So What?," 220.

19 See Lee Ang, *On Not Speaking Chinese: Living Between Asia and the West* (London: Routledge, 2001); Ang, "Together-In-Difference."

20 Ang, "Together-In-Difference," 141.

theologian, agrees with this notion of change in his proposal for a theology of culture. He writes, "It is in the experience of moving from one place to another, of cobbling together new identities out of the old ones, of negotiating multiple identities and logics that insight into where God is at work in a globalized culture will be found."[21]

The Third Space of intercultural contacts is not something we create. Rather, it occurs organically. Whether we choose or not, the Third Space exists all around us in this era of mass global movement of people, money, and ideas. We can experience it as an unpleasant, difficult change being forced upon us or as a fact of life which is to be actively pursued and shaped with a positive intent. Those who intentionally enter this liminal space must do so by purposefully distancing self from their own culture in order to draw nearer to cultural other. When we intentionally partake in this space for better, it brings multi-ethnic communities closer together.

It is important to remember that multi-ethnic mission teams are not just international project groups; rather, they are communal interstices centered on Christ. The ones who put aside their cultural preferences in deference to cultural other are likely to build thriving Jesus communities, witnessing to the reconciling work of Christ (John 13:35). This is how multi-ethnic communities in mission are faithful witnesses to Christ in any culture—by embracing the reality of the Third Space and actively seeking changes by striving for newness.

Theology of marginality

Another emergent theme that we need to pay attention to is a theology of marginality developed by Jung Young Lee, a Korean immigrant theologian in the United States. It is noteworthy that Lee's theological reflections have much in common with Bhabha's theory of hybridity. According to Bhabha, the creative powers of culture are not confined within essentialized "cultures." They are located, and even thrive, in the interstitial space of hybridity. Bhabha recognizes the significance of the ambivalent positions of minorities and migrants. He observes that the marginalized position of minorities and colonial subjects gives them the basis for their "subaltern agency" which subverts dominant powers.[22]

---

21 Robert J. Schreiter, *The New Catholicity: Theology Between the Global and the Local* (Maryknoll, NY: Orbis 1997), 59.

22 Bhabha, *The Location of Culture*, 265.

Though Bhabha's claims of hybridity and the notion of the Third Space are quintessentially postcolonial, they are surprisingly reminiscent of Lee's non-centralist theology of the margin.[23] Hybridity entails marginality, which is, as Lee suggests, the basis for agency. He sees marginality as "deeply rooted in the life and mission of a marginal Jew, Jesus of Nazareth, who is known to marginal people as the margin of marginality."[24] Lee's thesis, closely aligning with Bhabha's notion of hybridity as a subaltern agency, suggests how intentional marginality needs to be included in discussions of leadership in global mission.

Migrants, members of diaspora communities, and cross-cultural missionaries are by nature marginalized people. There is a great deal of pain and humiliation in their lives. However, pains of marginality have a potential for agency, which cannot be experienced by those who are at the center of power and privilege. This is a point that needs to be further explored in Christian mission today. For too long, Christian leadership models have lopsidedly leaned toward strength rather than weakness, centrality than marginality. In this era of rapid global cultural flows, an imaginative marginality will be a key to emerging leadership in Christian mission.

Global concepts of culture

Multi-ethnic leadership in Christian mission needs to be grounded in a culture model that incorporates the reality of globalization and cultural hybridization. Schreiter calls such a model, "globalized concepts of culture."[25] He explains, "Culture is something to be constructed rather than discovered, and it is constructed on the stage of struggle amid the asymmetries of power. It is mapped out on the axes of sameness and difference, comparability and incommensurability, cohesion and dispersion, collaboration and resistance."[26] Building on post-colonial theories, Schreiter presents a salient culture model that includes the marginalized in its articulation and pays attention to their agency. Similarly, Rynkiewich argues, "Culture is contingent, culture is

---

23 Jung Young Lee, *Marginality: The Key to Multicultural Theology* (Minneapolis, MN: Fortress), 1995.

24 Ibid., 173.

25 Robert J. Schreiter, *The New Catholicity: Theology Between the Global and the Local* (Maryknoll, NY: Orbis, 1997), 53.

26 Ibid., 54.

constructed, and culture is contested," and Rynkiewich emphasizes that we consider the fine nuances of the world in which we engage in mission.[27]

On the contrary to the global concepts of culture, the dominant model of culture currently found in missions texts is what Schreiter calls "integrated concepts of culture."[28] Also called "the system view of culture" by some social psychologists,[29] this view is widely spread in multiculturalteam and leadership literature.[30] It tries to quantify thematic categories called "dimensions of national cultures." For example, this model insists that the cultures of Japan and Korea are more "high-context" and "high-power distance." They suggest that in these cultures people do not communicate directly to their superiors about their inner thoughts and feelings. On the contrary, cultures of the United States and Canada are "low-context" and "low-power distance." People in these cultures speak more directly, have more egalitarian views, and expect others to also speak their minds. The biggest problem with this model is that it ignores cultural diversity within each nation or region and erases socio-cultural nuances by simplifying them into manageable numbers.

This model of culture was, however, deemed seriously flawed and subsequently abandoned by anthropologists during the late twentieth century.[31] Even within the field of organizational management, which has long promoted this model, it is being criticized for its inadequate theoretical and empirical grounding.[32] At the current point in time,

---

27 Michael H. Rynkiewich, "The World in My Parish: Rethinking the Standard Missiological Model," *Missiology* 30, no. 3 (July 2002).

28 Schreiter, *The New Catholicity*, 51.

29 Chi-yue Chiu, Angela K., Leung, and Ying-yi Hong, "Cultural Processes: An Overview," in *Cultural Processes: A Social Psychological Perspective*, edited by Angela K.-Y Leung, Chi-yue Chiu, and Ying-yi Hong (New York: Cambridge University, 2011), 3–22.

30 For example, see Hofstede, *Culture's Consequences; Trompenaars and Hampden-Turner, Riding the Waves of Culture; House et al., Culture, Leadership, and Organizations.*" These works are heavily cited and used in cross-cultural leadership and organization management literature.

31 See Kuper, *Culture*; Clifford and Marcus, *Writing Culture*; Abu-Lughod, "Writing Against Culture"; Featherstone, *Undoing Culture*; Gupta and Ferguson, "Beyond 'Culture'"; Shore, "Taking Culture Seriously."

32 For example, McSweeney, "Cultural Diversity within Nations"; McSweeney, "Hall, Hofstede, Huntington, Trompenaars, GLOBE: Common Foundations, Common Flaws"; McSweeney, "Collective Cultural Mind Programming"; McSweeney, Brown, and Iliopoulou, "Claiming Too Much, Delivering Too Little"; Brewer and Venaik, "The Ecological Fallacy in National Culture Research"; Nathan, "A Non-Essentialist Model of Culture"; Venaik and Brewer, "National Culture Dimensions."

many scholars from multiple disciplines do agree that an integrated model of culture is not an adequate representation of the cultural and social reality of any society.

Unfortunately, missionaries have been slow to make a course correction. In general, literatures on missionary training, leadership, and multicultural teams uncritically utilize this integrated culture model and often describe culture as fixed and bound.[33] By essentializing cultures, it perpetuates stereotypical view of cultural others and creates an unnecessary gap between team members. While it may be enlightening to some, and even helpful to others to a certain degree, this way of viewing cultures negatively affects the health of a multi-ethnic community by imposing an essentializing view, which is far removed from the reality and maintaining stereotypes of cultural groups.[34] It widens the gap by focusing on differences rather than commonalities and encouraging "othering" of people. The integrated model impedes formation of deep relationships within multi-ethnic teams by reducing complexities of people and incorrectly assuming cultures to be fenced-in and immutable.

A leadership framework that utilizes an integrated culture model is inadequate for Christian mission. Several contemporary missiologists, most notably Michael Rynkiewich, have challenged this model.[35] Schreiter rightly maintains, "In a time when pluralism is more widely assumed, such absorptive strategies of integrated concepts of culture cannot be justified. Totalizing approaches muffle the voices of the dissident and the minority, and of those who find no home in the integrated whole."[36] It neither provides the tools to understand ongoing

---

33 See Lingenfelter and Mayers, *Ministering Cross-Culturally*; Plueddemann, *Leading Across Cultures*; Moreau et al., *Effective Intercultural Communication*; Hibbert and Hibbert, *Leading Multicultural Teams*.

34 The typical practice by mission agencies is to emphasize the importance of becoming aware of distinct cultural characteristics. They erroneously suggest that if a missionary or a leader understands these cultural differences, he or she can overcome many cross-cultural issues and lead multi-ethnic teams more effectively.

35 See Rynkiewich, "The World in My Parish"; Rynkiewich, "Corporate Metaphors and Strategic Thinking"; Rynkiewich, "Mission in 'the Present Time'"; Rynkiewich, "'Do Not Remember the Former Things'"; Tiénou, "The Invention of the 'Primitive' and Stereotypes in Mission"; Tiénou, "Reflections on Michael A. Rynkiewich's 'Do Not Remember the Former Things'"; Howell, "Globalization, Ethnicity, and Cultural Authenticity"; Howell, "Contextualizing Context-Exploring Christian Identity in the Global Church Through Six Contemporary Cases"; Howell, "Multiculturalism, Immigration and the North American Church"; Priest, "Afterword: Concluding Missiological Reflection"; Nehrbass, *God's Image and Global Cultures*.

36 Schreiter, *The New Catholicity*, 51

cultural processes of hybridization nor resolves issues of power and privilege that go back to the historical entanglements of colonialism but still run deep in the currents of present day narratives.[37]

International mission organizations face many challenges. On the surface, there are issues of leadership, teamwork, and partnership. At a deeper level, however, issues of power, inequality, and prejudice are found. Tendencies of "Orientalism" and "Occidentalism" rise to the surface in unexpected times and places, deepening the divide between the majority world and the Western world.[38] These are systemic issues that cannot easily be resolved by a simple call for "unity in diversity."[39] Appealing to the realities of hybridizing cultures, however, has a potential to provide a way for multi-ethnic teams to move beyond historical and cultural issues that have stifled them for so long.

Further Questions for Hybridity and Multi-ethnic Leadership in Mission

Incorporating hybridity perspectives in mission theories would require further reflections and research. Leadership theories will need to be founded upon understanding hybridity, marginality, and global concepts of culture. More empirical studies need to be conducted to learn from lived experiences that articulate cultural processes in various mission contexts. The following questions might help direct our attention for future missiological research.

First, how can we better understand the hybridization process in various mission contexts? Processes of hybridization are perhaps influenced by social relationships of missionaries; their multi-ethnic team may be a mediating factor in these processes. What do these social networks do to the missionary, the multi-ethnic team, the mission organization, and the local people whom the missionary encounters? Secondly, in what ways can we increase cultural awareness among mission workers without being reductionistic? How can we harness this awareness to improve relationships within multi-ethnic ministry teams? Thirdly, how can a framework of cultural hybridity recognize and encourage agency of the marginalized within global mission, namely, those who do not have economic power or social status?

---

37 Ibid., 52.

38 Said, *Orientalism*; Buruma and Margalit, *Occidentalism*.

39 Ang, "Beyond Unity in Diversity."

Conclusion

Some years ago, I had a revealing conversation with a veteran missionary from East Asia. While discussing cultural differences between non-Westerners and Westerners and ways for us to work together, she said, "Westerners just don't get it. So we non-Westerners have to try to understand them, help them, and let them do things in their way. This is really the best way." While this career missionary's frustrations are understandable, there is another way for us to live "together-in-difference". We need to allow room for probing complex, and oftentimes messy, historical entanglements in Christian mission. We cannot reduce the reality, resort to incomplete solutions or settle for one-sided deferments. We must not let superficial diversity compartmentalize unity that has already become a reality in Christ's death and resurrection.

We would do well to reject all-too-easy meta narratives and grand strategies that do not take cultural complexity seriously.[40] Instead, we need to embrace realities of a globalizing, hybridizing world and strive to shape the Third Space of globalizing mission where the marginalized may speak. As Bhabha points out, significance of hybridity is found only in a marginalized position that renounces claim to privilege.[41] This point resonates with Lee's remarks. He uses the language of hybridity when he states:

> The ultimate victory of suffering love transforms central-group people to marginal and marginal people to new marginal people, so all become marginal people of God. When all are marginal, all become servants to one another in Jesus-Christ, who is the servant of all servants (Matt 20:28; Phil 2:5–11). By becoming servants to one another, tears of sorrow change to tears of joy, an in-between is transformed into an in-both, and suffering is overcome in the fellowship of suffering. When all become servants to one another, the dualistic, exclusive, and dominant ideology of centrality is overcome.[42]

His conclusion meaningfully sums up the kind of multi-ethnic framework required of Christian leadership in this era of globalization and hybridization.

---

40 See Lee and Park, "Beyond People Group Thinking."

41 Homi K. Bhabha, "Foreword," in *Debating Cultural Hybridity: Multi-Cultural Identities and the Politics of Anti-Racism*, edited by Pnina Werbner and Tariq Modood, 2nd ed. (London: Zed, 2015), ix–xiii.

42 Lee, *Marginality*, 173.

BIBLIOGRAPHY

Abu-Lughod, Lila. "Writing Against Culture." In *Recapturing Anthropology: Working in the Present*, edited by Richard G. Fox, 137–62. Santa Fe, NM: School of American Research, 1991.

Ang, Len. "Beyond Unity in Diversity: Cosmopolitanizing Identities in a Globalizing World." *Diogenes* 60, no. 1 (2013): 10–20.

———. *On Not Speaking Chinese: Living Between Asia and the West*. London: Routledge, 2001.

———. "Together-In-Difference: Beyond Diaspora, Into Hybridity." *Asian Studies Review* 27, no. 2 (June 2003): 141–54.

Appadurai, Arjun. "Globalization and the Research Imagination." *International Social Science Journal* 51, no. 160 (June 1999): 229.

———. *Modernity at Large: Cultural Dimensions of Globalization*. Minneapolis: University of Minnesota, 1996.

Bhabha, Homi K. "Foreword." In *Debating Cultural Hybridity: Multi-Cultural Identities and the Politics of Anti-Racism*, edited by Pnina Werbner and Tariq Modood, 2nd ed., ix–xiii. London: Zed, 2015.

———. *The Location of Culture*. Routledge Classics ed. London: Routledge, 2004.

Brewer, Paul, and Sunil Venaik. "The Ecological Fallacy in National Culture Research." *Organization Studies* (01708406) 35, no. 7 (July 2014): 1063–86.

Burke, Peter. *Cultural Hybridity*. Cambridge, UK: Polity, 2009.

Buruma, Ian, and Avishai Margalit. *Occidentalism: The West in the Eyes of Its Enemies*. Penguin, 2004.

Chiu, Chi-yue, Angela K.-y. Leung, and Ying-yi Hong. "Cultural Processes: An Overview." In *Cultural Processes: A Social Psychological Perspective*, edited by Angela K.-Y Leung, Chi-yue Chiu, and Ying-yi Hong. New York: Cambridge University, 2011.

Clifford, James. *The Predicament of Culture: Twentieth-Century Ethnography, Literature, and Art*. Cambridge, MA: Harvard University, 1988.

Clifford, James, and George E. Marcus, eds. *Writing Culture: The Poetics and Politics of Ethnography*. Berkeley: University of California, 1986.

Featherstone, Mike. *Undoing Culture: Globalization, Postmodernism and Identity*. SAGE, 1995.

García Canclini, Néstor. "Introduction: Hybrid Cultures in Globalized Times." In *Hybrid Cultures: Strategies for Entering and Leaving Modernity*, translated by Bruce Campbell, xxiii–xlvi. Minneapolis: University of Minnesota, 2005.

Gupta, Akhil, and James Ferguson. "Beyond 'Culture': Space, Identity, and the Politics of Difference." *Cultural Anthropology* 7, no. 1 (February 1, 1992): 6–23.

Hibbert, Evelyn, and Richard Hibbert. *Leading Multicultural Teams*. Pasadena, CA: William Carey Library, 2014.

Hofstede, Geert. *Culture's Consequences: Comparing Values, Behaviors, Institutions and Organizations Across Nations*. 2nd ed. Thousand Oaks: SAGE, 2003.

House, Robert J., Paul J. Hanges, Mansour Javidan, Peter W. Dorfman, and Vipin Gupta, eds. *Culture, Leadership, and Organizations: The GLOBE Study of 62 Societies*. Thousand Oaks, CA: SAGE, 2004.

Howell, Brian M., "Contextualizing Context-Exploring Christian Identity in the Global Church Through Six Contemporary Cases." In *Power and Identity in the Global Church: Six Contemporary Cases*, edited by Brian M. Howell and Edwin Zehner, 2–25. Pasadena, CA: William Carey Library, 2009.

———. "Globalization, Ethnicity, and Cultural Authenticity: Implications for Theological Education." *Christian Scholar's Review* 35, no. 3 (April 2006): 303–21.

———. "Multiculturalism, Immigration and the North American Church: Rethinking Contextualization." *Missiology* 39, no. 1 (January 2011): 79–85.

Huddart, David. *Homi K. Bhabha*. London: Routledge, 2006.

Izenberg, Gerald. *Identity: The Necessity of a Modern Idea*. Philadelphia: University of Pennsylvania, 2016.

Kraidy, Marwan M., *Hybridity, or the Cultural Logic of Globalization*. Philadelphia: Temple University, 2005.

Kuper, Adam. *Culture: The Anthropologists' Account*. Cambridge, MA: Harvard University, 2000.

Lee, Jung Young. *Marginality: The Key to Multicultural Theology*. Minneapolis, MN: Fortress, 1995.

Lee, Peter T., and James Sung-Hwan Park. "Beyond People Group Thinking: A Critical Re-evaluation of Unreached People Groups." *Missiology* 46, no. 3 (July 1, 2018): 212–25. https://doi.org/10.1177/0091829618774332.

Lingenfelter, Sherwood G., and Marvin K. Mayers. *Ministering Cross-Culturally: A Model for Effective Personal Relationships*. 3rd ed. Grand Rapids, MI: Baker Academic, 2016.

McSweeney, Brendan. "Collective Cultural Mind Programming: Escaping from the Cage." *Journal of Organizational Change Management* 29, no. 1 (February 5, 2016): 68–80.

———. "Cultural Diversity within Nations." In *Remaking Management: Between Global and Local*, edited by Chris Smith, Brendan McSweeney, and Robert Fitzgerald, 61–89. Cambridge, UK: Cambridge University, 2008.

———. "Hall, Hofstede, Huntington, Trompenaars, GLOBE: Common Foundations, Common Flaws." In *Transculturalism and Business in the BRIC States: A Handbook*, edited by Yvette Sánchez and Claudia Franziska Brühwiler, 13–58. Farnham, England: Routledge, 2015.

McSweeney, Brendan, Donna Brown, and Stravroula Iliopoulou. "Claiming Too Much, Delivering Too Little: Testing Some of Hofstede's Generalisations." *Irish Journal of Management* 35, no. 1 (April 2016): 34–57.

Moreau, A. Scott, Evvy Hay Campbell, Susan Greener, and A. Moreau. *Effective Intercultural Communication: A Christian Perspective*. Grand Rapids, MI: Baker Academic, 2014.

Nathan, Ganesh. "A Non-Essentialist Model of Culture: Implications of Identity, Agency and Structure Within Multinational/Multicultural Organizations." *International Journal of Cross Cultural Management* 15, no. 1 (April 2015): 101–24.

———. "Hybridity, So What?: The Anti-Hybridity Backlash and the Riddles of Recognition." *Theory, Culture & Society* 18, no. 2/3 (April 2001): 219.

Nehrbass, Kenneth. *God's Image and Global Cultures: Integrating Faith and Culture in the Twenty-First Century*. Eugene, Oregon: Cascade, 2016.

Ortner, Sherry B. *Anthropology and Social Theory: Culture, Power, and the Acting Subject*. Durham, NC: Duke University, 2006.

Pieterse Nederveen, Jan. *Globalization and Culture: Global Mélange*. 3rd ed. Lanham, MD: Rowman & Littlefield, 2015.

Plueddemann, James E., *Leading Across Cultures: Effective Ministry and Mission in the Global Church*. Downers Grove, IL: IVP Academic, 2009.

Priest, Robert J., "Afterword: Concluding Missiological Reflection." In *Power and Identity in the Global Church: Six Contemporary Cases*, edited by Brian M. Howell and Edwin Zehner, 185–91. Pasadena, CA: William Carey Library, 2009.

Rutherford, Jonathan. "The Third Space: Interview with Homi Bhabha." In *Identity: Community, Culture, Difference*, edited by Jonathan Rutherford, 207–21. London: Lawrence & Wishart, 1990.

Rynkiewich, Michael A., "Corporate Metaphors and Strategic Thinking: 'The 10/40 Window' in the American Evangelical Worldview." *Missiology 35*, no. 2 (April 1, 2007): 217–41.

———. "'Do Not Remember the Former Things.'" *International Bulletin of Mission Research* 40, no. 4 (October 2016): 308–17.

———. "Mission in 'the Present Time': What About the People in Diaspora?" *International Journal of Frontier Missiology* 30, no. 3 (July 2013): 103–14.

———. "The World in My Parish: Rethinking the Standard Missiological Model." *Missiology* 30, no. 3 (July 2002): 301–21.

Said, Edward W., *Orientalism*. 1st Vintage Books ed. New York: Vintage, 1979.

Schreiter, Robert J., *The New Catholicity: Theology Between the Global and the Local*. Maryknoll, NY: Orbis,1997.

Shore, Bradd. "Taking Culture Seriously." *Human Development* 45, no. 4 (July 2002): 226–28.

Tiénou, Tite. "Reflections on Michael A. Rynkiewich's 'Do Not Remember the Former Things.'" *International Bulletin of Mission Research* 40, no. 4 (October 2016): 318–24.

———. "The Invention of the 'Primitive' and Stereotypes in Mission." *Missiology* 19, no. 3 (July 1991): 295–303.

Trompenaars, Fons, and Charles Hampden-Turner. *Riding the Waves of Culture: Understanding Diversity in Global Business*. 3rd ed. New York, NY: McGraw-Hill, 2012.

Venaik, Sunil, and Paul Brewer. "National Culture Dimensions: The Perpetuation of Cultural Ignorance." *Management Learning* 47, no. 5 (November 2016): 563–89.

Werbner, Pnina. "Introduction: The Dialectics of Cultural Hybridity." In *Debating Cultural Hybridity: Multi-Cultural Identities and the Politics of Anti-Racism*, edited by Pnina Werbner and Tariq Modood, 2nd ed., 1–26. London: Zed, 2015.

Young, Robert J. C. *Colonial Desire: Hybridity in Theory, Culture, and Race*. London: Routledge, 1995.

ABOUT THE AUTHOR

PETER T. LEE works with Operation Mobilization (OM) and is an ordained minister in the Presbyterian Church (USA). He served in North Africa for ten years, during which he led a multi-ethnic mission team and trained international business and development workers. He is currently working toward a PhD in intercultural studies at Trinity Evangelical Divinity School in Deerfield, Illinois.

APPENDIX 1

The Manila Statement on Hybridity in Diaspora Mission

Convening as theological educators and ministry leaders in diaspora mission at the Lausanne Consultation on Hybridity, Diaspora and Missio Dei, sponsored by the Global Diaspora Network and in partnership with the Biblical Seminary of the Philippines,

We recognize
That our sovereign God is at work among the diaspora peoples of the world,

That hybridity is the process by and through which God mixes ethnicity, culture, and identity,

And that before God we confess our prejudice against people who are different from us.

We affirm
The growing reality and implications of hybridity for the mission of God,

And the need for expanded vision, ongoing dialogue, and fresh perspectives to overcome our cultural, ethnocentric, and theological blind spots.

We challenge
The global Church to embrace God's heart for people on the move,

To address the opportunities and challenges for ministry that hybridity brings to families, congregations, and communities,

And to pray for hybrid peoples to be redeemed and unleashed for the mission of God.

Manila, Philippines
June 19-22, 2018

APPENDIX 2

THE CAPE TOWN COMMITMENT

Cape Town, South Africa
October 16-25, 2010

PART II For the world we serve: The Cape Town Call to Action
IIC. Living the love of Christ among people of other faiths

5. Love reaches out to scattered peoples

People are on the move as never before. Migration is one of the great global realities of our era. It is estimated that 200 million people are living outside their countries of origin, voluntarily or involuntarily. The term "diaspora" is used here to mean people who have relocated from their lands of birth for whatever reason. Some relocate permanently, and others, like three million international students and scholars, temporarily. Vast numbers of people from many religion backgrounds, including Christians, live in diaspora conditions: economic migrants seeking work; internally-displaced people because of war or natural disaster; refugees and asylum seekers; victims of ethnic cleansing; people fleeing religious violence and persecution; famine sufferers-whether caused by drought, floods, or war; victims of rural poverty moving to cities. We are convinced that contemporary migrations are within the sovereign missional purpose of God, without ignoring the evil and suffering that can be involved.[75].

A) We encourage Church and mission leaders to recognize and respond to the missional opportunities present by global migration and diaspora communities, in strategic planning, and in focused training and resourcing of those called to work among them.

B) We encourage Christians in host nations which have immigrant communities and international students and scholars of other religious backgrounds to bear counter-cultural witness to the love of Christ in deed and word, by obeying the extensive biblical commands to love the stranger, defend the cause of the foreigner, visit the prisoner, practice hospitality, build friendships, invite into our homes, and provide help and services.[76]

C) We encourage Christians who are themselves part of diaspora communities to discern the hand of God, even in circumstances they may not have chose, and to seek whatever opportunities God provides for bearing witness to Christ in their host community and seeking its welfare.[77] Where that host country includes Christian churches, we urge immigrant and indigenous churches together to listen and learn from one another, and to initiate co-operative efforts to reach all sections of their nation with the gospel.

INDEX

A

African Christian
46, 49, 51, 55

apartheid
190, 194

art-making
201–4, 206–14

arts
7, 58, 67, 69, 72–73, 118, 155, 179, 199, 201–11, 213–16

B

Babylonian exile
11, 34–35, 40

Biblical Theology
31, 33, 143, 155

bi-national marriage
159–65, 167–71

Brazil
1–9, 11–17, 19–29, 31–43, 45–55, 57–87, 89–99, 101–11, 113–31, 133–43, 145–57, 159–71, 173–227

bridge, bridge-builders
26, 97, 161, 163, 186

C

Chinese
Canadian church
156

Chineseness
101–103, 105, 107, 109–11

Diaspora
19, 111

Filipino
20, 25, 101–3, 105–11

Immigrant
103

Christian faithfulness
145–46, 151, 153–54

church network
23–24, 26–27, 181

Coconut Generation
133–37, 139, 141, 143, 184, 187

compartmentalization
110, 208, 227

compassion
140, 191, 194–99

contextualization
145–146, 150, 153, 155–56, 185

contextual theology
47–48, 154–55

Creatio Dei
21, 201–2, 206–8, 210, 213–14

creativity
2, 61, 97, 134, 142, 201–203, 206–8, 210, 213–16

cultural
anthropology
84–85, 102, 215

diversity
51, 224

hybridity
37–38, 41, 72, 107, 111, 131, 145, 147, 201–202, 206–207, 217–18, 220– 21, 226

identity
143, 221

logic
73, 155

mixing
102, 106–8, 219

D

dekasegi
113–19, 121, 123–24, 126–30

dialogue
48, 89–91, 94–97, 145, 155, 208–9, 212–13, 216

diaspora
community
1, 16, 31, 43, 71–72, 142, 171, 218, 223

missiology
1, 16, 31, 43, 71–72, 171

musician
142, 159, 184, 204, 206, 215, 219

people
142, 159, 184, 219

digital
16, 60–62, 72–73, 80, 213

discipleship, multiplying disciples
19–23, 25, 27, 29, 124–25, 145, 157, 168

displacement
138–40, 189–90

dominant culture
46, 90, 110–11, 125, 138, 192

E

ethnic group
26, 109, 111, 120

exilic era
6–7

F

families
11, 15, 25, 62–64, 75, 77, 82, 105, 123, 129, 162–63, 174, 178, 182–85, 187–88

fusion
106, 117, 125, 136, 204

G

Gentile mission
31, 33, 35–37, 39, 41, 43

global
church
16, 26, 51, 55, 64, 155, 173

mission, 155, 223, 226

globalization
16, 41, 55, 57–59, 61, 63, 65, 67, 69, 71–73, 105, 111, 114, 118, 122, 130–31, 136, 155–56, 171, 187, 218–19, 223, 227

Great Commission
16, 19, 28, 34, 40–41

H

heart language
129–30

Hindu
69, 206–9, 215

Holy Spirit
51, 96, 186, 197

home country
107, 115, 128, 170, 173, 177, 180, 185

host country
63, 103, 108–9

house church
23–24, 26–29

human dignity
195–96

hybrid
art
202–3, 216

children
173, 175, 177, 179, 181, 183, 185, 187

culture
5

identity
85, 114–15, 126

hybridity
theology
45–47, 49–55, 207, 211–212

theories
1–9, 11–17, 19–29, 31–43, 45–55, 57–87, 89–99, 101–11, 113–31, 133–43, 145–57, 159–71, 173–227

hybridization
47, 59, 66, 70–71, 84, 90, 95, 123, 139, 218, 223, 226–27

I

India
16–17, 26, 133, 142, 148, 170, 204, 207–8, 210, 212, 216

indigenous art
201, 205

intercultural
17, 55, 89, 97, 136, 138, 155, 178, 188, 216–17, 219, 221–22

intermarriage
75–79, 81, 83–87, 123, 138

international
55, 66, 69, 131, 143, 155, 159–162, 165, 168–71, 178, 183, 216, 218–19, 222, 226

international student ministry
1–9, 11–17, 19–29, 31–43, 45–55, 57–87, 89–99, 101–11, 113–31, 133–43, 145–57, 159–71, 173–227

J

Japanese

    diaspora
    116

    language
    125, 129–30

    migrant workers
    (See also *Dekasegi* and *Nikkei*), 126

Jesus
11–17, 20–28, 31, 33–42, 72, 77, 81–83, 86–87, 131, 139, 141–42, 160, 169, 182, 186, 191–93, 197, 206, 213, 222–23

Jewish

    Diaspora
    24, 39–40

    identity
    38, 76, 79–80, 84

intermarriage
75–76, 79, 83

millennial
79–80, 82

people
34, 77–78, 86

US Jews
76, 79, 86

K

King David
1–9, 11–17, 19–29, 31–43, 45–55, 57–87, 89–99, 101–11, 113–31, 133–43, 145–57, 159–71, 173–227

Korea
43, 51, 151, 184, 222, 224

L

Latin America
48, 51, 53, 90–92, 95–97, 131

Latino community
89–91, 97

Lausanne Movement
17, 29, 87, 143, 171, 185, 216

liminal
96–97, 108–9, 133, 135, 137, 141–42, 155, 186, 221–22

local

    church
    25, 180, 186, 190, 206, 211

    context
    127, 131, 211, 218

M

Malawi
50, 52–54

marginal people
223, 227

Matthew, Gospel of
12–15, 17, 23, 31, 33–37, 39–42, 155–56, 195

mestizaje
89–99, 139–40, 143

migrant worker
113, 120, 123, 126–27

migration
1, 4, 16, 26, 49, 54–55, 73, 130,
136, 187–88, 218

millennials
19, 79–82, 84–86

miscegenation
91–92, 137

Missio Dei
1–2, 8, 16, 19–23, 25, 27, 29, 159,
191, 201–2

missiological research
216, 226

missiology
1, 16, 31, 43, 48, 71–72, 86–87,
131, 155, 171, 187–88, 218

missional hermeneutic
32–33

missional theology
33

missions
9, 16–17, 19, 25–26, 28–29,
31–33, 35–37, 39, 41–43, 47,
55, 59, 71, 74, 81, 107, 110, 114,
127, 131, 133, 135, 137–43, 152,
154–56, 159–60, 163, 171, 177,
187, 201–7, 209–11, 213–27

mission teams
219–22

Mosaic era
4–5, 7

Moses
4–5, 7–8, 11–12, 140–41, 194

mulatez, mulato
92, 94–95, 98

multicultural
16–17, 19–20, 27, 45–46, 49,
54–55, 73, 93, 95, 97, 102, 153,
188, 225

multiethnic
leadership
217–18, 220, 223, 226
team
221, 225–26

N

New Testament
12–13, 17, 32–33, 39–43, 140–41,
155

Nikkei
113–15, 117–31

North American Church
161

P

Paul, the Apostle
12, 15–16, 19–25, 140–41, 143, 149

Pecha Kucha
65, 70–71

Peru
113–15, 117–30

pilgrim
55, 67, 98, 181–183, 198–99

Portuguese
90, 95–96, 114, 116, 125, 127,
129–30, 174, 184

prophetic critique
192, 199

public justice
198–99

pure
11, 37, 78, 90, 101, 108, 137–40,
211–12

R

reconciliation
73, 83, 168, 191–94, 196–99

remixing
49

Roman Empire
36, 38–39

S

silent exodus
152, 155

social media
73, 80, 178–79, 181–83

South Africa
69, 189–91, 193–94, 196, 198–99

spiritual harmony
83–86

storytelling
59, 64–66, 68–72

student ministry
159–60, 162, 170–71

syncretism
105, 109, 111, 156, 208, 216

T

third culture kids
1–9, 11–17, 19–29, 31–43, 45–55,
57–87, 89–99, 101–11, 113–31,
133–43, 145–57, 159–71, 173–227

third space
39, 137, 217, 219–23, 225, 227

tradition, traditions
1–9, 11–17, 19–29, 31–43, 45–55,
57–87, 89–99, 101–11, 113–31,
133–43, 145–57, 159–71, 173–227

Tsinoys
103–8

U

Unhomed
108, 110–11

unreached people group
16, 20, 26, 117, 130

V

virtual (world, places)
59–60

CPSIA information can be obtained
at www.ICGtesting.com
Printed in the USA
BVHW041032210521
607672BV00005B/12